'This book adds an important chapter to the world community's efforts to manage technological advances in harmony with demands for democracy and social justice. In discussing the transatlantic dispute over agricultural biotechnology, Murphy and Levidow show that trade liberalization is not a thing apart from national politics but rather involves making difficult choices among competing state-by-state political settlements. Their thoroughly researched and carefully argued account puts the governance of new technologies squarely on the agenda of globalization studies. It should be recommended reading for all concerned with the legitimacy of the emerging global order.'

Sheila Jasanoff
Pforzheimer Professor of Science and Technology Studies
Harvard University

'Anyone who has tried to grasp the politics of biotechnology and GM food knows that the problem is complex and not easily sorted out. For this reason, this new book by Joseph Murphy and Les Levidow is an important addition to the literature. They provide a wealth of information and a rigorous analysis that helps us better understand the tensions between the United States and Europe, including the conflicts between their respective citizens, experts, politicians and corporations.'

Frank Fischer
Professor of Political Science
Rutgers University

Governing the Transatlantic Conflict over Agricultural Biotechnology

Delays in approving genetically modified crops and foods in the European Union have led to a high profile trade conflict with the United States. This book analyses the EU–US conflict and uses it as a case study to explore the governance of new technologies.

The transatlantic conflict over GM crops and food has been widely attributed to regulatory differences that divide the EU and the US. Going beyond common stereotypes of these differences and their origins, this book analyses the conflict through contending coalitions of policy actors operating across the Atlantic. *Governing the Transatlantic Conflict over Agricultural Biotechnology* focuses on interactions between the EU and the US, rather than on EU–US comparisons. Drawing on original research and interviews with key policy actors, the book shows how EU–US efforts to harmonise regulations for agricultural biotechnology created the context in which activists could generate a backlash against the technology. In this new context regulations were shaped along different lines. Joseph Murphy and Les Levidow provide new insights by elaborating critical perspectives on global governance, issue-framing, standard-setting and regulatory science.

This accessible book will appeal to undergraduate and post-graduate students, academics and policy-makers working on a wide range of issues covered by political science, policy studies, international relations, economics, geography, business management, environmental and development studies, science and technology studies.

Joseph Murphy is a Senior Lecturer in the Sustainability Research Institute at the University of Leeds. His research focuses on environmental governance and regulation, and he has published widely on environmental issues.

Les Levidow is a Senior Research Fellow at The Open University, UK. He has been researching the innovation and regulation of agricultural biotechnology since 1989. His research encompasses the European Union, the United States and transatlantic relations. He is the Editor of the journal *Science as Culture*.

Genetics and Society

Series Editors:
Paul Atkinson, *Associate Director of CESAGen, Cardiff University*;
Ruth Chadwick, *Director of CESAGen, Lancaster University*;
Peter Glasner, *Professorial Research Fellow for CESAGen, Lancaster University*; and
Brian Wynne, *member of the management team at CESAGen, Lancaster University*

The books in this series, all based on original research, explore the social, economic and ethical consequences of the new genetic sciences. The series is based in the ESRC's Centre for Economic and Social Aspects of Genomics, the largest UK investment in social-science research on the implications of these innovations. With a mix of research monographs, edited collections, textbooks and a major new handbook, the series will be a major contribution to the social analysis of new agricultural and biomedical technologies.

Forthcoming in the series:

Governing the Transatlantic Conflict over Agricultural Biotechnology:
Contending Coalitions, Trade Liberalisation and Standard Setting
Joseph Murphy and Les Levidow (2006) 0-415-37328-X

The Public Debate about Transgenic Crops in Britain:
A Deliberative Future?
Tom Horlick-Jones, John Walls, Gene Rowe, Nick Pidgeon, Wouter Poortinga and Tim O'Riordan (2006) 0-415-39322-1

New Genetics, New Social Formations
Paul Atkinson and Peter Glasner (2006) 0-415-39323-X

New Genetics, New Identities
Paul Atkinson and Peter Glasner (2006) 0-415-39407-4

Local Cells, Global Science: Embryonic Stem Cell Research in India
Aditya Bharadwaj and Peter Glasner (2007) 0-415-39609-3

Growth Cultures: Life Sciences & Economic Development
Philip Cooke (2007) 0-415-39223-3

Governing the Transatlantic Conflict over Agricultural Biotechnology

Contending coalitions, trade liberalisation and standard setting

Joseph Murphy and Les Levidow

LONDON AND NEW YORK

First published 2006
by Routledge
2 Park Square, Milton Park, Abingdon, Oxon OX14 4RN

Simultaneously published in the USA and Canada
by Routledge
270 Madison Avenue, New York, NY 10016

Routledge is an imprint of the Taylor & Francis Group, an informa business

Typeset in Garamond
by Taylor & Francis Books

British Library Cataloguing in Publication Data
A catalogue record for this book is available from the British Library

Library of Congress Cataloging in Publication Data
Murphy, Joseph.
Governing the transatlantic conflict over agricultural biotechnology :
contending coalitions, trade liberalisation and standard setting / Joseph
Murphy and Les Levidow.

p. cm.

ISBN 0-415-37328-X (hardback)

1. Agriculture and state. 2. Agricultural biotechnology. 3. Genetic engi-
neering industry. 4. Genetically modified foods. 5. International trade. 6.
United States--Commerce--European Economic Community countries. 7.
European Economic Community countries--Commerce--United States. I.
Levidow, Les. II. Title.
HD1415.M88 2006
338.4'7664024--dc22

2005028807

ISBN10: 0-415-37328-X
ISBN13: 978-0-415-37328-9

Contents

Tables

Acknowledgements

This book builds on the results of a research project funded by the UK's Economic and Social Research Council between 2002 and 2004: 'Trading Up Environmental Standards? Transatlantic Governance of GM Crops' (Award Number: R000239460). It also draws on material collected for a research project funded by the European Commission at the same time: 'Precautionary Expertise for GM Crops' (FP5 Quality of Life Programme). Both of these projects were based at The Open University and we gratefully acknowledge the support of the funders and the university. We would like to thank the other members of the Trading Up project team (David Wield, Susan Carr and Simon Bromley), and all members of the Precautionary Expertise project team for providing insights into the regulation of agricultural biotechnology in the European Union.

Some of the following chapters bring together, benefit from or build on work that we have done with other researchers and published elsewhere. In particular we would like to point out that some of the material in Chapters 2, 3 and 7 was developed with Helen Yanacopulos and will be published as an article in *Geoforum* (Murphy and Yanacopulos, 2005). Material in Chapters 4, 5 and 7 was developed with Susan Carr and related articles will be published in *Social Studies of Science* (Murphy et al., 2006) and *Science, Technology and Human Values* (Levidow et al., forthcoming). In addition, Chapters 6 and 7 draw on work done with Joanne Chataway (Murphy and Chataway, 2005). Special thanks to various anonymous reviewers and editors of related publications, particularly Jenny Robinson, Michael Lynch, Ulrike Felt, Catherine Lyall and Joyce Tait.

Finally, we would like to thank all of the people who facilitated our research along the way. This book draws on interviews with over 50 policy makers, industry employees, regulatory officials and NGO campaigners. These were conducted between 1998 and 2005. The more recent ones in particular gave us valuable insights into the regulation of agricultural biotechnology and how this has been shaped by interactions between the European Union and the United States. We are very grateful for the time and support that interviewees have given and acknowledge that this book would not have been possible without it. Thanks also to Sarah Parry,

Marlene Gordon and Eileen Mothersole for reviewing chapters, providing administrative support and transcribing interviews. None of the people mentioned, however, are responsible for any errors that may be found in the following pages.

Abbreviations

ABPC	AgBiotech Planning Committee
ABSTC	Agricultural Biotechnology Stewardship Technical Committee
ACF	Advocacy Coalition Framework
ACGA	American Corn Growers Association
ACNFP	Advisory Committee on Novel Foods and Processes
AIA	Advanced Informed Agreement
APHIS	Animal and Plant Health Inspection Service
BEUC	Bureau Europ en des Unions de Consommateurs
BIO	Biotechnology Industry Organization
BSE	Bovine Spongiform Encephalopathy (degenerative brain disease in cattle)
Bt	*Bacillus thuringiensis* (toxin-producing bacterium)
BWG	Biotechnology Working Group
CAC	Codex Alimentarius Commission (also Codex)
CCGP	Codex Committee on General Principles
CEC	Commission of the European Communities
COC	Council on Competitiveness
CGG	Commission on Global Governance
CI	Consumers International
DCF	Discourse Coalition Framework
DDT	dichloro-diphenyl-trichloroethane (a pesticide)
DG	Directorate General
DNA	deoxyribonucleic acid (genetic information in cells)
EC	European Commission (sometimes European Community) (see also CEC)
ECJ	European Court of Justice
EEC	European Economic Community
EPA	Environmental Protection Agency
EU	European Union
EuropaBio	European Association for Bioindustries
FAO	Food and Agriculture Organization
FDA	Food and Drug Administration

FIFRA	Federal Insecticide, Fungicide, and Rodenticide Act
FoEE	Friends of the Earth Europe
G7/8	group of the world's richest countries
GATT	General Agreement on Tariffs and Trade
GM	genetically modified
GMO	genetically modified organism
ILSI	International Life Sciences Institute
IRM	Insect Resistance Management
ISO	International Organization for Standardization
LMO	living modified organism
MEP	Member of the European Parliament
NAFTA	North American Free Trade Agreement
NCGA	National Corn Growers Association
NRC	National Research Council
NTA	New Transatlantic Agenda
NTM	New Transatlantic Marketplace
NGO	non-governmental organisation
OECD	Organization for Economic Cooperation and Development
OSTP	Office of Science and Technology Policy
PIPs	Plant-Incorporated Protectants
PP	precautionary principle
RRI	Rowett Research Institute
SAP	Scientific Advisory Panel
SCF	Scientific Committee on Food
SCP	Scientific Committee on Plants
SPS	Agreement on Sanitary and Phytosanitary Measures
SS	sound science
StCF	Standing Committee on Foodstuffs
TABD	Transatlantic Business Dialogue
TACD	Transatlantic Consumer Dialogue
TAED	Transatlantic Environmental Dialogue
TAFTA	Transatlantic Free Trade Association
TBT	Agreement on Technical Barriers to Trade
TEP	Transatlantic Economic Partnership
TNC	transnational corporation
TRIPS	Agreement on Trade-Related Aspects of Intellectual Property Rights
UK	United Kingdom
UN	United Nations
UNCBD	United Nations Convention on Biological Diversity
UCS	Union of Concerned Scientists
US	United States
USDA	United States Department of Agriculture
USTR	Office of the United States Trade Representative

WHO	World Health Organization
WSJ	*Wall Street Journal*
WTO	World Trade Organization

Introduction

Introduction

In the late 1990s the European agri-food system was thrown into disarray by widespread public protests against genetically modified (GM) crops and foods. These protests led large food retailers to remove GM ingredients from their own-brand products. In 1999, in an effort to regain control, EU politicians imposed an unofficial *de facto* moratorium on the approval of new biotechnology products. They made it clear that this moratorium would remain in place until new and revised legislation restored public confidence. In the months and years that followed, however, the US continued to approve and commercialise new GM crops and foods and a regulatory gap opened up; products that were approved in the US could not be sold in the EU. Transatlantic trade was soon disrupted and in 2003 the US finally took a case to the World Trade Organization. This gave the WTO one of its most high-profile and politically difficult disputes.

Not surprisingly, the transatlantic conflict over biotechnology products has attracted the attention of many analysts and commentators. In their efforts to explain the dispute, most have identified, compared and contrasted internal characteristics of the EU and the US. These, they claim, explain why GM products were received differently in Europe and America and why regulatory frameworks diverged. For example, some claim that the origin of the dispute can be found in the fact that US regulation of GM products is based on 'sound science' while EU policy makers apply the 'precautionary principle'. (This account has been extended in partisan and simplistic ways: for example, the argument that the US approach to regulation focuses on risk issues and is rational and fair, while the EU's includes non-risk issues, accommodates politics and is irrational.)

Many comparative accounts have given us valuable insights into the transatlantic conflict over biotechnology products, but they have also neglected and obscured key characteristics. Most importantly, by treating each jurisdiction as a separate unit of analysis, and by focusing on 'endogenous' characteristics, they have neglected inter-jurisdictional dynamics. In practice, given sharp conflicts *within* the EU and the US, many policy actors have explored the extent to which they share a policy agenda with others *across* the Atlantic. Thus competing policy agendas are associated with contending transatlantic networks, alliances or coalitions, and they do not map onto a conflict between the US and the EU in a simple way, if at all. Such transatlantic interactions have also helped to shape intra-jurisdictional conflicts.

In this book we address some of the weaknesses and gaps in earlier research, by examining EU–US interactions and intra-jurisdictional conflicts and how these have been linked. We focus on how these dynamics have helped to shape regulatory frameworks and standards for biotechnology products in both jurisdictions. We avoid taking a comparative approach to the transatlantic conflict. And the EU and the US are not presented as places where an unlikely consensus around agricultural biotechnology has already emerged. The EU–US conflict is understood instead through transatlantic coalitions of policy actors who have been contending with each other in an effort to influence the policy agenda and standard-setting processes. The next section shows that these dynamics were present at the start of the EU–US conflict over agricultural biotechnology.

The origins of the EU–US conflict: transatlantic trade in biotechnology products

In 1996 soybeans became synonymous with the power of the US to impose GM food on Europe. In that year US farmers were already growing a GM soybean developed by Monsanto and policy actors in Europe were anticipating its arrival in mixed shipments from the US. These shipments would have been illegal unless the new variety was approved in advance under the EU's 1990 Deliberate Release Directive. During the approval procedure, however, some NGOs (non-governmental organisations) demanded that GM foods should be labelled so that consumers could decide for themselves whether or not to buy processed foods containing GM soya. In response the European Commission (EC) argued that it did not have the authority to require labelling for any purpose other than risk management. The safety of the product concerned was not being questioned and consequently most Commissioners (and member states) opposed labelling on the grounds that it could not be justified scientifically. The Monsanto GTS 40-3-2 soybean was approved for import and processing on 3 April 1996.

Conflicts over GM products intensified further with pressure to approve Ciba-Geigy's *Bt*-176 maize. The EC met on 13 November 1996 to discuss approval of this product, the day after Greenpeace had demonstrated at the port of Hamburg against shipments of GM soybeans. Under EU law, because the EU Council had failed to reach a decision on this product, the EC could approve *Bt*-176 maize itself. When the moment came, however, the Commissioners could not agree. Leon Brittan, a strong advocate of transatlantic trade liberalisation, argued that indecision in Brussels might anger Washington. Others successfully argued for a delay and the Commissioners decided to wait for the opinions of three EU-level scientific committees. The meeting also discussed whether approval should include a labelling requirement. Two Commissioners, Leon Brittan and Martin Bangemann, opposed mandatory labelling. They argued that it might be illegal under international trade rules and could draw the EU into a trade dispute at the WTO (Rich, 1997: 8).

To some extent the procedural delay over *Bt*-176 maize accommodated consumer groups. The consumer lobby had gained more political influence following the BSE scandal; politicians were keen to reassure consumers. In early December 1996 the UK's Environment Minister John Gummer robustly reassured everyone concerned about US maize shipments. He stated that they would not be permitted in the EU without prior approval of the GM maize they might contain and he linked this implicitly to the question of sovereignty:

> It is true that the Americans are trying to force this onto Europe without us making up our own minds about it. . . . One of the important reasons for the EU is that we are strong enough to say to the Americans that 'We decide what we want in our food chain and not you'.
>
> (ENDS, 1997: 41)

The problem that was emerging at this time is confirmed by the fact that in late November 1996 the EC warned national authorities that US maize shipments might contain GM maize not authorised for sale in the EU. They instructed them to hold these shipments at European ports until a regulatory decision was taken.

At this time the media began to cover the GM debate in more detail. Amongst other issues they focused on risks to human health and the environment, and they drew attention to disagreements amongst experts. For example, in relation to Ciba-Geigy's maize, the EU's Scientific Committee for Food advised the EC on 13 December 1997 that 'The possibility that the product would add significantly to the already widespread occurrence of ampicillin resistance bacteria in animals and man is remote' (SCF, 1997: 25). The UK's food safety committee, however, had opposed approval of *Bt*-176 maize on this basis. According to one member of that committee, speaking at the time, and quoted in the popular science journal *New Scientist*, 'No one has yet looked at the effect of feeding a gene to lots of animals, day in and day out for years' (Cohen, 1997: 8). Some experts were concerned that the antibiotic-resistance gene in the *Bt*-176 maize might enter pathogenic microbes and jeopardise the clinical use of the corresponding antibiotic.

The EU system denied any possible risks associated with this product. The EU's Scientific Committee for Food had already rejected safety concerns about antibiotic resistance. Likewise, the Environment Commissioner, Ritt Bjerregaard, as the Commissioner responsible for the EU's Deliberate Release Directive, dismissed all the safety concerns: 'The scientific advice provided a sufficiently strong basis to go ahead and approve this product' (cited in Bates, 1996). Greenpeace anticipated a decision to approve the product and threatened to mount a legal challenge.

On 23 January 1997 the EC approved Ciba-Geigy's *Bt*-176 maize, despite opposition from all EU member states except the French rapporteur (CEC, 1997a). The Environment Commissioner supported approval. Her colleague said on the day, 'We have awaited the scientific opinions for six months and now it is difficult for us not to accept them' (Rich, 1997: 8). Bjerregaard also made a public statement in which she attempted to refute the various risk arguments. These had been restated recently by the Bureau Europ en des Unions de Consommateurs (BEUC) in a letter to the EC. In this letter BEUC identified several risks that had already been raised by some member states as a basis on which to oppose approval. The Commissioner also tried to deflect demands for product labelling by arguing that existing laws did not allow the EC to require it, although a new law soon would.

Soon after the approval of *Bt*-176 maize, disagreements within the EC were revealed by leaked minutes. The minutes showed that when the decision was actually taken, US maize shipments were creating a strong pressure on the EU to grant approval as quickly as possible; the product potentially made up 0.6 per cent of those shipments. Some European Commissioners were anticipating a compensation claim from the US if they failed to authorise the maize. However, the Consumer Affairs Commissioner, Emma Bonino, expressed regret that the approval decision was responding to economic pressures of this kind. She believed that the EC should reflect on consumer concerns and their desire for transparency. Mentioning the BSE crisis, Commissioner Neil Kinnock said that consumer confidence must be re-established. He pointed out that maize is widely used and that GM maize would be difficult to identify in derived products (Rich, 1997: 1, 8).

The EC's decision to approve *Bt*-176 maize was attacked in various ways by different critics. Its minutes were leaked to the Belgian newspaper *Le Soir* and reported with the headline 'After mad cow, recidivism with transgenic maize' (Rich, 1997: 1). One Green MEP (Member of the European Parliament) claimed, 'Despite mad cow, they have learned nothing!' The Pesticides Action Network argued, 'This is crazy. They have started a gigantic experiment with us as the guinea pigs' (Rich, 1997: 8). In this way the EC was criticised for favouring market pressure over safety. In the same vein, in April 1997 the European Parliament voted overwhelming to denounce the EC for its approval decision. MEPs criticised the EC specifically for prioritising commercial considerations. An EC statement rejected the criticisms, and, moreover, Commissioner Bjerregaard claimed that the approval of a GM product could not be withdrawn unless the scientific committees involved changed their opinions (Agence Europe, 1997).

These developments were part of the context for the unprecedented backlash against agricultural biotechnology in Europe during the late 1990s. A range of small opposition groups from around Europe took the initiative, for example Gen-ethisches Netzwerk in Germany, NOAH in Denmark, Genetics Forum in the UK, Ecoropa in France, Global 2000 in Austria. They linked GM food with a wide variety of issues, including unknown risks to the environment and human health, corporate control of the food chain, globalisation and threats to sovereignty and democracy. Such arguments were taken up by the mass media and mainstream NGOs, particularly environment, consumer and development groups. Some started to organise consumer boycotts, as a way to 'vote' against GM food, implying that conventional forms of democracy had failed in this case. Large European food retailers had initially accepted the grain exporters' claim that it would be impossible to segregate GM and non-GM products, but by 1999 these retailers accommodated the protests by finding non-GM sources of soybeans. These sources allowed them to keep their own-brand products 'non-GM' (Levidow and Bijman, 2002).

Regulatory blockages and the intensification of conflict

By the late 1990s agricultural biotechnology was a highly controversial issue across Europe. Arguments for and against the technology were taking place far beyond the relatively well-defined areas of risk and product labelling. It became clear that public protest undermined the legitimacy of product approvals, particularly in EU member states like the UK and France. In the view of some industrialists, the governments had lost control of the issue.

In this context some governments began to ban GM products that had already been approved at the EU level. This was a serious development for the EU, not least because it struck at the heart of the EU ideal of a single European market – trade liberalisation within the EU. Other countries had greater difficulty justifying why they were continuing to support the commercial use of GM crops and foods. As EU regulatory procedures became more controversial, industry diagnosed a governance problem: 'The old regulations are not really working well. The system is stuck, and this is not how it is meant to be', stated EuropaBio, the European trade association for the biotechnology industry (cited in Hodgson, 1999).

In June 1999 a group of politicians in the EU's Environment Council agreed to block the regulatory procedure for GM products. Many of them signed one of two similar statements, making it known that they would not consider additional GM crops or foods for approval until the EU had made significant changes to its regulatory framework in order to address various weaknesses. To justify this move they cited 'the need to restore public and market confidence' (FoEE, 1999). Together these statements became known as the EU's unofficial *de facto* moratorium. It was an agreement not to consider further products for approval. This was possible because a minority of countries could prevent the 2/3 majority needed in the Environment

Council for straightforward approval of a product. The EC still had the legal authority to approve products, after a period of time, if the European Council failed to do so, and in previous cases it had done so. However, after the European Parliament denounced it in 1998, and the members of the EU's Environment Council signed their statements in 1999, it was clear that doing so again could make the situation worse.

In their statements the members of the EU Environment Council listed the changes to the existing regulatory framework that they believed were necessary. Support for these changes – amongst politicians, officials and NGOs – had been growing for some time. The list included applying precaution as the basis of risk assessment, and traceability and labelling of all GM products and derived products. Some member states added further conditions later, including liability legislation (possibly with mandatory insurance) to make producers financially responsible for future adverse effects, and rules for segregating GM from non-GM crops during cultivation. In addition, although the EC had argued that existing law provided no authority for such a requirement, some member states were already demanding post-market monitoring, particularly where there were uncertainties about risks. These developments set in motion regulatory divergence across the Atlantic and in time all these demands were accommodated in European legislation to some extent.

Meanwhile, as the list of products waiting for approval grew longer, the trade conflict with the United States intensified. Given the delays associated with the EU product approval procedure, US farmers were cultivating more and more varieties that were approved in the US but not in the EU. As a result, by the late 1990s, US maize shipments plausibly contained approximately 0.6 per cent GM maize that could not legally be sold in the EU. Before 1997 the US exported 1.75 million tons of maize to Spain and Portugal annually. This amount filled a tariff-free quota agreed when Spain and Portugal joined the EU. Before the conflict this represented 4 per cent of total US corn exports. However, following the EU *de facto* moratorium, this figure dropped to less than 0.1 per cent in 2002 (Pew, 2003a). The US stopped exporting maize to Spain and Portugal because shipments might contain 'illegal' varieties. Or, if you are on the other side of the argument, Spain and Portugal stopped importing maize from the US. Estimates suggest that US exporters lost between $200 and $300 million per year in maize exports to the EU from the late 1990s onwards.

In time the trade conflict encouraged new transatlantic networks to emerge and become involved in the issue. In many cases their agendas challenged those of the transatlantic networks that had promoted regulatory harmonisation and transatlantic trade in GM products earlier in the 1990s. Earlier in the 1990s the Transatlantic Business Dialogue, a transatlantic network of businesses trading across the Atlantic, had argued for 'approved once, accepted everywhere'. In the late 1990s the Transatlantic Consumer Dialogue, a recently established network of consumer groups, argued for stricter regulation in both jurisdictions and for the 'right to know, right to choose' in relation to GM foods. Another sceptical voice was the American Corn Growers Association. This group questioned the benefits of GM maize, and representatives visited European organisations of small-scale farmers who held a similar view. Its position was an alternative to the one adopted by the US National Corn Growers Association, which represented larger producers. Jose Bov , the controversial French farmer and anti-globalisation campaigner, went on a speaking tour in the US and gave speeches at rallies during the ill-fated WTO meeting in Seattle in 1999.

By the time the new century dawned, biotechnology products had joined an increasingly long list of products that were causing problems for the world's largest trade relationship. Other products on the list included beef, steel and bananas. US politicians and officials criticised the EU in increasingly strident terms, especially after the election of President George Bush. US officials argued that there was no sign that the EU was ever going to lift the moratorium, which was either irrational or protectionist. The EC responded by arguing that new EU legislation, such as that which would create a traceability and labelling regime to facilitate consumer choice, was the key to unblocking the European approvals process. In practice this argument did very little to reassure advocates of biotechnology in the US. They anticipated more barriers to trade as a result of new EU rules on traceability and labelling of GM products. In addition, even representatives of the EC, such as Environment Commissioner Margot Wallstr m, raised the possibility that member states would 'move the goalposts' when new rules were in place (AgraFood Biotech, 2002).

In 2003, after nearly five years of tension and threats, the US government finally led a multi-country complaint to the World Trade Organization regarding EU regulation of biotechnology products. The US case focused on delays in the EU approval process, despite positive assessment by EU-level scientific committees, and member-state bans on products already approved at the EU level. Some argued that this action was the only way to restore transatlantic trade but there were other motives as well. One of the most important was the desire to discourage other countries from restricting agricultural biotechnology by adopting the EU's increasingly demanding approach to regulating the technology. The US government also indicated that it was time to challenge the EU's tendency to restrict trade for reasons that were not based on science (ENDS, 2003). In response to the WTO complaint, important US NGOs denounced their own government. Several of them also made links across the Atlantic to submit *amicus curia* – friends of the court – briefs in which they argued how the WTO should judge the case. The WTO itself was placed in the position of having to judge a case that it had hoped would never come before it, at a time when it was suffering from legitimacy problems of its own.

The EU–US conflict: comparative approaches and their limitations

This outline of key events draws our attention to important and related aspects of the conflict over biotechnology products. First, although transatlantic conflict and trade barriers have attracted the most attention, there are also examples of transatlantic cooperation and consensus amongst policy actors. The Transatlantic Business Dialogue and the Transatlantic Consumer Dialogue are good examples of this. Second, although there is a tendency to stereotype the EU and the US, and to imply that a consensus has emerged in each one, in practice we see intra-jurisdictional conflicts as well as transatlantic conflict. This is seen in disputes between EU-level institutions and between governments and NGOs. In this book we explore the relationship between these two aspects and how they have shaped the regulation of agbiotech products. This focus is important because existing research on the regulation of GM crops and foods in the US and the EU does not draw attention to these influences. We will illustrate this point by briefly reviewing recent work by Grant Isaac (2002), Thomas Bernauer (2003), David Toke (2004) and Sheila Jasanoff (2005).

Isaac (2002) is concerned about regulatory divergence and its implications for international political and economic integration. Increasingly, he argues, it is possible to identify examples of 'regulatory regionalism', whereby regulations in different places are underpinned by different 'rationalities'. He also argues that it is beyond the means of trade diplomacy, as it currently operates, to overcome these differences. In relation to the EU–US conflict over GM crops he concludes:

> It has been shown that the domestic regulatory approach for GM crops is, in fact, a function of endogenous political-economy factors. These include various interests and events, along with the traditional regulatory role of the state and the competitiveness of the jurisdiction in respect of the particular regulatory issue. While there is a transatlantic consensus that the risk-analysis framework is the most appropriate framework for developing GM-crop regulations, there are divergent views on how to implement the risk-analysis framework properly.
>
> (Isaac, 2002: 251)

In this quote Isaac makes it clear that US–EU regulatory differences arise from domestic influences on policy processes, that is 'endogenous political-economy factors', and he assumes that these jurisdictions can be treated separately in this regard.

Bernauer (2003) focuses on the problem of 'regulatory polarisation', a concept that echoes Isaac's 'regulatory regionalism'. He argues that such polarisation underlies the transatlantic conflict where we see 'An increasing gap . . . between agri-biotech promoting and agri-biotech restricting countries, both in terms of approval and labelling regulation and at the market level'

(2003: 8). Bernauer argues that the current US–EU conflict is one outcome of this polarisation. To explain its origins he argues against simplistic analysis of 'regulatory culture' and the use of stereotypes. He also dismisses explanations that focus on technophobia or protectionism in Europe. Instead, in his own explanation of the case, he focuses on two dynamics: the struggle of interest groups for political and market influence; and the interactions between sub-political units within the EU and the US and their ability to influence regulatory frameworks at the higher level. In relation to these processes, Bernauer states:

> In the European Union, both processes have worked in ways that have driven agri-biotech regulation towards greater stringency. In the United States, they have worked in ways that have sustained agri-biotech promoting regulation.
>
> (Bernauer, 2003: 10)

David Toke (2004) uses discourse analysis to compare the regulatory systems of the US, the UK and the EU in the area of agricultural biotechnology. He focuses on the relationship between risk assessment and cultural attitudes in each jurisdiction, as a basis on which to explain transatlantic differences and conflicts. He argues that in the US the dominant policy framework viewed agricultural biotechnology as a more precise extension of traditional plant breeding and on this basis minimised any special regulation. This policy frame marginalised more cautious perspectives, of the kind which eventually became mainstream in the EU policy framework. In his account, Toke identifies the 1996–97 conflict over Ciba-Geigy's *Bt*-176 maize as a turning point. As described above, this approval decision was widely attacked by European critics, who drew analogies to the BSE scandal. After this event, various US–EU interactions further polarised the two jurisdictions; both sides accused each other of prioritising commercial objectives over scientific evidence. Like Bernauer, Toke also draws attention to intra-jurisdictional conflicts, for example US industry divisions over pharmaceutical crops and the threat they might pose for the corn market, and EU regulatory conflicts over approval of GM products.

Finally, Sheila Jasanoff (2005) analyses biotechnology policy to inform a discussion of democracy. She explores agricultural biotechnology as one of several related technologies, as an entry point to examine policy in the US, the EU and some member states. According to her analysis, 'Democratic engagement with biotechnology was shaped and constrained by national approaches to representation, participation, and deliberation that selectively delimited who spoke for people and issues, how those issues were framed, and how far they were actively reflected upon in official processes of policy-making' (Jasanoff, 2005: 287). In each country, she argues, institutional boundary work demarcated some issues as being separate from ordinary politics. This rendered them invisible or designated them as appropriate only for expert analysis. She also analyses extra-democratic sources of authority and how they vary across countries. Although her book does not emphasise the late 1990s transatlantic conflict, it appears to arise from jurisdictional divergences in the framing of biotechnological innovation and risk. Divergence itself is explained largely in relation to the domestic characteristics of countries, which in broad terms can be understood as political culture.

These brief accounts indicate how diverse the existing studies of the regulation of biotechnology in the EU and the US are. Isaac's interest in trade theory and diplomacy, for example, can be contrasted with Toke's focus on the link between discourse and policy, as well as with Jasanoff's interest in democracy and the boundary that is drawn around expert issues. Each account adds to our understanding of the case in different ways. Bernauer and Toke draw our attention to some important intra-jurisdictional conflicts. Toke and Jasanoff highlight the role that issue-framing can play in shaping regulation and risk assessment. Isaac's analysis draws attention to the different 'rationalities' explicit and implicit in different international agreements. We will return to each of these contributions at various points, but for now we will note their limitations in order to clarify the contribution we make in the following chapters.

Perhaps the most significant gap in the existing literature is that it neglects transatlantic interactions and coalitions, and particularly their role in generating the transatlantic conflict. By exploring transatlantic interactions we can identify extra dynamics and cast a new light on issues that others have already raised primarily from a jurisdictional and comparative standpoint. Starting in the mid-1990s we will highlight cooperative interactions between businesses, politicians and policy makers in the EU and the US around their shared agenda of regulatory harmonisation and trade liberalisation. From the late 1990s we will highlight cooperative transatlantic interactions involving NGOs and critical scientists. We use the transatlantic conflict, therefore, to explore competing policy agendas but do not assume that those agendas can be mapped onto the EU or the US or that this conflict should be understood primarily as one between these jurisdictions. By focusing on interactions we complement research that takes a largely comparative approach.

In other accounts, then, EU–US regulatory divergence and conflict are explained largely in relation to domestic factors. In the chapters that follow, we challenge such explanations as incomplete and even misleading. We argue instead that transatlantic regulatory divergence occurred because of interactions between the EU and the US and the way such interactions were linked to intra-jurisdictional conflicts.

The arguments and structure of this book

This book analyses the EU–US conflict over agricultural biotechnology as a way to study 'global governance'. At the transatlantic scale, contending coalitions framed the new technology and defined policy problems in different ways. These framings and definitions had implications for regulatory frameworks, standard setting and government legitimacy. As the two jurisdictions diverged, the EU and the US then presented different regulatory models to countries around the world. This raised the stakes associated with transatlantic regulatory differences and required the EU and the US to develop governance strategies at the global level. For our purposes, therefore, analytical perspectives on 'global governance' can be explored through the transatlantic dynamics associated with this dispute. We do this particularly by analysing policy coalitions and their interactions, both within and across jurisdictions.

We believe that our analysis has important implications for policy but we do not make policy recommendations. Instead we try to show how all policy actors and agendas favour certain ways of framing the issue and certain accounts of the problem to be solved. In this way they influence what is understood as a solution and what policy and regulatory interventions are thought to be necessary. Issue-framing and the definitions of collective problems are therefore central concerns for policy making. We also emphasise the need for a critical understanding of such processes and their role in conflict. Most importantly, global governance can be understood as a process of redefining the collective problem as a way of dealing with conflict. A new collective problem can include some policy actors in the policy process whilst at the same time marginalising others.

The transatlantic conflict over biotechnology products began in the late 1990s and was ongoing as we completed this book (March 2006). In order to understand this conflict, Chapters 2–6 describe developments from the mid-1980s onwards. Thus, although we focus on the period from the mid-1990s onwards, we are interested in EU–US interactions and intra-jurisdictional dynamics over a period of 20 years. To help us analyse the complex transatlantic dynamics involved and draw out links across chapters, we focus on four narrative questions:

- How did policy actors try to advance particular policy agendas?
- How were expertise and knowledge used to influence policy making?
- How were regulatory standard-setting processes and trade conflict linked?
- How were EU–US interactions and intra-jurisdictional conflicts linked?

These questions have two main roles. They are the starting point from which we develop theoretical concepts and pose questions in Chapter 1. They also focus our preliminary analysis in the conclusions to Chapters 2–6.

The main theoretical perspectives of this book are developed in Chapter 1 – 'Global governance of new technologies'. Critical accounts of 'global governance' suggest that it is a way of dealing with legitimacy problems that arise with a specific form of political-economic globalisation. Central to this process is the definition of 'collective problems', or the identification of problems as collective ones. To elaborate this argument, we focus on the role that 'issue framing' plays in policy-making and how issue-frames bind policy actors together in coalitions and underpin their engagement with policy processes. Building on these arguments we examine the relationship between trade liberalisation and regulatory standards, a key issue in globalisation debates. To do this we discuss standard-setting through regulatory harmonisation and judicial review. More specifically we explore the concept of 'trading up', which suggests that trade liberalisation can lead to the adoption of higher regulatory standards in some circumstances. In the final section of this chapter we examine regulatory science. Here we focus particularly on understanding how the boundary between science and policy is contested and shifted, and the relationship between the content and context regulatory science. A table in the conclusion gives the book's overarching issues, analytical perspectives and pertinent questions.

Chapter 2 – 'Approved once, accepted everywhere' – is the book's first empirical chapter. In it we focus on EU–US networks of policy actors involved in transatlantic trade liberalisation and their efforts to shape the regulation of GM products from the mid-1990s onwards. The 1995 New Transatlantic Agenda (NTA) promoted trade liberalisation between the EU and the US and created a policy context for these networks. Against this background we examine two complementary networks and their involvement in agricultural biotechnology. The Transatlantic Business Dialogue (TABD) is a network of businesses that trade across the Atlantic and the Transatlantic Economic Partnership (TEP) is a network organised by US and EU trade officials. These networks identified 'barriers to transatlantic trade' as their collective problem, thus creating a transatlantic coalition of policy actors that included businesses, politicians and policy officials. Coalition members framed agricultural biotechnology along similar lines and shared frames helped to cement relationships across the Atlantic. However, the basis of this transatlantic coalition in the GM products area was undermined by developments in the late 1990s, such as the public backlash against GM crops and foods in Europe, the commercial and political response to this, and controversies around new biotechnology products. These difficulties led to fractures in the transatlantic coalition and to a new US coalition largely based at the domestic level.

Chapter 3 – 'Right to know, right to choose' – focuses on transatlantic civil society and expert networks. In the late 1990s, critics of the NTA argued that EU–US trade liberalisation was being pursued in the interests of business and without sufficient concern for consumer or environmental protection. These arguments were applied specifically to biotechnology products. Such criticism led to the creation of the Transatlantic Consumer Dialogue (TACD) and the Transatlantic Environmental Dialogue (TAED), as civil society counterparts to the TABD. Consumer groups in the US and the EU were able to build a transatlantic coalition around a shared frame of 'consumer rights'. This gave TACD members a common basis on which to intervene in policy, while also helping them to ignore or downplay differences of opinion on other issues. For GM food, members of this coalition emphasised the 'right to know, right to choose'. This was particularly effective in Europe, where reframing by consumer groups played a central role in the move towards traceability and labelling legislation. In practice this policy change addressed a new collective problem of 'restoring public/ consumer/market confidence'. Environmental groups, in contrast, operated within the TAED for only a short period. They had more profound concerns about transatlantic trade liberalisation and more difficulty in identifying the basis of a coalition across the Atlantic. The EU–US Consultative Forum on Biotechnology was formed later as a multi-stakeholder group to find ways beyond the transatlantic conflict over agricultural biotechnology. As a governance process it could help to overcome legitimacy problems by incorporating some policy actors whilst marginalising others.

In Chapter 4 – 'Environmental risks of GM crops' – we explore the relationship between regulatory standards and regulatory context for the case of *Bt* maize. This crop produces an insect toxin and it was expected to replace agrichemical sprays and bring about environmental improvements as a result. Regulators in the EU and the US approved commercial cultivation on this basis. In the mid- to late 1990s, however, controversy arose in relation to two environmental risks: non-target harm and insect resistance to the toxin. In the context of this controversy regulatory assumptions and standards were challenged. Normative judgements were opened up for further negotiation and optimistic assumptions about risk were turned into questions requiring further research. Different transatlantic networks of scientists sought to highlight or downplay the risks involved. European scientists played a significant transatlantic role by challenging the basis on which US regulators had approved *Bt* maize. Citing various criticisms raised by them, US NGOs successfully pressed the US regulatory system for significant changes in expert advisory bodies and regulatory standards. Ultimately the EU–US trade conflict added an additional element to the context and provided further pressure for regulatory changes. The case of *Bt* maize shows that transatlantic interactions have been an important resource in intrajurisdictional conflicts and that both the US and EU generally moved towards more stringent standards for risk assessment and management.

Chapter 5 – 'Health risks of GM foods' – focuses on the risk assessment and regulation of GM foods and the concept of 'substantial equivalence'. In the early 1990s an OECD expert consultation recommended that substantial equivalence could underpin the risk assessment of GM foods. By the mid-1990s this concept had been incorporated into EU and US regulatory frameworks, thus serving their shared policy agenda of establishing a harmonised regulatory framework across the Atlantic. The process of agreeing and implementing substantial equivalence involved efforts to depoliticise GM food through science, for example by downplaying uncertainties and casting various questions as purely scientific ones. However, substantial equivalence was criticised from the outset by some scientists and NGOs, and their criticisms gained greater prominence with the public backlash against GM food in Europe. This stimulated a 'scientification' process as policy makers became more dependent on science to defend their policy choices. At the same time, however, the science involved was increasingly open to conflicting interpretations. Ultimately the public-scientific controversy around GM food broke the earlier link between science and policy. In response, the concept of substantial equivalence was recast to accommodate criticisms, which pre-dated the conflict, and to address scientific weaknesses. The negotiations of the Codex Alimentarius Commission were particularly important as was the role played by consumer groups. Thus the 'science/policy boundary' was contested and shifted in association with a new policy agenda.

In Chapter 6 – 'The WTO agbiotech dispute as a global contest' – we examine EU–US interactions in relation to the World Trade Organization. In the mid-1990s the dispute over hormone-treated beef became a test case for interpreting the WTO Agreement on Sanitary and Phytosanitary (SPS) Measures. Although the EU lost the case, the judgement left scope for the EU to justify trade restrictions in future cases. From the late 1990s onwards various developments added momentum towards a formal WTO dispute over biotechnology products and this process began in 2003. The second half of the chapter examines EU and US strategies in the WTO dispute over biotechnology products. In their submissions to the WTO, the complainants and the defendant (EU) disagreed over the basis of the dispute, in particular: whether applications to market GM products in the EU had faced 'undue delays'; whether the EU had a '*de facto* moratorium' in place; whether official EU-level expert advice provided an adequate basis on which to approve prod-ucts in the late 1990s and thus a basis for judging the WTO dispute; and whether the Dispute Panel needed its own expert advice. The EC tried to maximise its scope for discretion within WTO rules in various ways, for example by appealing to the Biosafety Protocol to justify long approval timescales, by framing EU regulatory procedures as a sovereignty issue and by warning that the WTO would encounter greater legitimacy problems if its judgement ignored scientific uncertainties. With these arguments the EC successfully persuaded the WTO to establish its own expert group and then cited disagreements amongst experts as evidence of scientific uncertainty. This provided a plausible defence for the slow/blocked approval process in the EU.

In Chapter 7 – 'Global governance of agricultural biotechnology' – we analyse the transatlantic trade conflict over agricultural biotechnology as a domestic, transatlantic and global governance process. We use the concepts and arguments introduced in Chapter 1. Each section answers the theory questions from the corresponding section in that chapter. Overall we show that governance in the case of GM crops and foods can be understood as a way of dealing with the legitimacy problems that accompany a particular – neoliberal – form of political-economic globalisation. In the late 1990s agricultural biotechnology became a technology to be contested for a variety of reasons including risks to health and the environment, but it also became a symbol of an ominous form of globalisation and its related problems and threats. Businesses and governments in Europe and America had pursued transatlantic trade liberalisation from the mid-1990s but civil society groups challenged this process and biotechnology products became a focus for the conflict. We examine the contending coalitions involved and how redefining the collective problem and making changes to regulatory standards helped to manage the conflict.

1   Global governance of new technologies

Introduction

The EU–US conflict over genetically modified crops and foods is a valuable opportunity to study the politics of a new technology. This opportunity exists because the conflict itself reveals practices and relationships that would otherwise remain hidden. Before the late 1990s, the regulation of biotechnology products took place in a relatively narrow world, involving a small number of experts. The backlash against the technology in Europe, however, changed that to a significant extent. It was followed by a commercial boycott and the *de facto* moratorium and a much wider range of actors engaged with the regulation of biotechnology products. Social scientists can exploit this opportunity. In this chapter we begin the process by developing concepts and arguments that we will use to analyse the case. We draw on a range of different social sciences, including International Relations, Political Science, Policy Studies and Sociology (Science and Technology Studies).

Our entry point for this chapter, and for the book as a whole, is the concept of 'global governance'. We explore the relationship between the state and society through this concept. In the first section we develop a critical understanding of global governance, focusing especially on how collective problems are defined. In the second section we focus on public policy and post-empiricist approaches to policy analysis. To explore post-empiricist accounts of public policy in detail we examine the relationship between issue-framing and stakeholder coalitions. The third section focuses on trade liberalisation, particularly the relationship between regulatory harmonisation and standard-setting, and the role of judicial review in the event of a trade dispute. In the final section we discuss regulatory strategies to manage technological risk, especially the role and shaping of regulatory science.

Global governance: civil society and collective problems

Hajer and Wagenaar (2003) observe that 'governance' is part of a new vocabulary in International Relations, Political Science and Policy Studies. They speculate that this might be explained by academic fashion but ultimately conclude otherwise. The use of this vocabulary, they argue, reflects actual changes in politics and policy making, from the late 1980s onwards, which are empirically observable:

> The new vocabulary seems to capture changes in both the nature and topography of politics. A new range of political practices has emerged between institutional layers of the state and between state institutions and societal organizations. The new language is rooted in an appreciation of the importance of these new political practices.
>
> (Hajer and Wagenaar, 2003: 1)

The concept of governance, more than any other, tries to capture these changes. In this book we are primarily interested in political practices at the international level, rather than those that exist within countries, so to begin we can ask: what are the analytical and policy meanings of 'global governance'?

Global governance: functionalist versus critical accounts

A valuable starting point is the use of global governance to refer to relations between governments at the international level. In practice, although there is no global government, legal authority and power have passed beyond the level of nation states. To a greater or lesser extent, the Organization for Economic Cooperation and Development, the United Nations and the World Trade Organization are all examples of this. These organisations, therefore, play a mediating role in the relations between states, and to account for them concepts like global or transnational governance are necessary (Lipschutz, 1996: 249). Interestingly, this use of global governance draws attention to the differences between political practices at the national level compared to those at the international level. At the national level, governments do exist, and to some extent decisions can still be taken and implemented based on their authority alone. At the international level, however, there is no authoritative global government. This suggests that cooperation between governments, rather than a superior political authority, is needed to solve common problems.

Beyond purely inter-governmental relations, global governance is also used to refer to the inclusion of transnational non-state actors in international decision-making processes (e.g. Young, 1997: 284). The actors involved can be from the private sector or civil society. When the concept of global governance is used in this way it begins to resemble the most common use of the concept of governance at the national level – diverse actors making policy in complex networks. Global governance in this sense is often defined in a procedural way. It refers to the establishment and operation of rules and institutions, which define responsibilities and manage cooperation between international policy actors, so that a shared objective can be reached. Increasingly the concept of global governance denotes the involvement of transnational non-state actors in policy making, in addition to interactions between governments. This terminological usage is replacing the narrower use of the concept to denote only relations between states.

How can the emergence of governance, including global governance, be explained? Why has this concept become so widely used over the past decade? From a functionalist perspective governance can be understood as a response by governments to problems of overload and complexity (Raman, 2003). Governance, therefore, from an instrumental point of view, is the way that governments deal with an increasing number of responsibilities and novel problems. Given the focus of this book it is significant that Hajer and Wagenaar (2003: 3) note:

> It is probably no coincidence that these practices are more developed in 'new' spheres of politics such as the environment and the 'life politics' of food and technology.

A related view is that a key driving force behind governance is the poor performance of public policy in specific areas. It is argued, for example, that governance involves drawing more actors into the policy process because more perspectives on complex problems will produce better policies. From this perspective, global governance means reforming institutions and practices to make them more effective, while taking for granted the problem to be addressed. In relation to global environmental issues, Paterson has described this strategy as follows:

> . . . a programmatic, reformist orientation to the institutional arrangements in global politics, principally the UN system. . . . How to reform the UN machinery to deliver more effective environmental governance . . . [in such debates governance is] expressed in terms of concerns about the fragmentation of existing environmental agreements into different issue areas, lack of sufficient authority to enforce compliance, and local coordination of the various environmental governance mechanisms.
>
> (2003: 1–2)

Such functionalist accounts and agendas of global governance are a valuable starting point, but more critical accounts also exist. The latter focus on the legitimacy problems that some international organisations, and the governments who support them, began to experience in the 1990s. Some critics attribute these legitimacy problems to the pursuit of trade liberalisation and a neo-liberal form of political-economic globalisation. In her book *Naming the Enemy*, Amory Starr identifies this agenda as the enemy:

> Corporations are busy dismantling economic boundaries to their operations, busting open new markets (which may not require moving fixed assets), homogenising consumer tastes, and harmonising civic standards

downwards – while persuading citizens to interiorise their necessary flexibilisation, abandon social goals in pursuit of 'international competitiveness', and reorganise their human aspirations into something called 'consumer choice'.

(Starr, 2000: 7)

From this perspective, trade liberalisation and political-economic globalisation created a legitimacy crisis out of which emerged the concept of global governance. Evidence of the legitimacy crisis is found, of course, in the 'anti-globalisation' protests that have regulatory challenged meetings of the EU Council, WTO, World Bank, G7/8 and others. As some political scientists argue, 'economic globalisation and political change have created a crisis of the old hegemonic structures and forms of political consent, which are now coming apart . . . ' (Lipschutz, 1996: 55; citing Gill, 1993: 22–33).

This more critical understanding of global governance has been developed specially around environmental issues. From a political-economy perspective, global environmental governance

. . . can be seen as a product of two phenomena: the pursuit of neoliberal forms of globalization; and the resistance to such centralization of power . . . neoliberal globalization involves the centralization of power to a mix of public and private organizations such as transnational corporations (TNCs), the WTO, the G7, the International Organization for Standardization (ISO), or the World Economic Forum. Environmental questions are a key part of legitimizing such a project, with neoliberals keen to display their environmental credentials through organizations like the Business Council for Sustainable Development or via the promotion of innovative governance mechanisms such as emissions trading. But at the same time such governance is deeply problematic in environmental terms and is increasingly resisted across the world, in part because of such problematic aspects. There is thus also a 'governance from below' comprising both direct protests against institutions such as the World Bank or WTO, and the myriad of diverse activities by NGOs and social movements attempting to shape TNC practice and to regulate their power directly.

(Paterson et al., 2003: 2)

From a critical perspective on global governance, therefore, new political practices, such as participation in policy making and even the discourse of governance itself, express a legitimacy crisis. They also provide strategic ways to manage that crisis. In their governance role, states can influence the meanings of issues for non-state actors as well as their engagement with decision making. A state-like governance system can then include 'alliances between coalitions in global civil society and the international governance arrangements associated with the UN system' (Lipschutz, 1997: 96).

Based on this discussion we can say that social, political and economic developments at the global level in the 1990s created the context from which (global) governance could emerge as an analytical concept *and* a policy prescription. As an analytical concept it has been used in critical and uncritical ways, and as a policy prescription it offers a strategy to deal with problems of complexity and legitimacy. Protests against environmental destruction, Third World debt and loss of jobs, amongst other issues, have challenged a diverse range of policy actors. Governance has emerged as a way of understanding and dealing with this. As a result we have seen a rapid increase in references to governance in academic and policy documents, and international bodies and governments have consulted more and developed more participatory forms of decision making. In the following section we look at how global governance involves defining and redefining problems.

Global governance: the definition of collective problems

The legitimacy crisis being experienced by the WTO, World Bank, G7/8, OECD and more recently the European Union has created an opportunity for new transnational networks to form in an effort to influence global rules and institutions. Examples of global networks from the development arena include Jubilee 2000, Drop the Debt and Make Poverty History. New transnational networks like this can be rainbow coalitions; and they are often closely linked to international inter-governmental institutions (Lipschutz, 1997: 96). This proximity offers the opportunity to influence policy. At the same time, however, it also draws NGOs and others into a global governance process that they do not control. This opportunity, therefore, comes with political risks, which depend on how a governance process frames policy issues and structures stakeholder relations.

In the political-science literature, governance is often understood as co-operation to deal with collective problems. For example:

> . . . governance involves the establishment and operation of social institutions . . . capable of resolving conflicts, facilitating cooperation, or, more generally, alleviating collective-action problems in a world of interdependent actors.
>
> (Young, 1994: 15)

This focus on the role of collective-action problems, however, can easily lapse into naive functionalism. This would happen if we assume that such problems exist consensually and separately to the policy process.

In practice global governance processes frame collective-action problems in particular ways. As a result we must analyse the work involved in the definition of collective problems, or, perhaps more accurately, the definition of problems as collective ones. In practice some actors often seek to define 'the problem' before other stakeholders are involved. Consequently they may be incorporated into agendas which are not their own, or they may struggle to define collective problems differently, or pose different collective problems. These processes can increase conflict. From this perspective the process of defining problems as collective ones becomes a key concern for the analysis of global governance.

A useful starting point is 'process management', which indicates that problem-definitions can be expanded or changed through an interactive process involving different views. Young (1997: 286) has argued further that 'The idea of process management also helps us to grasp the role that regimes can play in deepening or even transforming our understanding of the problems that led to their creation'. Although this account describes inter-state relations, the concept of 'process management' can also encompass governance relations between the state and civil society. We explore related processes further below by focusing on the role of issue-framing in policy-making processes.

Global governance of agricultural biotechnology

Relatively little critical research has been done on the global (or trans-atlantic) governance of agricultural biotechnology. In broad terms this justifies our focus on it in this book. That said, before concluding this section we will outline some critical accounts of the global governance of agricultural biotechnology along the lines discussed above (Buttel, 2000; Newell, 2003). Newell addresses global governance explicitly while Buttel's contribution is relevant because he makes observations on the role of civil society in conflicts around globalisation and international economic integration. In Chapter 7 we will explore some of the points raised by these authors further.

Buttel (2000) tries to explain why the trajectory of agricultural biotechnology was undermined in the late 1990s. He begins by pointing out that by the mid- to late 1990s the scene was set for the widespread and rapid adoption of this technology. Various agreements of the World Trade Organization in particular were in place and suggested this would happen – for example, the agreements on Sanitary and Phytosanitary Measures, Technical Barriers to Trade and Trade Related Aspects of Intellectual Property Rights. Things did not, however, go smoothly. To explain this Buttel identifies agricultural biotechnology as the issue that bridged the gap between the specific concerns of various NGOs, particularly environmental groups, and their emerging and wider concern over trade liberalisation. With this in mind Buttel (2000: 1) wonders ' . . . whether GMOs might be the Achilles Heel of the globalization regime, or conversely whether the globalization regime is the Achilles Heel of GMOs'.

Buttel's argument has a theoretical underpinning – the concept of the 'globalization regime', a regime of accumulation which includes a food regime. He argues that the globalization regime

> ... consists of a set of institutions and regulations to govern the profitable movement of financial and industrial capital, as well as goods and services, across world borders. The basis of the coincidence of interest underlying the globalization regime is partly that of adherence to notions of the mutual benefits of trade through the economics of comparative advantage. But this coincidence of interest is based most fundamentally on several common or coincident interests of states, international financial institutions, multinational enterprises, and has led to the establishment of the World Trade Organization as well as regional trade blocs ... [However] it is apparent that the globalization regime has serious weaknesses that threaten its long-term future. Many of these weaknesses pertain to agriculture and agricultural biotechnology.
>
> (Buttel, 2000: 2)

This approach suggests that institutional and regulatory arrangements are explained by the need to create the conditions under which capital will accumulate. However, this theory also suggests that regimes of accumulation tend to make themselves vulnerable in various ways. In particular, Buttel identifies agricultural biotechnology as a weak link of the globalisation regime.

In the chapters that follow we will focus on the role of civil society in challenging institutions and regulatory frameworks rather than discussing the challenge to the globalisation regime more generally. As mentioned above, Buttel argues that concerns over agricultural biotechnology intersected with nascent concerns over trade liberalisation to create a potent basis for protest. It served to ' ... greatly expand the traditional anti-trade liberalization coalition ... ' (2000: 6). He argues that US environmental groups were particularly important in this process. By 1999 not a single major US environmental NGO publicly supported the WTO, and most were actively opposed. This was a significant shift from the early 1990s when only a minority opposed the creation of NAFTA, which had a similar agenda. This shift was stimulated partly by various WTO dispute judgements that appeared to undermine environmental or consumer protection. On this basis, agricultural biotechnology is described as 'a bridging issue' – something that is contested in itself and as a symbol of a wider policy agenda.

Newell (2003) also discusses the relationship between the governance of agricultural biotechnology and globalisation processes. He focuses on production, investment, regulation and political authority; he examines how 'global economic forces circumscribe the scope for effective environmental regulation in particular issue areas' (2003: 60). In relation to regulation of agricultural biotechnology, after critically discussing such controversial ideas and processes as sound science, substantial equivalence and regulatory harmonisation, he argues:

> The point here is not that the different regulatory forms have been hegemonically constructed in commercial terms. Clearly, in Europe

particularly, the role of NGOs has been key in contesting the benefits of biotechnology and providing support to a precautionary approach. But emphasizing commercial considerations [in the analysis] has provided an account of why some discourses of regulation are privileged, both at the national level and in activities of the principal international bodies. This privileging reflects both the salience of corporate strategic concerns, and their relationship to governments' own priorities, underscoring the importance of a political economy approach to understanding the governance of biotechnology.

(Newell, 2003: 65)

This important observation will be explored in the chapters that follow, by showing in detail how corporate strategic concerns and government priorities combined in relation to the trade in GM products.

In this section we have identified important concepts and arguments which we will explore further in the chapters that follow. First, we have established global governance as a concept that deals with conflicts over economic globalisation (in critical and uncritical ways). Such conflicts have undermined the legitimacy of a particular model of international integration and global governance can be understood as a response to this problem. Through the conflict over agricultural biotechnology we have an opportunity to study this further. We have also established that engagement with civil society around particular definitions of problems is central to global governance processes. It seems likely that we can use the conflict over agricultural biotechnology to explore the struggle to define a collective problem as the basis for collective action and policy interventions.

Drawing on this section, and to guide our analysis in Chapter 7, we can ask the following questions: How did agricultural biotechnology become a governance problem, or a legitimacy problem that required a governance solution? In order to govern GM products, what collective problems have been identified, or how have problems been defined as collective ones?

Issue-framing: policy making and stakeholder coalitions

Global governance is a valuable starting point for our discussion. It gives us a way of understanding interactions between state and non-state actors in policy-making processes at the international level. In this section we develop our understanding of governance further by focusing specifically on the links between issue-framing, stakeholder coalitions and public policy. We discuss a variety of related issues, including: the relationship between issue-framing and the evidence that a problem exists and requires a policy intervention; the role that issue-framing plays in cementing relationships between actors so that they can form coalitions; and how policies change through the process of re-framing issues. In broad terms our focus on issue-framing helps to extend our understanding of the role of collective problems in governance.

Policy processes: going beyond empiricism

As Fischer (2003) has argued, the failure of various flagship policy interventions in the 1960s and 1970s forced scholars and policy makers to reflect on their assumptions about the policy process. Until then it had been assumed that policy making could, with sufficient effort and resources, be pursued in an objective and logical way. The dominant model of the policy-making process proposed a series of steps, including the identification of the problem, the identification of the solution, the formulation of policy interventions, and ultimately implementation and feedback. Policy making in practice, however, rarely corresponded with this model, and policy outcomes were rarely what policy makers intended. Well-known policy mishaps include nuclear power 'too cheap to meter' and agrichemicals used to 'clean' fields of weeds, eventually threatening a 'silent spring'.

That problems rarely speak for themselves is perhaps the most difficult challenge to the logical ideal of policy making. In practice, the evidence of a problem is significantly shaped by the context within which it is gathered and interpreted. So 'the problem', as such, is not obvious. Indeed evidence may not be required to drive the policy process in a given direction; a problem claim may be enough. As Yearley (1991: 49) has argued:

> No one would now argue that the objective conditions in themselves . . . are enough to promote awareness of a social problem. The subject of dispute is whether the actual existence of the objective conditions is necessary before a social problem can arise.

Post-empiricist approaches to policy analysis have their origins in problems of this kind, argues Fischer (2003). The broad category of post-empiricist (or post-positivist) approaches includes all analytical perspectives that do not start with an obvious policy problem, or evidence of it. As he explains:

> . . . [post-empiricism] accepts the idea that something called 'reality' exists, and that parts of it lend themselves to objective analysis. But this reality can never be fully understood or explained, especially in the social world, given the multiplicity of causes and effects and the problem of social meaning . . . Given the multitude of causes and meanings involved, none of which speak unambiguously for themselves, the post-empiricist orientation emphasizes the social construction of theories and concepts and qualitative approaches [to] the discovery of knowledge.
>
> (Fischer, 2003: 121)

In broad terms our analysis of policies for agricultural biotechnology in the chapters that follow is consistent with this position.

Issue-framing, stakeholder coalitions and policy change

Post-empiricist perspectives generally analyse the role of issue-framing in policy making; some analysts call this 'interpretive framing' (Fischer, 2003), which includes 'cognitive and normative framing' and 'discursive framing'. Laws and Rein (2003: 174) characterise such framing as follows: 'The more general phenomena . . . is that of distinguishing between what demands attention and what can be neglected, and of giving stable shape by providing structure, even when that structure cannot be directly observed.' In addition they argue that issue-framing may be particularly significant in governance situations because such situations increase awareness of the number of issue-frames and the related conflicts.

Issue-framing is particularly important for the creation and maintenance of coalitions of stakeholders involved in policy-making processes but there are different ways of understanding this process. They can be illustrated by comparing the Advocacy Coalition Framework (ACF) with the Discourse Coalition Framework (DCF). The ACF proposes that any policy problem will be associated with a small number of advocacy coalitions (1–4). Actors in these coalitions will ' . . . share a set of normative and causal beliefs and . . . engage in a non-trivial degree of co-ordinated activity over time' (Sabatier, 1998: 103). Although the actors involved in a coalition might be very diverse, the ACF suggests that a shared belief system binds them together. 'Deep core beliefs', which are ontological and normative, determine the way the policy problem is understood, and the belief system provides the basis of the coalition (see also Sabatier, 1988; Sabatier and Jenkins-Smith, 1993).

The DCF, in contrast, suggests that issue-framing is done through story-lines and discourses and it is these, rather than beliefs, that bind a coalition of stakeholders together. Storylines are ' . . . narratives on social reality through which elements from many different domains are combined and that provide actors with a set of symbolic references that suggest a common understanding' (Hajer, 1995: 62). Whole discourses are ' . . . a specific ensemble of ideas, concepts, and categorizations that is produced, reproduced, and transformed in a particular set of practices and through which meaning is given to physical and social realities' (Hajer, 1995: 60). Consequently, although ACF and the DCF both propose that coalitions of stakeholders are the best analytical unit for the purpose of policy analysis, they offer different ways of understanding the basis on which they are constituted and the role that issue-framing plays in policy making.

In the chapters that follow our goal is not to identify which of these frameworks is better or worse. Instead we use them both to provide different insights into the role that issue-framing plays in coalition formation and policy making. This may appear to be a somewhat lax approach because, as Hajer (1995: 71) has argued,

> . . . the cement of advocacy coalitions is the shared beliefs of individuals. Sabatier takes these beliefs as *a priori*, although they are changeable

through social learning. In both cases language is seen as a means . . . [to express stable values or for rational reflection]. In the argumentative approach both language and context help to constitute beliefs. People are not seen as holding stable values but as having vague, contradictory, and unstable 'value positions'. New discourses may alter existing cognitive commitments and thus influence the values and beliefs of actors.

However, despite these differences between ACF and DCF perspectives, we can combine their insights. This is possible because discursive approaches emphasise discourse but do not deny the existence of beliefs (Fischer, 2003: 102).

In this discussion so far we have explored the relationship between issue-framing, stakeholder coalitions and the definition of policy problems – which are central concerns of this book. We have also suggested links between these aspects and global governance. Most importantly, our discussion of issue-framing gives us additional insights into a governance process of identifying problems as collective ones. In a situation involving multiple coalitions of stakeholders, with competing framings of an issue, the identification of a collective problem may require efforts to reconcile some competing frames.

Surel (2000) has surveyed perspectives that focus on the role of cognitive and normative framing in policy making – for example, paradigms (Hall), beliefs (Sabatier) and r f rential (Jobert and Muller). Based on his review Surel is able to identify the work performed by frames:

> Beyond their differences, all [such approaches] in fact posit the existence of an ensemble of general principles and values defining the relations and identities of actors, in particular through forms of thought which delimit, hierarchically rank and legitimate social distinctions, all the while setting priorities for action in a given community. In addition, the consequences of these different cognitive and normative societal frames are to legitimate some groups rather than others, mark out the terrain for public action, as well as define the possibilities for change in a particular subsystem. They thereby determine as much the world views themselves as the practices that follow from them.
>
> (2000: 499)

As suggested above, framing can help to manage tension and conflict. Surel argues that the dominant frame helps to contain conflict by providing a causal explanation of the current state-of-affairs: our collective problems exist for reasons x, y and z. In addition, because it gives a causal account, the dominant frame provides a basis from which to decide on practical action. At the same time, however, other coalitions may sustain competing frames. For these reasons, Surel (2000: 502) argues, 'A cognitive and normative frame thus marks out the terrain for social exchanges and disagreements, rather than simply supporting an unlikely consensus.'

Given that issue-frames play a central role in containing conflict, how can policies change, sometimes radically? To begin to answer this question, we can focus on policy change through learning, as understood by the ACF and the DCF. From the ACF perspective policy change can take place through learning, and such learning is understood as ' . . . relatively enduring alterations of thought or behavioural intentions which result from experience and/or new information and which are concerned with the attainment or revision of policy objectives' (Sabatier, 1998: 104). Through learning across coalitions and their policy frames, there may be a change in secondary aspects of policy. From this perspective policy change occurs as a result of a better understanding of the problem. In the ACF, technical knowledge, provided by scientists and policy analysts, is seen as particularly important in the learning process.

With this emphasis on new empirical information and better analysis of problems, the ACF raises many questions. Most importantly, how do these relate to the beliefs of actors and their coalitions? Also, conversely, how do these beliefs shape the gathering of evidence and problem definitions? According to the ACF, secondary aspects may be readily changed, while changes to core beliefs would be similar to religious conversion. How such a change is linked to new empirical evidence is unclear. In addition, we should note that the ACF's emphasis on new empirical information places it somewhere between empiricist and post-empiricist approaches to policy analysis.

Unsurprisingly, the DCF suggests a radically different view of policy change through learning. Placing little importance on technical information, instead it emphasises the need for stakeholders to debate different ways of defining the problem. In the consensual setting of environmental mediation, a limited group deliberates possible decisions, and to allow the practice to work, this procedure may need to delimit the problem-definition. By contrast, reflexive institutional arrangements would consider the socio-cognitive basis of knowledge and 'can therefore never be based on preconceived problem definitions'. Reflexive practices should 'be oriented towards constructing the social problem' that needs a solution (Hajer, 1995: 285–7; cf. Fischer, 2003: 111). In this process, evidence is demoted to the role of a discursive resource. This DCF understanding of policy change through learning is more consistent with our focus on issue-framing and it provides another important link back to the earlier discussion of governance and the definition of collective problems.

Amongst the above perspectives, there is more consensus on explaining radical change in policies, which can only result from a crisis of some kind. Crisis raises questions about the dominant frame. It is associated with ' . . . the growing incapacity felt by actors to view changing social relations according to previous frames' (Surel, 2000: 505). The inability of a dominant frame to manage social tensions and offer satisfying and legitimate public policy solutions can result in a re-evaluation of the frame. In the case of agricultural biotechnology, at least in Europe, such a crisis took the form of public protest, attacks on crops in fields and a commercial boycott of GM grain by food retailers. Undoubtedly this had profound implications for policy and these have been well documented. Less well documented, however, are how change through learning and crisis proceeded together, and stakeholder conflicts were governed.

Policy processes and agricultural biotechnology

To conclude our discussion of issue-framing and stakeholder coalitions we can outline contributions by Toke (2004) and Jasanoff (2005) who have used similar concepts specifically in relation to agricultural biotechnology. In his comparison of the regulation of GM products in the EU, UK and the US, David Toke identifies discourse-paradigms which frame agri-biotechnology in quite different ways across and within those jurisdictions. He also identifies policy networks 'relying on sometimes changing storylines for their cohesion'; through network analysis, he analyses 'a discourse or storyline to which an alliance of groups are committed, rather than imagining a set of "real" group interests which underpins the ideas' (Toke, 2004: 49).

By drawing on aspects of Foucault and Hajer, Toke also shows how socio-cultural framings explain why different risks became problematic in each country and how scientific-regulatory criteria can be understood as cultural. His analysis implies the linear elaboration of a policy framework into science, whereby regulatory agencies recruit scientists or expert advisors who reflect the basic policy aims, which are then translated into facts. This argument inverts the driving assumption of empiricist approaches to policy analysis. In Chapter 7 we explore some aspects of this argument further, which may have some validity, although it downplays the roles played by experts – for example, in raising new risk issues, in challenging safety assumptions, and thus in providing discursive resources for civil society actors.

Jasanoff (2005) links different approaches to regulating agricultural biotechnology to earlier divergences in risk-framings between the US and EU, as well as among EU member states. In the US, she argues, a 'product' framing of biotechnology reinforced a more general view: technology as an instrument of progress, and nature providing new commercial products which could meet increasingly diverse needs. This also constructed the citizen as an entrepreneurial adopter. The policy implications of this framing were a *laissez faire* approach toward private initiative and risk-taking, significantly lowering the threshold barriers to biotechnological innovation. By contrast to the USA, however, the EU framed agricultural biotechnology as a novel process which generated scientific uncertainty, thus warranting a precautionary approach to policy. This perspective implies that framing played a central role in the transatlantic conflict between the US and the EU, although Jasanoff does not examine this conflict as such. In the following chapters we do explore the EU–US conflict and as a result are able to build on this work.

At the national level the UK government elaborated the EU framing by making public appeals for expert claims to be supported by empirical evidence. Sceptical voices were encouraged to contribute to the UK policy debate in an effort to build a stronger consensus in support of agricultural biotechnology. In practice 'this effort to broaden politics led to a more extensive unpacking of scientific unknowns', argues Jasanoff (2005: 277). In Germany, also operating within the EU's overarching frame, biotechnology was presented as a programmatic alliance between science and the state, which might lead to abuses of power unless the technological development was tightly controlled. Consequently, the German Rechtstaat was expected to specify legal and moral absolutes as a basis for preventing such abuse, as well as a basis for regulators to make purely technical-administrative decisions within those statutory parameters.

Drawing on this section, and to guide our analysis in Chapter 7, we can ask the following questions: In relation to agricultural biotechnology, what role did issue-framing play for actors engaged in the policy process? How did policies for GM crops and foods change?

Standard-setting: regulatory harmonisation and judicial review

Earlier in this chapter we outlined a link between a particular form of political-economic globalisation, legitimacy problems, global governance and the definition of collective problems. We explored the definition of collective problems further by examining issue-framing and stakeholder coalitions. These are central concerns of the chapters that follow. In this section we add to our understanding of economic globalisation by exploring the link between standard-setting, regulatory harmonisation and judicial review. Trade liberalisation and regulatory harmonisation have been accused of lowering regulatory standards. We discuss this issue because regulatory standards for GM crops and foods are central to the EU–US conflict over agricultural biotechnology. We also discuss related research on the regulation of agricultural biotechnology in the EU and the US (Young, 2001; Princen, 2002), which have implications for our analysis.

Trade liberalisation and regulatory harmonisation

In recent years there have been fierce debates over whether trade liberalisation favours higher or lower regulatory standards. This formulation of the question, however, can be misleading, because it reifies a complex socio-political process as an independent variable which has effects elsewhere. Consequently, it is important to raise questions that open the black box of trade liberalisation. How does trade liberalisation take institutional forms which favour those who advocate or oppose higher standards? How are these institutional forms related to processes of issue-framing and the definition of collective problems? To investigate these questions, the stereotypical relationship between trade liberalisation and regulatory standards might be reversed: how do standard-setting processes shape trade liberalisation? Overall, in order to avoid reifying trade liberalisation, we must examine standard-setting processes, as well as higher/lower standards themselves.

This task is complicated because popular 'globalisation' and 'anti-globalisation' discourses have both reified trade liberalisation and in doing so they have hidden standard-setting processes from view. In both cases this is a strategy to influence policy. Neoliberal militants have invoked objective imperatives associated with globalisation, such as economic competitiveness, market efficiency or WTO rules, in an effort to restrict national (or European Union) procedures for setting regulatory standards. It is often said, 'such-and-such regulatory criteria would threaten globalisation/trade liberalisation/ free trade, and it may even be illegal'. Partly as a response to this strategy, anti-globalisation activists, along with many NGOs, have opposed trade liberalisation. They have negatively stereotyped international regulatory harmonisation as inherently antagonistic to democracy, sovereignty and higher standards. Discursive framings of both kinds have become forces in policy making and institutional change.

Perhaps in response to such polarisation, some scholars have tried to unpack the complex relationship between trade liberalisation and regulatory standards. The concept of 'trading up', also known as the 'California effect', tries to do this. It has been applied mainly to product-related regulatory standards which aim to protect the environment or human health. Products are the main focus because these are often traded internationally and thus are dependent upon internation-ally agreed product standards. The concept has, however, also been applied to production processes and domestic regulatory standards, which are set by governments with limited formal or direct influence from abroad. Since research in this area was initiated by David Vogel (1995, 1997) others have explored the concept (Young, 2001; Princen, 2002; Bernauer and Caduff, 2004).

According to David Vogel (1995: 5), ' . . . trade liberalisation can just as easily be achieved by forcing nations with lower standards to raise them as by forcing nations with higher standards to lower them'. After examining various sectors and liberalising contexts, such as agriculture and food and the World Trade Organization, he concludes: 'To the extent that trade liberaliza-tion has affected the level of consumer and environmental protection, it has more often strengthened than weakened it' (Vogel, 1995: 5). Vogel identifies various mechanisms to explain why trading up rather than levelling down can occur, in order to analyse the contingent role of trade liberalisation. On the whole, these mechanisms involve political power or economic rationality. For example, he argues that domestic producers can campaign for higher standards as a source of competitive advantage. Vogel focuses mainly on powerful states interacting with less powerful ones through formal institu-tions and processes associated with trade liberalisation.

In our discussion of global governance we focused particularly on the role of civil society groups, which Vogel has also identified as important in trading up. Beyond political power and economic rationality as trading-up mechanisms, Vogel has argued that:

> ... when rich nations with large domestic markets ... enact stricter product standards, their trading partners are forced to meet those standards in order to maintain their export markets. This in turn often encourages consumer and environmental organizations in the exporting country to demand similar standards for products sold in their domestic markets.
>
> (1995: 6)

Here Vogel identifies transboundary dynamics involving civil society. Similarly, Vogel (1997) argues that negotiations to achieve trade liberalisation can create new opportunities for NGOs to campaign for higher standards – opportunities that would not otherwise be available to them. From this it is clear that Vogel sees NGO influences as largely dependent upon governments and inter-governmental arrangements, almost as if they can only support one government's stance against another. In the chapters that follow, by examining EU–US interactions in relation to agricultural biotechnology, we challenge this view and extend the understanding of trading up in this sector.

Vogel also discusses the role of science and risk assessment in trade liberalisation and trading up. For example, in relation to the EU–US conflict over hormone-treated beef (see below), he asks:

> ... what standards of scientific proof should be required to justify a regulation that interferes with trade? In the case of the EU hormone ban, should the EU be obligated to prove that the consumption of meat from cattle which have been fed on hormones is *unsafe*, or must the United States prove that meat from hormone-fed cattle is *safe*? In other words, what makes a regulation that restricts trade 'necessary'? And on whom does the burden of proof of demonstrating that it is necessary or unnecessary fall?
>
> (Vogel, 1997: 16–17)

Such observations are particularly important for agbiotech, because of the central role played by risk assessment in the regulation of GM products in the US and the EU, and the focus on it in the transatlantic dispute. However, as we discuss further below, the trading-up literature has offered little analysis of scientific knowledge and expertise. By linking the trading-up debate to work on regulatory science from Science and Technology Studies, we are able to take both perspectives further.

Judicial review: legitimacy and democracy

The 'trading up' concept focuses our attention mainly on the regulatory standards that emerge from inter-governmental negotiations. In the chapters that follow we discuss various examples, including the provisions of the Biosafety Protocol to the UN Convention on Biological Diversity and standards of the Codex Alimentarius Commission. In addition to such formal and consensus-based standard-setting processes, however, there are more conflictual ones. In this section, therefore, we will briefly explore the relationship between standard-setting and judicial review by a higher authority, focusing particularly on the World Trade Organization. This is particularly important because of the US decision to bring a formal complaint to the WTO regarding EU regulation of biotechnology products.

The WTO is increasingly called upon to make judgements regarding the legality of measures that restrict global trade. As trade negotiations lead to the removal of more and more tariff barriers – taxes, charges and subsidies – disputes increasingly involve non-tariff barriers such as health and safety regulations. The WTO encourages governments to seek a mutually acceptable bilateral solution to a trade conflict in the first instance. If this is not possible, however, then the WTO can produce a judgement. In Chapter 6 we discuss the hormone-treated beef case, which set criteria relevant to the subsequent case on biotechnology products. In this section, however, we sketch the shrimp–turtle dispute to illustrate broader issues.

In the area of environmental protection a number of important cases have come before the WTO. In the shrimp–turtle dispute, in May 1998, a WTO Dispute Panel found against the US and the Appellate Body clarified the ruling later. At the centre of the dispute was a US law restricting shrimp imports from countries where Turtle Excluder Devices were not fitted on shrimp nets. Significantly, the ruling accepted the conservation objective of the US, and justified this by referring to the UN Convention on International Trade in Endangered Species (CITES), which classifies sea turtles as endangered. However, the WTO rejected the US action for various procedural reasons. For example, it argued that WTO member states have an obligation to attempt to resolve trade disputes multilaterally before taking unilateral action. The US had not tried to do this. Also, the US had not taken into account other methods that may be used to protect sea turtles. It had simply tried to force countries to adopt the methods included in its own law (DeSombre and Barkin, 2002).

As a legal precedent, this WTO judgement focused on international relations rather than regulatory standards *per se*:

> In Shrimp/Turtle, famously, the AB [Appellate Body] did not second-guess the policy objectives of the United States. On the contrary, it adopted a permissive stance . . . Emphasis was laid upon the manner in which the United States had behaved vis- -vis its trading partners in the operationalization of its sea turtle conservation regime. It might be thought that the United States was condemned for being insufficiently 'other-regarding' in its attitude to those situated outside of the polity, but affected by decisions adopted within it.
>
> (Scott, 2004: 14)

This case is useful for our purposes because it draws attention to the central dilemma facing the WTO in relation to standard-setting and judicial review. It raises most clearly the following question: how should the preferences of the public within a jurisdiction be weighed against obligations to those outside? It is a political risk for the WTO that it may be perceived as a threat to democracy if it challenges trade barriers. As Scott (2004: 9–10) says:

> This judicial review function may be performed in respect of executive or administrative acts, but it bites also in respect of legislative acts, including those adopted by democratically elected parliaments within the Member States. In performing this task the AB [Appellate Body] enjoys extensive interpretative room for manoeuvre. It is called upon to exercise judgment. This fact of judicial review at the level of the WTO presents a profound challenge to the legitimacy of this organization from the perspective of democracy. The challenge is not unique to the WTO. It inheres in the institution of judicial review more generally.

This author analyses the WTO's democratic dilemma as follows:

> . . . 'judicial review' may, in this setting, be conceived as re-enforcing rather than negating democracy, by enhancing accountability, and in particular the external accountability of states . . . [however] as the Appellate Body of the WTO comes to elaborate stronger substantive benchmarks for review – rationality or proportionality type tests – 'judicial review' also raises a democracy dilemma for the WTO . . . This democracy dilemma presents an audacious challenge for the WTO, and one which admits of no easy or absolute answers.
>
> (Scott, 2004: 2–3)

The question of whether or not the WTO enhances or undermines democracy – and thus its own legitimacy – is an important one for the EU–US dispute over biotechnology products, as we explore in Chapters 6 and 7.

Trade liberalisation and agricultural biotechnology

Young (2001) provides a detailed and well-researched account of the EU–US conflict over GM foods. He is particularly interested to find out if higher regulatory standards have been adopted in the US as a result of higher standards and regulatory blockages in the EU. His work draws on the 'trading up' concept discussed above. He writes:

> . . . 'trading up' is taking place in response to the learning by and mobilisation of US consumers and to business adaptation to the EU's rules and changing domestic market conditions. There are limits to this

process, however, and limited 'trading up' by the US (even combined with reform in the EU) is insufficient to end the dispute.

(Young, 2001: 3)

In 2001 Young correctly predicted that there would be 'protracted tension' between the EU and the US and that the dispute would 'simmer for some time to come'. As Young points out, 'Because the EU insists on approving all varieties itself, "trading up" by the US was never going to be sufficient to end the dispute . . . ' (2001: 37).

At the end of his paper Young (2001) explicitly tries to identify the mechanisms that are responsible for the limited amount of trading up he observes in the area of GM food. The following passage captures the important arguments:

> Although the US reforms have been limited, the preceding analysis stresses that 'trading up' occurs even when international institutions do not favour it and that it is a phenomenon that affects actors even as economically and politically powerful as the United States. There are two key aspects to this conclusion. The first is the importance of the transmission of political mobilisation as a mechanism for 'trading up'. By raising awareness of US consumers and consumer and environmental organisations, the EU's rules on GM food provided a catalyst to political mobilisation and limited policy change. An important caveat is that domestic institutions play a pivotal role in shaping how political mobilisation translates into policy change. In this instance, the prevailing approach to regulation and the legal framework in which it is situated dampened the impact of political mobilisation. The second aspect is the importance of exceptions to multilateral trade rules to diffusing 'trading blows'. The acceptance in multilateral rules of legitimate obstacles to trade undermines aggressive trade policies and creates incentives for cooperative solutions.

(Young, 2001: 38)

Young's emphasis on 'transmission of political mobilisation' as a mechanism for 'trading up' is particularly interesting here. In his analysis, although it is not mentioned in the quote given above, he touches on the roles played by transatlantic networks of policy actors in this process, particularly the Transatlantic Consumer Dialogue and the Transatlantic Environmental Dialogue (see Chapter 3). Here there is a further suggestion, therefore, that civil society might be a neglected part of trading-up research. Young also identifies 'exceptions to multilateral trade rules', by which he means reasons for blocking trade which are acceptable under trade law, as a driver of trading up. He believes they create an incentive to accommodate rather than challenge higher standards. This suggests the need for more research on lower-profile, perhaps informal interactions, beyond formal negotiations or dispute resolution processes.

Princen (2002) also examines trade in GM foods and EU–US relations in order to explore trading-up processes. Drawing on Vogel, he understands the California effect as follows: 'For a California effect to take place, two things have to occur. First, the exporting country has to strengthen its standards and, second, this strengthening has to be attributable to the regulatory trade measures of the importing ("initiator") country' (Princen, 2002: 256). This precise account sets a high threshold for identifying related processes.

In relation to GM foods Princen argues that the EU and the US had similar regulatory approaches until the mid-1990s, at which point the EU began to develop more stringent standards of various kinds. He then focuses on the US response and concludes:

> In general, the regulatory developments [in the US] . . . have probably been driven primarily by domestic political processes. There have not been any direct negotiations between the EC . . . and the US on their respective regulatory frameworks . . . Moreover, the reactions of regulatory agencies seem to have been a reaction to domestic political pressures from consumer groups and, sometimes, producers, rather than to the trade effects of the EC measures . . . Still, the changes in the US and Canada can be linked to the EC measures in at least two ways. First, the EC measures may have had an effect on the public debate in the US and Canada, and on the position and strength of consumer and environmental groups within it . . . The links between US and EC groups have been facilitated by the existence of global groups . . . and by the establishment of formal links in the TAED and TACD . . . The fact that the EC adopted more stringent measures in the late 1990s, may have provided an extra impetus to these groups in both the US and Canada, in that it lent credibility to their position and proved that a powerful government could be persuaded to act upon their concerns. In this indirect sense, the EC measures and their trade effects can be said to have contributed to changes in the US . . . The second way in which the EC measures may have influenced the US . . . regulatory framework is through debates and negotiations in multilateral forums [e.g. OECD, Codex, WTO, Cartegena Protocol] . . . outcomes have not been the same in all forums . . . [but] the Cartegena Protocol seems to be closer to the European approach.
>
> (Princen, 2002: 259–60)

There are important similarities between this analysis and Young's. Most importantly, Princen also identifies indirect and informal transatlantic influences as important; in particular, when he suggests that European measures influenced public debate in the US and thus strengthened consumer and environmental groups there. Further support for US NGOs came via formal

NGO links such as the Transatlantic Consumer Dialogue and the Transatlantic Environmental Dialogue. Although this is similar to a mechanism identified by Vogel, Princen is reluctant to conclude that this is a case of trading up, based on his own way of operationalising the concept. He argues that European measures are only indirectly responsible for changes in US regulatory standards and that 'This is a somewhat stretched use of the concept of a California effect . . . ' (Princen, 2002: 331).

For reasons that are not entirely clear, but perhaps relate to the fact that formal negotiations and an international agreement are involved, Princen more confidently concludes that the Cartegena Protocol is an example of trading up in practice. The Protocol 'appears' to be closer to the European approach, though interpreting this is difficult because of the US's ambiguous relationship to it, and the uncertainty surrounding its practical meaning.

As another trading-up mechanism, Princen mentions the decision of US farmers not to produce soya beans lacking authorisation in the EU but again he argues that this is a 'weak effect in terms of regulatory change' because it will presumably be reversed when such products are authorised. He also points out that US maize producers have not made the same decision (though some later did so, as outlined in our Chapter 6). In conclusion he states:

> The GM foods and food products issue therefore shows some strengthening of regulatory standards in the US . . . but this strengthening is fairly limited and only partly the result of EC regulatory trade measures.
>
> (Princen, 2002: 332)

Drawing on this section, and to guide our analysis in Chapter 7, we can ask the following questions: In the case of agricultural biotechnology, how have standard-setting and trade liberalisation shaped each other? How have civil society groups used trade liberalisation and trade conflict to stimulate higher regulatory standards for agbiotech products?

Regulatory science: the science-policy boundary and risk assessment

In the final section of this chapter we focus on regulatory science, i.e. the knowledge used in risk regulation. This is important because risk assessment has played a central role in public debate and regulatory disputes around GM products. This section draws on research and writing from Science and Technology Studies (a sub-discipline of Sociology). We explore three aspects: the contested and movable boundary between science and policy; links between the context and content of regulatory science; and the role of science in trade disputes.

The boundary between science and policy

In public debate over contentious technologies, the term 'risk' has acquired meanings that are far broader than technical calculations, and these meanings have in turn limited or undermined the authority of expert claims. According to Ulrich Beck, risk debates generate 'conflicts of accountability' over risks and their consequences – how they 'can be distributed, averted, controlled and legitimated' (1996: 28). In practice, risk conflicts involve expert disagreements: 'Risk society is tendentially a self-critical society . . . Experts are relativised or dethroned by counterexperts' (Beck, 1996: 32–3). The dynamics of this situation are, however, more complex than simply experts versus counter-experts – a distinction which is readily blurred and challenged.

When scientists take on the role of risk experts, they necessarily address practical problems and try to make predictive judgements. In so doing, however, they make statements which go beyond their own expertise, or which even transgress the limits of scientific knowledge. They therefore become 'the more or less conscious advocate of a cause' (Roqueplo, 1995: 177), for example a policy agenda. Politicians may cite expert advice as if it is a scientific truth, and thus justify their decisions, but this strategy can be challenged by expert disagreements and alternative expertise. In practice this contest has generated what might be called 'public expert appraisal'. Consequently, 'true scientific expertise' is more 'contained within the space opened and articulated by public debate between experts than in the statements made by any of them, no matter how scientific' (Roqueplo, 1995: 176–7).

Focusing on the boundary between facts and values, or science and policy, is a valuable way of exploring these dynamics further. Whenever expert advice is presented as objective knowledge, the boundary between these can be easy to render visible and challenge. In risk controversies, especially those that feature great uncertainty, the putative boundary between facts and values is readily challenged. Indeed, the stereotypical distinction between 'hard facts and soft values' is effectively inverted: 'Thus the traditional scientific inputs have become "soft" in the context of the "hard" value commitments that will determine the success of policies . . . ' (Funtowicz and Ravetz, 1993: 751).

Any line drawn between facts and values is specific to an institutional purpose and subject to change. Official experts play a crucial role in this process because they help to present advice as science-based, that is not value-laden. In the US regulatory context, for example, advisory bodies have attempted to define 'good science', so that an agency decision can be sufficiently supported by evidence. For this task, they have strategically shifted the boundary between science and policy (Jasanoff, 1990). Following Gieryn (1995), we can say that boundary-work is done as people contend for, legitimate or challenge the cognitive authority of science.

What, then, is the relationship between science and policy? In practice, when actors try to build a bridge between science and policy, the actual outcomes may differ from what they intend. We can illustrate this by focusing on three dynamics: scientisation of politics, scientification of politics and politicisation of science.

The 'scientisation of politics' involves strategies to depoliticise risk issues and regulatory science. From the 1970s onwards, governments began to justify contentious decisions about new technologies on 'objective, scientific' grounds. This move sometimes had the effect of depoliticising the issue but could just as well increase conflict and undermine the role of science in decision making more generally.

Research and analysis has now unravelled some of the complexities associated with the scientisation of politics. As B ckstrand (2004: 4) has argued, it 'implies that political and social issues are better resolved through technical expertise than democratic deliberation'. When politicians effectively evade responsibility in this way, experts 'maintain their monopoly claim to rationality against the non-specialised public sphere' (Beck, 1992: 159). Not surprisingly, therefore, the scientisation of politics can inadvertently politicise science. Even where science appears to have depoliticised an issue, it is possible that this outcome depends more directly on politics than it does on scientific knowledge, for example by one actor exercising power over rival interests (Nelkin, 1979: 19).

Unintended outcomes of the scientisation of politics have been explained in various ways. For example, in a technological controversy, protest may be aimed 'less against specific technological decisions than against the declining capacity of citizens to shape policies that affect their interests; less against science than against the use of scientific rationality to mask political choices' (Nelkin, 1979: 11). Opposition groups often develop and use their own experts, who can show that technical data are uncertain and/or open to different interpretations. The existence of conflicting data and different interpretations then generates political activity and implies the need for more publicly accountable and legitimate decision making (Nelkin, 1979: 15–17).

Risk issues are particularly difficult to depoliticise through science for a number of reasons. Weingart (1999) has discussed these in relation to a dynamic that he has called the 'scientification of politics'. In this process, expertise can play two related roles: (i) its instrumental role is to clarify scientific problems through more reliable knowledge; (ii) its legitimation role is to absorb scientific uncertainty into expert advice and in so doing support policy decisions. As distinct from the scientisation of politics, however, the scientification of politics means that regulatory authorities become more dependent upon progress in scientific knowledge in relation to risk questions. The result can be an abundance or proliferation of science, which remains open to diverse interpretations. Scientific perceptions can also put new issues onto the agenda and define new policy problems for which further knowledge and expertise are required.

In practice, Weingart (1999) argues, this process readily goes hand-in-hand with the 'politicisation of science'. One aspect of this is a competition for the latest scientific evidence which can support or undermine a specific regulatory policy. Competition for expertise intensifies controversies and thus potentially de-legitimises science as a basis for decisions. When experts disagree in public then the knowledge that underpins policy is widely understood to be uncertain. In the battle for authority there can be an inflationary use of expertise, which increasingly pushes debate and policy towards the realm of uncertain knowledge and towards the disputed boundary between unreliable and reliable scientific information. This can be understood as democratising in the sense that existing or new knowledge becomes more widely available to all groups in the political system, thus providing a stronger basis for non-expert views about policy.

Regulatory science has been linked with governance in many STS analyses, especially by treating science as an inherently value-laden way of framing uncertainties. From the broad historical perspective, De Marchi and Ravetz (1999: 754) argue that 'At stake here is the Enlightenment project, where objective science and representative democracy are combined to provide a new legitimation of the State.' From the controversial cases of the BSE crisis and Ciba-Geigy's *Bt* maize (see our Introduction), they diagnose difficulties of governing potential hazards. Even speculative hazards can undermine public trust in risk regulation. 'Here it is the uncertainties which dominate, and which require the reference to explicit values' (De Marchi and Ravetz, 1999: 755). As a governance solution already under way in some contexts, they advocate wider public participation, conceptualised as 'extended peer review' of official expert judgements. However, NGO involvement requires a somewhat 'self-contradictory balance between their functions as critics and as stakeholders' (De Marchi and Ravetz, 1999: 756).

From this discussion it is clear that there is no fixed or stable link between science and policy. Instead we see complex dynamics and tendencies with diverse possible outcomes – scientisation of politics, scientification of politics, politicisation of science. Each involves drawing or destabilising the boundary between science and policy (or facts and values) in a different way. In the chapters that follow we will link these processes to institutional strategies, which have both intended and unintended outcomes.

Regulatory science: content and context

STS scholars have studied science and its role in risk assessment in great detail. In particular they have analysed how values and interests frame the generation and interpretation of scientific evidence. As Jasanoff (1993: 129) has argued: 'We can hardly order, rearrange, or usefully supplement our knowledge about risk without incorporating these issues into a clear, framing vision of the social and natural order that we wish to live in.'

The knowledge referred to here, which is used in risk assessment and is often generated specially for this purpose, has been called 'regulatory science' (or 'mandated science'). One early commentator described 'trans-science' as a 'new branch of science . . . in which norms of proof are less demanding than are the norms in ordinary science', particularly because of the need to predict potential effects (Weinberg, 1985: 68). Although also emphasising its predictive role, later commentators argued that it is impossible to make a straightforward distinction between regulatory and academic science. They focused instead on the complex contingent relationship between these two.

In an important contribution Jasanoff distinguished between regulatory and research science by focusing on their 'content', 'context' and relationships between these. She argued that the content of regulatory science involves three types of activities: the production of knowledge which fills gaps in the knowledge base; the synthesis of knowledge, more so than original research; and the prediction of potential effects. As regards context, she pointed out that regulatory science is often carried out by the private sector, which can keep the results confidential, and that, moreover, 'Science carried out in non-academic settings may be subordinated to institutional pressures that influence researchers' attitudes to issues of proof and evidence' (Jasanoff, 1990: 77–9). This account hints at how the context can shape the content of regulatory science.

Such observations focus our attention on peer-review processes in all their forms and the special ways in which regulatory science can be held accountable. Here we also see significant differences between regulatory science and research science. As Jasanoff (1990: 80–2) has observed, peer review of regulatory science can involve methodological assumptions that have their origins in the compositional biases of expert advisory bodies. This is somewhat different (although related) to the problem of disciplinary biases shaping academic science. In a regulatory setting, peer review by an expert advisory body plays an important role in gate-keeping, for example by judging what science is adequate or even relevant for regulatory purposes. Here again we see how the context can shape regulatory science.

Building on earlier approaches, Irwin et al. (1997) have also analysed regulatory science. They confirm its 'significance for future research and policy-making' (p. 30) but argue that researchers must avoid one-dimensional approaches. The two most common, they suggest, are the 'concerns' and 'context' approaches. The first suggests that regulatory science is different from research science simply because it deals with different questions and has a different purpose. The second approach suggests that special contextual factors shape regulatory science in ways that they do not shape research science. Irwin et al. (1997: 22) argue that neither approach on its own does justice to the complex nature of regulatory science. Instead they link concerns with context in order to highlight its *'heterogeneous and hybrid character'* (emphasis original). They draw attention to the many different types of regulatory science that exist, such as speculative research and the development and validation of regulatory tests.

Irwin et al. (1997: 20) also argue that public-sector involvement in regulatory science can mean that it sometimes resembles academic science. They suggest that this is more often the case in the Europe than the United States. Using the case of agrochemicals regulation in the UK, they emphasise the 'private' world of government–industry–academia relationships which shape regulatory science. In their conclusion they say:

> ... the implications ... for environmentalist and 'public interest' groups deserve serious attention: it seems possible that regulatory science effectively disenfranchises groups which cannot play an intimate role in the largely confidential negotiations discussed so far.
>
> (Irwin et al., 1997: 28)

Regarding peer review in this context, they wonder 'whether the institutional context of regulatory science will hinder external scrutiny and hence diminish the quality of scientific work' (Irwin et al., 1997: 29).

From this survey we can see that accounts of regulatory science emphasise that it is provisional and often remains vulnerable to challenge. This is consistent with our broader discussion of the science-policy boundary. In particular, risk assessment depends on science done 'at the margins of existing knowledge, where science and policy are difficult to distinguish', and where there is little agreement on research methods (Jasanoff, 1990: 77–9). New knowledge in this context can provoke further disputes among policy actors. More fundamentally the policy demand of predicting risk means that regulatory science 'has to transgress its own cognitive boundaries and limitations' (Irwin et al., 1997: 19). Such accounts also emphasise interactions between the context and content of regulatory science, and between regulatory and research (or academic) science.

Science in trade disputes: the case of biotechnology products

Before closing our discussion of the science-policy boundary and regulatory science we will explore how the issues discussed so far bear on the use of science in trade disputes. Here we build on the earlier discussion of judicial review in the context of the WTO.

Observations made by Isaac (2002), specifically in relation to the transatlantic conflict over GM crops and foods, are a useful starting point. Isaac begins by arguing that all regulations have essentially two functions. Their economic function is to improve the efficiency of the market system; their social function is to ensure that market activity takes place in a way that is consistent with the preferences and expectations within jurisdictions. Although these two functions are often found operating simultaneously in any given international agreement, their theoretical foundations are quite different:

> International economic integration adopts economic principles to explain appropriate regulatory development and regulatory integration strategies for a jurisdiction. Accordingly, rational, optimizing behaviour fulfilling the economic function governs policy development, shapes social regulations and forms the basis for dealing with social regulatory barriers through trade diplomacy. Alternatively, international social integration adopts a perspective that argues that markets are embedded in normative constructs so that the economic perspective is meaningless if separated from social realities.
>
> (Isaac, 2002: 13)

To develop this distinction further, Isaac (2002) discusses the treatment of science and technology in processes and institutions of international integration. Here he draws attention to different rationalities involved:

> [The] economic perspective generally assumes that technology and innovation are vital factors of economic growth and welfare. As a result, it supports a regulatory framework that encourages technological progress. For instance, it is quite common for economic analysis to support 'scientific-rationality' approaches to regulating the risk of new technology . . . The economic- and scientific-rationality perspectives are similar, in that they decompose complex behaviour and actions into causal-consequence models, which are then used to forecast outcomes. . . .
> . . . [The] 'social-rationality' approach holds that it is insufficient to view new technology and innovations simply as a positive force in economic growth. Instead, the social implications of science must be considered and, under this consideration, new technology may not always be greeted without reservation – despite its potential to improve economic growth.
>
> (Isaac, 2002: 16–17, 21)

From this basis Isaac is able to distinguish between different institutions, regulatory frameworks and international agreements, based on the values that underpin them and their treatment of technology and risk. This is useful in the case of agricultural biotechnology where overlapping agreements may conflict with each other: the UN Biosafety Protocol; the WTO's SPS Agreement; WHO/FAO Codex Alimentarius Commission. Of these the Biosafety Protocol is understood to be informed by social rationality to the greatest extent, whereas the SPS agreement is informed mainly by economic and scientific rationality. This analysis, therefore, helps us to understand why the US and the EU emphasise different international agreements and different interpretations of those agreements.

In the event of a dispute, how do judicial review procedures at the WTO deal with risk and scientific expertise? In a way that is consistent with Isaac's description of the linking of economic and technical rationality in the SPS Agreement, one critic has argued that expert judgements are made in a technocratic world 'in which the contingency of scientific knowledge is denied, and in which the values which enter law through science remain obscured' (Scott, 2000: 157). Consequently, WTO procedures demand 'not merely that Members report as to the content of their measures, and as to the epistemic basis upon which they rest, but also that there be a "rational" or "objective" relationship between the premises said to underpin the measure and the measure itself' (Scott, 2000: 20).

Whilst the discipline that the WTO's SPS Agreement imposes is important it has had complex and unanticipated outcomes. This has led to controversy regarding the legitimate role of dispute panels and expert scientific evidence in WTO dispute resolution. Christoforou (2000: 642–3) has argued that:

> It would also appear that panels, with the unfortunate endorsement of the Appellate Body, are allowed to pick and choose from the different views they receive from scientists who are consulted in their individual capacities . . . If the evidence is divergent or conflicting, panels claim that they may assess, weigh and accept one or the other scientific view as they see fit.

Drawing on Isaac (2002), this raises the problem of the WTO assessing scientific evidence in a way determined by economic/scientific rationality. Indeed the WTO has been accused of doing just this. Critics point out that in practice the WTO and dispute panels have been facilitated in their pursuit of an economic agenda by plural and conflicting advice from individual experts from which they have been able to select certain perspectives. As an alternative, however, it has been proposed that expert advice at the WTO could focus on credible scientific disagreements rather than definitive judgements:

> In the long run, allowing panel members who do not have scientific expertise to make choices as to the 'correct' scientific approach is likely to harm the WTO system by reducing the legitimacy and social acceptability of its dispute-settlement rulings. A more promising alternative is for panels to establish expert review groups and seek to identify whether the scientific views presented to it by the parties and the consulted experts constitute plausible scientific alternatives.
>
> (Christoforou, 2000: 648)

At least implicitly, this proposal addresses some of the legitimacy problems of the WTO. As the same author has argued, moreover, expert disagreements can be interpreted as scientific uncertainty and thus as a defence for trade-restrictive measures:

The basic legal definition of scientific uncertainty reflects the potential for error inherent in science and scientific information. In law, uncertainty indicates evidence showing credible scientific disagreements among experts, which prevents the judge from rendering an informed decision on the scientific basis of the dispute . . . courts do not and cannot judge science.

(Christoforou, 2003: 208)

Drawing on this section, and to guide our analysis in Chapter 7, we can ask the following questions: In relation to agricultural biotechnology, how have policy agendas and scientific uncertainties been linked? What is the relationship between the context and content of regulatory science in the case of GM products?

Conclusion

In this chapter we have introduced the theoretical concepts and arguments that we will use to analyse the transatlantic conflict over GM crops and foods. Our entry point was the concept of global governance and much of the chapter has involved elaborating on important aspects of it. We have also explored existing research on the regulation of agricultural biotechnology in the US and the EU and at the global level. Much of this work intersects with our own. Although none of the above authors specifically focus on the transatlantic conflict as such, they have developed ideas and insights which we can develop in new ways. Table 1.1 summarises the discussion in this chapter and restates the pertinent questions we derived along the way. In Chapter 7 we take this table as the starting point for our analysis and discussion.

Table 1.1 Overarching Issues, Analytical Perspectives and Pertinent Questions

Overarching Issues	Analytical Perspectives	Pertinent Questions
Global Governance	Functionalist versus critical accounts, inter-governmental relations and non-state actors, political-economic globalisation and legitimacy problems.	How did agricultural biotechnology become a governance problem, or a legitimacy problem that required a governance solution?
	Governance as cooperation to solve collective problems, transnational networks of civil society, governance through defining problems as collective ones, process management.	In order to govern GM products, what collective problems have been identified, or how have problems been defined as collective ones?

(*continued on next page*)

Table 1.1 (Continued)

Overarching Issues	Analytical Perspectives	Pertinent Questions
...and GM products	Globalisation, limiting regulatory options, anti-globalisation opposing those limits, agricultural biotechnology as a bridging issue.	
Issue-Framing	Empiricist versus post-empiricist approaches to policy; policy problems speaking for themselves versus constructed problem-definitions.	In relation to agricultural biotechnology, what role did issue-framing play for actors engaged in the policy process?
	Issue/interpretive framing, stakeholder coalitions, discursive framing, conflict management, policy change through issue-reframing and learning.	How did policies for GM crops and foods change?
...and GM products	Discourse-paradigms for agri-biotechnology, socio-cultural framings, expert-policy links, divergent risk framings within and across jurisdictions.	
Standard-Setting	Trade liberalisation and regulatory harmonisation, regulatory standard-setting processes, trading up, civil society mobilisation.	In the case of agricultural biotechnology, how have standard-setting and trade liberalisation shaped each other?
	Judicial review, the role of science, inter/intra-jurisdictional obligations, WTO's legitimacy problem and democratic dilemma.	How have civil society groups used trade liberalisation and trade conflict to stimulate higher regulatory standards for agbiotech products?
...and GM products	Political mobilisation and influence between jurisdictions, informal interactions, indirect and weak trading up.	
Regulatory Science	Science-policy boundary, boundary work, scientisation of politics, scientification of politics, politicisation of science.	In relation to agricultural biotechnology, how have policy agendas and scientific uncertainties been linked?
	Regulatory science, framing visions, content and context, peer review, the 'private' world regulatory science and public scrutiny.	What is the relationship between the context and content of regulatory science in the case of GM products?
...and GM products	Economic versus social rationalities, scientific expertise in WTO judicial review, credible expert disagreements versus definitive judgements.	

2 'Approved once, accepted everywhere'

Biotechnology products and transatlantic trade networks

Introduction

Journalists have become accustomed to reporting on transatlantic trade disputes in dramatic terms. Recent BBC reports, for example, include 'EU opens new front in trade war' (1 March 2004) and 'Who will win the EU–US trade war?' (1 May 2005). These articles discuss corporation tax on foreign sales and subsidies to aerospace companies; similar articles have been written about steel products and bananas. The transatlantic conflict over GM products has been treated in the same way. BBC articles include 'New US–EU trade war looms' (2 December 2002) and 'US escalate GM trade war' (25 June 2003). All of these articles raise concerns about a growing number of disputes between the world's largest trading partners.

Such articles are valuable but they are also misleading. They are valuable because they draw our attention to complex interactions between the EU and the US. It is indeed striking that so many trade conflicts are emerging at this time. They are misleading, however, because they rarely analyse transatlantic interactions and instead present a world of stand-offs, where the only options are win or lose. Even articles that attempt a more subtle analysis, perhaps focusing on regulatory divergence or grey areas, usually ignore cooperative interactions. They also offer little historical or contextual detail to enable the reader to understand the conflicts involved.

To begin a more subtle analysis here, Chapters 2 and 3 focus on key transatlantic networks that attempted to shape the regulation of GM crops and foods from the mid-1990s onwards. In this chapter we examine networks that have been promoting trade liberalisation, particularly the Transatlantic Business Dialogue (TABD) and the Transatlantic Economic Partnership (TEP). We analyse the involvement of these networks in discussions about the regulation of GM products before and after the backlash and *de facto* moratorium in the European Union, focusing particularly on how their roles changed.

Transatlantic trade liberalisation agenda

In the mid-1990s politicians in the EU and the US reflected on the fact that global politics had changed dramatically over the previous decade. Many believed that this had significant, and possibly profound, implications for the EU–US relationship. Most importantly, with the end of the Cold War, the defence and security function of that relationship appeared to be less important. At the same time, however, following the conclusion of the Uruguay round of trade negotiations, and the creation of the World Trade Organization, a new agenda and common purpose was emerging – trade liberalisation.

On 3 December 1995 at the EU–US Summit in Madrid, EC President Santer, Spanish Prime Minister Gonz lez (as President of the European Council) and US President Clinton signed the New Transatlantic Agenda (NTA) (EU/US, 1995). The NTA is still central to the effort of redefining the EU–US relationship in the post-Soviet era. Reflecting the shock in Europe at the instability of the Balkan region at this time – particularly the war in the former Yugoslavia – the promotion of peace, stability and democracy were given a high priority. Beyond this, however, the NTA emphasises the expansion of world trade, partly through a closer EU–US economic relationship, and more generally the building of various kinds of links across the Atlantic.

For our purposes the emphasis that the NTA places on a closer economic relationship between the EU and the US, and building bridges across the Atlantic, are particularly important. With respect to the first of these the rationale and spirit of the NTA is captured in the following:

> Analyses which suggest that either party may turn away from the Transatlantic Relationship rarely take into account the economic glue which binds Europe and the US. The EU is America's largest trading partner and vice versa, with a combined trade worth $213 billion in 1994. Around 3 million US workers are employed by European-owned companies. Around 51% of foreign direct investment in the US comes from the Union, and 42% of foreign direct investment in the Union comes from the United States. The relationship generates wealth and jobs on both sides of the Atlantic.
>
> (CEC, 1995 in association with objective 3)

In the NTA this statement precedes a call to 'deepen economic and commercial ties'. To achieve this objective EU and the US negotiators agreed to cooperate in two areas: (1) the strengthening of the multilateral trading system; (2) the removal of regulatory and other obstacles to the flow of goods, services and capital between them.

The emphasis that the NTA places on trade liberalisation is justified in various ways in the document. These justifications are both economic and political in nature. Drawing on the basic tenets of trade theory the argument is made that trade liberalisation will make everyone richer. Politically the justification is that trade liberalisation will bring the EU and the US closer together thus emphasising their common political project. However, the NTA document also acknowledges that overall the new transatlantic agenda is more clearly aligned with the interests of some stakeholders rather than others, particularly the business community. It states: 'It is no coincidence . . . that the Agenda's priorities closely resemble those recommended by European and American business leaders who participated in the first meeting of the Transatlantic Business Dialogue in Seville in early November' (CEC, 1995 in association with objective 3).

In the area of building bridges across the Atlantic it is much less clear what the NTA's purpose is. The text suggests a desire on both sides to ensure that the EU and the US do not drift apart at various levels, particularly culturally, commercially and politically. The NTA states:

> For more than 40 years, transatlantic ties were firmly underpinned by a security relationship whose values and importance to both Western Europe and the United States were clearly understood and supported by the broad mass of their populations. With that dimension now much altered, the task is to encourage a similar allegiance to the transatlantic community among current and future generations, so that it draws additional strength from vibrant networks of individuals, groups and institutions of many kinds.
>
> (CEC, 1995 in association with objective 4)

Concerning the process of actually building bridges across the Atlantic, the NTA makes it clear that the creation of transatlantic networks of various kinds is important. At this time, in late 1995, an example already existed in the form of the Transatlantic Business Dialogue (see below). Politicians and policy makers raised the prospect of encouraging a range of other similar networks, made up of scientists, policy makers and civil society groups, amongst others. The TABD, therefore, in the eyes of some, provided a template that could be used by others. Thus, in addition to the 'economic glue' that binds the EU and the US together, the NTA proposed that the transatlantic relationship could be cemented further through the creation of additional transatlantic 'dialogues' of various kinds.

With this brief overview we have established the context for much of what is discussed in the rest of this book. This section situates politicians and policy makers in 1995, in the EU and the US, in a context of profound geo-political and economic changes. The NTA was a response and a contribution to these changes. What purpose should (or could) the EU–US relationship have from the mid-1990s onwards? Peace and security and trade liberalisation are given in the NTA as answers to this question. It also encourages the strengthening of the transatlantic relationship through the creation of various transatlantic networks. Put simply, policy makers argued for a deepening of EU–US interactions of various kinds. It is important to keep in mind that agricultural biotechnology, a new and controversial technology, was introduced into the EU and the US in this context and through related processes and interactions.

The Transatlantic Business Dialogue and GM products

Given their priorities it is not surprising that many business leaders in the EU and the US are vocal supporters of transatlantic trade liberalisation. In the early to mid-1990s, accompanied by some politicians, they argued for the creation of a Transatlantic Free Trade Association (TAFTA) (Isaac, 2002). This idea, however, failed to gain a foothold on the political agenda. France, amongst others, was antagonistic to the idea, fearing its implications for sovereignty and the protection of key sectors of its own economy. However, in 1995, at a conference in Seville (Spain) organised by US Secretary of Commerce Brown and EC Commissioners Brittan and Bangerman, over 100 leaders of EU and US companies launched the Transatlantic Business Dialogue to promote the cause of EU–US trade liberalisation.

Today the TABD is one of the main mechanisms for communicating the priorities of business to EU and US politicians and policy makers. Its aims are clearly in line with those of the New Transatlantic Agenda:

> The TABD's goal is to help establish a barrier free transatlantic market which will serve as a catalyst for global trade liberalisation and prosperity. Unified markets are needed to create a business environment which will stimulate innovation and economic growth, more investment and create new jobs.
>
> (TABD, 2005)

The TABD is chaired by a US and European CEO for a period of two years and they identify priority areas (in early 2005 these positions were held by the CEO of the Coca-Cola Company and the Chairman of Reuters Group Plc). In addition, various technical and longer-term projects are dealt with by a series of working groups. Representatives of business in the EU and the US must agree on policy recommendations to the EU and US governments, and these recommendations emerge from the ongoing activities of working groups, mid-year conferences and the annual CEO Conference, which alternate between EU and US cities.

The TABD is active in most areas of transatlantic trade and its aim in relation to products is captured in the phrase 'approved once, accepted everywhere'. This phrase first appeared in a TABD document in 1996. It has been restated in many publications since with a request that the EU and US governments should officially endorse the principle. Although some policy makers and politicians are sympathetic to the idea, as a group they have so far refused the invitation. The TABD's more strategic goal, however, is the creation of the 'barrier-free transatlantic market' (e.g. TABD, 2004). In many ways the idea of the 'barrier-free transatlantic market' is similar to the TAFTA proposal from the mid-1990s.

For this book TABD's work in the area of agri-food biotechnology is particularly important. The formation of a TABD Working Group on Agri-Food Biotechnology was announced at the CEO Conference in Chicago in 1996 (TABD, 1996). The working group began with a series of industry consultations and industry–government workshops in order to identify areas where recommendations could be made. Specific proposals began to emerge in 1997. The 'Rome Communiqu ' from the 1997 CEO Conference focuses on the risk assessment of GM products and states:

> . . . future trade barriers can be avoided if the final safety assessment criteria are fully shared among the authorities and mutually accepted by political decision-makers. Industry concludes that the ultimate goal should be to arrive at compatible regulatory requirements leading to full consensus on and mutual recognition of safety assessments. To get action in the short term, the industry recommends formation of a joint EU–U.S. Industry and Government group to work on predictable and transparent regulatory requirements and mutual sharing of safety data and assessments.
>
> (TABD, 1997: 4)

The joint EU–US industry and government group mentioned met for the first time in April 1997 and focused its attention on sharing information about approval procedures and safety assessment.

By 1998 TABD work in the area of agri-food biotechnology had progressed further, although it was still focused entirely on pre-market risk assessment. General calls for greater transparency in the regulatory process and the need for 'science-based' decision making were combined with more specific proposals. The 'Statement of Conclusions' from the CEO Conference in Charlotte shows how more specific requests were starting to be made which were consistent with the TABD's broader vision:

> . . . U.S. and EU authorities are invited (1) to define the terms of reference of a review of their respective risk assessment and data requirements in early 1999 and (2) to develop terms of reference to conduct a pilot project to review risk assessments for one or more products. Industry will identify products for possible inclusion in the study. The goal of the review and pilot project are to identify opportunities for possible U.S. EU regulatory cooperation.
>
> (TABD, 1998: 6)

Drawing on this brief history we can make a number of observations. We must note, first of all, that the TABD began to develop its position on trade in agri-food biotechnology products before the public controversy surrounding them emerged in Europe around 1998. Consistent with its broader position TABD members wanted to ensure that the US and the EU developed compatible – and if possible centralised – regulatory procedures so that mutual recognition of safety assessments would be possible. Second, it is implicit in TABD documents, because no other issues are discussed, that the only regulatory problem that exists in relation to agri-food biotechnology products is pre-market safety assessment. Although other stakeholders would try to broaden the regulatory debate to include such things as traceability, labelling and liability, particularly in Europe after 1998/99, the TABD does not discuss these issues.

The Transatlantic Business Dialogue after the backlash

Agricultural biotechnology was one of the TABD's priority issues from the mid-1990s onwards. However, events in Europe in the late 1990s made TABD's work difficult for a number of reasons. First, it made it increasingly unlikely that there would be significant progress on its policy proposals. Second, the TABD itself began to be scrutinised more closely by NGOs and criticised for its efforts to shape regulatory frameworks in various areas. NGOs often highlighted its work in the area of agri-food biotechnology as evidence of an unacceptably close relationship with EU and US policy makers and the promotion of a specific economic agenda. Third, given the commercial implications of the backlash in Europe, and potential problems with new biotechnology products, the TABD itself ultimately found it impossible to maintain a consensus amongst its own members in this area. In this section we will briefly outline developments following the backlash against GM crops and foods in Europe.

The report of the fifth TABD CEO Conference (Berlin, 1999) explores two related issues which do not feature in earlier documents, the idea of an 'early warning' system to alert governments and industry about potential trade problems, and the precautionary principle. The emergence of both of these can be understood in the context of the emerging trade conflict between the EU and the US over biotechnology products.

'Early warning' involves the identification of issues that might lead to a trade dispute in the future so that differences of approach can be dealt with. The TABD argues that problems only tend to get dealt with when a crisis actually emerges and that it is very difficult to make progress at this point. The Transatlantic Economic Partnership (see below) is identified as a mechanism that should help to avoid trade disputes. In relation to its proposal for an 'early warning' system the TABD acknowledges progress made by politicians at the June 1999 EU–US summit. However, as with other TABD initiatives, this one was also controversial with civil society groups. A representative of a European consumer group outlined their concerns:

I think it was and is just another way of business trying to downward harmonise and get rid of as many regulations as possible . . . So with the early warning system, it's not that we're looking at what they're discussing and saying: 'OK. We should follow that issue and that issue.' We're just looking at the early warning system itself and saying, 'This is isn't transparent and all it is a way of getting rid of regulations and its damaging consumer interests'.

(Interview, 15 November 2002)

In the late 1990s the precautionary principle (PP), and its use by the European Union, was identified by the TABD as key issue for early warning. It gets extensive treatment in the Berlin recommendations on the PP (TABD, 1999: 3–4):

> The concept of the precautionary principle, which is under further development in the EU, permits regulators and policymakers, in the absence of full scientific certainty or 'zero risk', to invoke precautionary measures to prevent harm to the environment or health/safety of consumers. However, the definition itself is the subject of much debate, as is when to use the principle and who should apply it.

The TABD advises that the principle should be based on 'sound science' and warns:

> Arbitrary use of the precautionary principle will cause trade conflicts; add to the cost of doing business; stifle innovation; and drive away investment from those countries that use it arbitrarily.

At this time the idea of the EU–US early warning system is also extended to the area of individual approvals of agri-food products. The following illustrates a number of points in relation to biotechnology products:

> The industry requires Government actions in order to obtain progress towards a transparent and predictable science-based approval system on both sides of the Atlantic. Continued and active cooperation between the authorities involved is necessary for the exchange of safety data and assessments.
>
> The TABD supports the idea of an early warning system for new regulatory requirements for individual product approvals. The longer-term objective remains the creation of centralized and compatible approval procedures in which the public has confidence on both sides of the Atlantic and which are consistent with OECD and Codex principles.
>
> Industry is, at the same time is [sic] committed to engage in a dialogue with society to address the concerns and needs of the population. The current debates in several countries in the transatlantic

marketplace, demonstrate that the end-users of the products should be more actively informed about the potential benefits of the products as well as the rigor of the health and environmental safety assessments during the approval procedures.

(TABD, 1999: 7)

In this quote we see a response from TABD to the emerging problems facing agri-food biotechnology in Europe. Whilst restating the overall goal of a centralised approval process for GM products, it is admitted that in the short term there may be difficulties around approving specific products. TABD members feared the emergence of new regulatory criteria and requirements at this time, particularly in Europe in the context of the back-lash against GM products, and they were therefore keen to emphasise the use of an early warning system at the level of product approvals, so that differences of approach between the EU and the US could be ironed out. At the same time, this passage is interesting because it includes a diagnosis of the problem now facing agri-food biotechnology – lack of information and understanding about potential benefits and public confidence in safety assessment procedures. This diagnosis appears very limited in context of the debate that was happening at the time.

After the 1999 Berlin meeting of TABD, the backlash against agbiotech products in Europe intensified in combination with additional food-chain problems, for example foot and mouth disease. The TABD then began to pay much less attention to this issue. The Working Group on Agri-food Biotechnology became much less active, largely because it could no longer identify a practical basis for consensus across the Atlantic. For the TABD the backlash in Europe was problematic because various European retailers began to reject GM grain for their own-brand products. This blockage undermined the business case for GM products, which TABD discussions had previously taken for granted, namely that GM was essential for economic competitiveness.

In addition to these problems, new products and issues created further internal divisions for TABD, particularly between biotechnology companies and companies involved in the food chain. While biotechnology companies tended to see new GM products as the high-value future of agriculture, food processors and retailers identified them as a threat to the food chain and profits. For example, after the decision by agbiotech companies to insert pharmaceutical genes into corn, consumer groups warned that pollen (gene) flow could lead to 'drugs in your cornflakes'. At this point the Grocery Manufacturers Association, a group who had played an integral part in the TABD, denounced GM pharmaceutical corn. Moreover, US farmers warned that Monsanto's plans for GM wheat could undermine wheat export markets – far greater than corn markets. The US Biotechnology Industry Organization (BIO) found it difficult to deal with such divisions, even outside of the context of TABD.

As TABD involvement in biotechnology products faltered, a US network eventually emerged and became more important. The AgBiotech Planning Committee (ABPC) was created to lobby Washington directly on issues relating to agricultural biotechnology. This network comprised over 20 organisations including groups like the National Corn Growers Association (NCGA) and the Biotechnology Industry Organization (BIO). ABPC lobbied on a variety of issues. In late 2001, for example, they supported the US Government's Biotechnology and Agricultural Trade Program as a 'necessary and critical tool to ensure the acceptance and adoption of important agricultural biotechnologies in world markets'. They argued that this measure should be retained in the final version of the US Farm Bill (ABPC, 2001). As discussed further in Chapter 6, ABPC also argued that the US should make a formal complaint to the WTO regarding the EU's *de facto* moratorium on biotechnology products. In 2003 they argued further that the US should also submit a formal complaint to the WTO regarding the EU's traceability and labelling rules.

A policy officer of a major trade association involved in the US food chain, and member of TABD and ABPC, reflected on some of the developments discussed in this section as follows:

> The TABD includes all actors in the food chain. They are differently willing to assume the [commercial] risk of GM products . . . Your interests and perspectives depend on where you are in the food chain. In the late 1990s a TABD Ag-Food Working Group would have taken place in the transition of GM products to the marketplace in Europe. TABD discussions focused on this situation but were set aside as US-EU differences became apparent . . . The TABD takes a business-strategic approach. In this case TABD discussions could not be managed towards direct results . . .
>
> For this sector, TABD discussions were initiated in 1998 by Niall Fitzgerald of Unilever and Robert Shapiro of Monsanto. It became clear that the European food industry was not going to use GM grain, and neither would farmers. Yet the technology providers wanted a market. So what would keep an Ag-Food Working Group together? The reality was that the market would do what it would do, so it was difficult to see a common project in the TABD.
>
> [TABD discussions on ag-food biotechnology were halted at the end of 2000.] We faced the question of how best to advance industry interests. It mattered little whether discussions were held in the TEP [see next section] or in a TABD Ag-Food Working Group; the main difference would be the absence of government officials in such a working group. After TABD discussions we established a new policy vehicle, the Ag-Biotech Planning Committee, which represents US interests across the food chain.
>
> (Interview, 14 October 2003)

The Transatlantic Economic Partnership

Following agreement on the NTA in 1995 the business community, through the TABD, began to argue for the creation of an EU–US government-to-government network to work systematically on the removal of transatlantic trade barriers. Business saw this as an essential part of the implementation of the New Transatlantic Agenda. The EU and US governments acted in 1998 by creating the Transatlantic Economic Partnership (TEP). This is a government-to-government network run by trade officials from the US and EU. In this section we will describe the background to the TEP and how it works. In the following sections we focus on the work of the TEP in the agricultural biotechnology sector.

A declaration at the EU–US Summit in May 1998 (London) outlined an initiative to intensify multilateral and bilateral cooperation in the areas of trade and investment (TEP, 1998a). The EU and US governments stated: 'In keeping with our leading role in the world trading system, we reaffirm our determination to maintain open markets, resist protectionism and sustain the momentum of liberalisation.' The Transatlantic Economic Partnership was launched at this meeting as one of the ways of sustaining the momentum of liberalisation.

In an interview with an official from the EC, the history and nature of the TEP was described succinctly as follows:

> Originally the TEP was the son of failure. Sir Leon Brittan had a vision for transatlantic free trade . . . It didn't get through the [European] Council . . . and the fallback was a Transatlantic Economic Partnership. It was a mixed agenda. There were some issues, like the lack of a structured dialogue between stakeholders on either side of the Atlantic that needed addressing. There were other TEP issues that related not to dialogue but to market opening, including regulatory convergence.
>
> (Interview, 2 April 2003)

Perhaps the most striking omission from this description is the extent to which the TEP's history was linked to the TABD. In many ways the TEP was conceived as a way of acting on TABD recommendations. For example, the TABD held its fourth annual conference in 1998 and shortly before this meeting the EC outlined its 'priorities for this conference' as follows:

> To reconfirm business support for the Transatlantic Economic Partnership (TEP). Negotiations on a joint Action Plan for this major EU/US initiative are nearing completion. The TEP is designed to be supportive of TABD objectives to facilitate EU/US trade and economic relations . . .

> The TEP Action Plan with its concrete timetable for achieving results is expected to provide a new impulse to bring forward the implementation of TABD recommendations.
>
> (CEC, 1998a)

A similar sentiment was included in the TEP declaration made by the EU and the US:

> The EU and US recall the imaginative and practical approach of EU and US business in the Transatlantic Business Dialogue which has contributed to many of the NTA's successes . . . We urge the TABD to continue and extend its valuable contribution to the process of removing barriers to trade and investment.
>
> (TEP, 1998a, para. 15)

Following the political launch of the TEP in mid-1998 the task of turning it into a reality, particularly by drawing up a programme of work, fell to trade officials in the EU and the US. The output of this process became the TEP Action Plan (TEP, 1998b), which was agreed between the EU and the US in November 1998. One EU trade official described the process and made a link with the Transatlantic Free Trade Association agenda as follows: 'In the Commission it was generated bottom up. People said: "Help. TAFTA is dead and now we've got to invent a TEP. What can we put in it?" So it was generated by securing suggestions from people in specific policy areas. What can we usefully do with the Americans?' (interview, 2 April 2003). This description suggests that the process of drawing up the TEP Action Plan was a fairly ad hoc one, and this may be accurate, but TABD priorities and proposals were nevertheless written into the TEP's work plan at this stage. We show this in relation to GM products below.

The TEP Declaration and the TEP Action Plan, both agreed in 1998, identify various ways in which the TEP can help to 'sustain the momentum of liberalisation'. In broad terms, and in a wide variety of areas, the list includes such things as the mutual recognition of testing and approval procedures, agreement on the equivalence of technical and other requirements, intensification of dialogue between scientific experts, standard-setting bodies and regulatory agencies. More generally, although the TEP is primarily concerned with EU–US trade liberalisation, early documents make it clear that it will also serve as a way of influencing the international trade liberalisation agenda. From the outset the EU and the US intention was to use the TEP to agree common positions before presenting them to the world at large. The ill-fated WTO ministerial meeting in Seattle in 1999, where the WTO failed to launch a new round of trade negotiations, is identified in the 1998 TEP documents as a key target.

In operation the TEP is a novel and unusual transatlantic network. Prior to its existence EU and US officials did discuss trade and regulatory issues with each other but there was no structured dialogue that brought officials of different kinds together to discuss common problems. In part the TEP is an attempt to deal with this problem. One European official involved with the TEP Environment Working Group described the situation before the TEP as follows:

> It was less structured in any given field and not structured at all between fields. On environment, for example, our environment people talked to EPA [US Environmental Protection Agency] from time to time. Trade people talked to USTR [Office of the US Trade Representative] from time to time. But . . . [DG Trade] never talked to EPA and our environment people seldom talked to USTR. So the missing link was the joining up of thinking between policy areas.
>
> (Interview, 2 April 2003)

The TEP and biotechnology products before the moratorium

It is clear from the above that throughout the early and mid-1990s the EU–US trade liberalisation agenda gained momentum. Although the Transatlantic Free Trade Association was rejected in the early part of the decade, the basic idea was soon taken up. The creation of the Transatlantic Business Dialogue, followed by agreement on the New Transatlantic Agenda and the formation of the Transatlantic Economic Partnership, intensified efforts around EU–US trade liberalisation. This coincided with the commercialisation of agricultural biotechnology and trade in related products. The fact that these developments coincided with each other is important. In the following two sections we examine the TEP's work in the area of biotechnology products before and after the moratorium in Europe in the late 1990s.

Agri-food biotechnology was on the TEP agenda from the outset. The 1998 TEP declaration identified it as a key area of TEP activity and this ensured that it featured in the TEP Action Plan released later that year. The TEP Action Plan argued for the creation of an 'over-arching group' (TEP, 1998b: § 3.5.2(a)):

> to monitor progress of the dialogue on the various technical issues carried out in existing groups, and to take into account their potential trade effects with the objective of reducing unnecessary barriers to trade; to seek to increase and enhance scientific and regulatory cooperation and information exchange and promote transparency and information of consumers [sic].

A more concrete action in the area of biotechnology is identified in the TEP Action Plan as follows (TEP, 1998b: § 3.5.2(b)):

> An early step towards accelerating the regulatory process would be to encourage simultaneous applications for scientific assessments in the US

and in a Member State; the possibility of a pilot project to this effect is under consideration.

For this specific action the target date given is 'as soon as an appropriate new application is in preparation by industry'.

From this list of activities it is the pilot project on simultaneous scientific assessment of a GM product that is most striking in retrospect. In practical terms this activity was aimed at ensuring that EU and US regulators, faced with the same application for approval from industry, would conduct the risk assessment in the same way and, by extension, come to the same conclusion. This proposal makes a number of assumptions – for example, that risk assessment is a purely objective process.

Ultimately such an activity is driven by the desire to reduce the costs incurred by industry when they apply for approval of a product in different jurisdictions. It also seeks to reduce barriers to trade between jurisdictions. Such a pilot project could be followed by a proposal for mutual recognition of safety assessments, which would then remove the need for both the EU and the US to conduct their own safety assessments in all cases. More generally, it is striking that the TEP Action Plan acknowledges no other regulatory issues beyond risk assessment. For example, at this time no TEP discussions were proposed on the labelling of GM foods, even though different approaches to labelling can create a trade barrier; indeed, mandatory GM labelling in the EU was becoming an issue at this time.

Where did the proposal for a pilot project on simultaneous assessment come from? Enthusiasts and sceptics can be identified. The TABD had proposed such a project earlier in 1998, as discussed above, and US officials had already done similar work with Canada. One EU official involved in TEP work on biotechnology described the second of these influences as follows:

> That was an American idea. USDA [US Department of Agriculture] and APHIS [Animal and Plant Health Inspection Service] had done that with Canada. They said 'OK. Let's try extending it to Europe as a first step in real regulatory convergence.' I would say that on both sides the technicians were open to the idea but the policy officials were reluctant. People with a stake in the TEP process adding value, which I would characterise as DG Trade and DG Relex [External Relations], had to push the officials in charge of regulatory policy to allow the technicians to do the cooperative work.
>
> (Interview, 2 April 2003)

A US official involved in TEP's work on biotechnology gave a similar account:

> APHIS, and their Canadian counterparts, eventually worked out an MOU [memorandum of understanding], which led to closer cooperation.

So we tried to reduce duplication of testing requirements on companies in different countries. What you had was Canadian and US authorities spending enough time together and understanding each other's systems that they became comfortable enough to say, 'OK. If company x has commercialised product y in Canada, Canada's examined the whole data package and assessed its safety, we at APHIS USDA are willing to accept the results of the Canadian assessment and not require the company to go through duplicate assessments here.' In the TEP we asked, 'Can we move in the same direction between the US and the EU? Why not?'

(Interview, 15 October 2003)

With a skeleton agenda provided by the TEP Action Plan, a TEP Biotechnology Working Group was created in the late 1990s. It was co-chaired by representatives of DG Trade of the EC and USTR of the US government, and meetings were attended by a long list of other officials and regulators from both sides. The EU side included DG Trade, DG Consumer Affairs, DG Environment and DG Research and the US side included USDA (US Department of Agriculture), APHIS (Animal and Plant Health Inspection Service), USFDA (US Food and Drug Administration), USEPA (US Environmental Protection Agency), US Department of State, and USTR (Office of the United States Trade Representative). It thus served the purpose of creating a dialogue amongst officials who would not otherwise be directly in contact with each other. One participant in the discussions of the TEP Biotechnology Working Group classified the list of participants into three groups:

You have three groups. You have those who make regulatory policy. They typically don't want anybody to look at what they're doing . . . Then you've got the technicians. They're honest seekers after scientific knowledge and efficient ways of doing things. They were keen to share their work and talk. Then you've got people who have a stake in making TEP work and resolving and avoiding disputes. In this case they were more on the side of the technicians.

(Interview, 2 April 2003)

Although this membership appears diverse from one perspective, it can also appear quite limited from another. There was no input from civil society into the TEP's agenda nor any of its ongoing discussions. Businesses, in contrast, through TABD, had played a large part in setting the TEP's agenda and were involved in its work in various ways.

In 1999, therefore, the TEP Biotechnology Working Group intended to pursue an agenda that was both general and specific – general discussions on regulatory convergence and specific work on simultaneous assessment. These different strands were described by a US trade official involved as follows:

> [The TEP Biotechnology Working Group] was an attempt to have a better dialogue on biotechnology, where we obviously had some significant differences, and . . . in the first instance to keep each other informed of what was going on in our respective jurisdictions.
>
> (Interview, 15 October 2003)

And more practically:

> It is unlikely that any two jurisdictions at any point in time could have exactly the same products approved . . . So we thought it might be worthwhile to try to work out a system to deal with that. We spent some considerable time on that but, at the end of the day, didn't succeed.
>
> (Interview, 15 October 2003)

The final sentence above hints at the trouble that lay ahead for the TEP Biotechnology Working Group. In practice its work on simultaneous assessment was soon thrown into disarray. In June 1999 several members of the EU Environment Council signed statements that effectively blocked approval of any more GM products – this became known as the *de facto* moratorium.

The TEP and biotechnology products after the moratorium

After the backlash against agbiotech products in Europe, and the response by European politicians, the agenda and role of the TEP Biotechnology Working Group had to change. Put simply, European trade officials were no longer in a position to pursue the liberalisation of trade in GM crops and foods. However, the working group discovered a new role as a rare venue to continue a dialogue about the trade conflict, by separating cooperative efforts from the increasingly inflamed rhetoric of both EU and the US politicians and high-level officials. In this section we will outline the activities of the TEP from the late 1990s onwards, focusing on the pilot project on simultaneous assessment, discussion of new regulatory issues and efforts to overcome 'the corn ban'.

The EU's *de facto* moratorium on new biotechnology products becalmed the TEP Biotechnology Working Group's project on simultaneous scientific assessment of a GM product. Even if the biotechnology industry identified a candidate product, the EU was unable to assess it properly for approval. As a result the working group became much less ambitious. It worked simply to agree on such issues as how a GM product should be described – molecular genetic characterisation – and what was required in a data set before a risk assessment could be done. In an interview one EU official described the activities of the TEP Biotechnology Working Group in this area as follows: 'We agreed on the data set. We were never trying to agree what the regulatory authorities should do with it. We were simply trying to arrive at a single set of papers for American and Community regulators' (interview, 2

April 2003). Yet the TEP Biotechnology Working Group had been set up to achieve more than this. However, as the transatlantic conflict over agricultural biotechnology became more acrimonious, problems arose in relation to the TEP agreeing too much – rather than too little, as had previously been the case. Having agreed on the data that was required for a risk assessment, the US could demand that EU regulators come to the same decision about approval based on that information; this was a political risk from the EU perspective.

Although it became impossible to pursue the original agenda of the TEP Biotechnology Working Group, new developments gave the group further issues to discuss. For example, in the late 1990s, in response to the public backlash, European politicians instructed the EC to develop legislation on traceability and labelling of GM products. The proposals were drawn up and circulated by the Commission; in 2000–2002 they began to work their way through the EU's legislative process. US industry and the US government vehemently opposed this legislation from the outset. They argued that traceability is technically impossible to achieve and prohibitively expensive; they criticised mandatory GM labels as misleading and as a barrier to trade – indeed, a 'skull and crossbones' in the eyes of consumers. The EU went ahead anyway and the TEP became a place where European officials could explain their approach to their US counterparts and try to minimise trade conflict.

Following the EU *de facto* moratorium on approval of new biotechnology products, the TEP Biotechnology Working Group faced another new problem – 'the corn ban', as the US side called it. As outlined in the introduction to this book, the US lost a market for its maize in Spain and Portugal in the late 1990s, partly because not all GM maize approved in the US had been approved in the EU. The US has a bulk commodity system of production which involves routine mixing, so US exporters could not guarantee that exports to Europe would not contain maize that could not legally be placed on the market there. A solution to this problem would involve some form of identity preservation in the US system, with EU-approved maize being kept separate in the supply chain for export. Some form of testing and verification would also be needed.

Work on these issues began seriously in the TEP Biotechnology Working Group in 2000 and continued until 2003. Eventually these efforts, which included US businesses, reached an impasse. Here an EU official and a US official involved in these negotiations reflect on the difficulties:

> We also looked at whether we could overcome current problems that have led American suppliers not to tender for corn shipments to Europe. In this area US business put things on ice. Unlike soya, where the only event [GM trait] planted in the US is approved in Europe, for corn some of the events planted in the US are not approved in Europe. So far they account for less than 20 per cent of production in any given year. Either

GM-free or approved GM accounts for the rest. But there is no systematic identity preservation. As a result the Americans decided that once
corn was in the supply chain they could no longer safely ship it to
Europe. The rather small tariff quota allowing a certain amount to be
shipped to Europe, 200,000 or 300,000 tons, is now taken up by Argentine
suppliers rather than the US. So there has been no change in terms of
EU imports. It isn't a protectionist measure. But it is a loss of a market
by the Americans. We've always said to the Americans: 'That's your
choice. Nobody is forbidding American corn to come in but, yes, you
would have to identity-preserve it in order to supply the market.
However, we believe that we could agree a framework or protocol on
sampling and testing which would enable you to certify that a given
shipment is conforming to EU regulatory requirements before you ship
it. Then you would reduce the risk of having a given shipment turned
away at the European end.' The American industry and administration
wanted to restore the trade but wanted to address two problems they saw
in our proposal. One was that the cost of the segregation and sampling
and testing would be too high for it to be a commercially viable activity.
The second was that we couldn't reduce to zero the risk that somebody,
if only for audit purposes, would want to check a shipment once it
arrived here. We got to the stage where the Americans were due to make
a further proposal to us about how to take this forward and their
industry said: 'No. Don't make a proposal at this stage. We don't want
you to go down this road.' That was last summer. At that point we said
to [the] Americans: 'We don't have an agenda. We know where we are in
terms of the regulatory pipeline. We have a good understanding of
where we are on the legislative process. On corn you can't move so let's
wait until you can.' That's still not the case.

(Interview, 2 April 2003)

We looked at it. Could we provide assurances to the EU that any given
shipment did not contain varieties that were not approved there? It
proved to be a huge problem because of the nature of corn and
commodity products. There was no market need to segregate biotech
corn from non-biotech corn, and we have so much biotech corn in this
country that it's unlikely that any given shipment has no biotech corn in
it. But to be able to say that the only varieties in a shipment are the ones
approved in the EU, obviously that would involve some sort of testing
process to validate that. [There are numerous practical, technical and
economic problems.] We did a fair amount of work on the issue. [An
official from DG Trade] came here and made a presentation to representatives of our grain companies who were willing to explore this, but they
were deeply sceptical, partly because of the politics of the European
Union. Part of the feeling was that, even if the governments could reach
agreement on all the protocols, and the technical details of a system like

this, how could Europe guarantee that some ship at whatever port could actually unload, and you're not going to have some sort of public protest and the government system stopped? How could you guarantee that you wouldn't have some group like Greenpeace who would attempt to stop unloading? It couldn't really be guaranteed. So from a trader's point of view it's a high-risk business and why do it? . . . We haven't seen a whole lot of courage by political authorities to stand up to these groups. Ultimately, I think it was down to the scepticism of companies that in the current climate in Europe you could have a workable system . . . At this point we had, I don't know the exact numbers, but Europe had approved four or five varieties of biotech corn, and we had like seven or eight, so we had two or three more. There was one variety that accounted for something like 90 per cent of the unapproved and we discussed it with the Commission: 'If you could just get this one through your approval system then the odds of finding unapproved varieties in your shipment drops way down.' They were aware of that, but they couldn't do anything to the system . . . sometimes they drafted things, sometimes we drafted things, it was kind of a joint effort to see if we could put this together . . . my general recollection is we were both kind of working cooperatively here, coming up with ideas on both sides . . . We felt we were working with really good people at that time. It wasn't for a lack of goodwill or effort. It was just that [at] the end of the day it was hard to bring guys to think it could actually work . . . The most senior political people were interested in seeing whether the TEP could come up with a workable solution, so they were certainly supportive of and interested in this effort . . . The trade were obviously involved as well. We had a TEP biotech working group meeting in Washington with representatives from NAEGA. That's the North American Export Grain Association. So we had the president of that association plus some members, representatives of some of the companies. There were four or five people from NAEGA who came in. There was some scepticism in the industry so I said [to DG Trade]: 'Why don't we have them in, let them hear directly from you, and you can make the best sales pitch on this?' But the trade were sceptical and they thought: 'These are nice guys but they're bureaucrats, they don't run grain ships and we do.'

(Interview, 15 October 2003)

Ultimately, the TEP was unsuccessful in its efforts to overcome barriers to importing US maize into the EU.

The US government acknowledged European commercial pressure to identify specific varieties of GM corn, as a basis on which to have identity preservation of US exports: 'US trading partners had created a need for product differentiation in the marketplace,' noted the Department of Agriculture. Several companies were developing lab tests for this purpose and the USDA offered to evaluate and validate their test methods. This meant specificity for the 'transformation event' of several biotech-derived grains and oilseeds (USDA–GIPSA, 2002). However, the grain trade generally showed little interest in segregation. According to a USDA (GIPSA) official involved:

> As far as I know, there is no testing that is being done in order to gain access to the European market . . . Since we have several corn [GM transformation] events that are commercialised, and some of them are approved in the EU and some of them are not, and all of our corn essentially is co-mingled, there is a small niche market for non-biotech corn. And we do have some markets where we sell non-biotech corn, but that's not trying to differentiate between EU-approved and unapproved events; that's just total biotech and non-biotech.
>
> (Interview, 15 October 2003)

Thus new techniques to identify GM varieties made little difference for overcoming the corn ban, mainly because the problem was not fundamentally a technical one. Indeed, US farmers and traders generally declined to accept responsibility for solving the segregation problem – which had been created by the EU, in their view.

Given the EU *de facto* moratorium on new agbiotech products, then, the TEP was unable to make significant progress on its Action Plan. The problems were political, rather than regulatory or technical. There was a meeting of the Biotechnology Working Group in March 2002 but officials from the US side reported little incentive to discuss issues because it was virtually impossible to influence practice anyway. In an interview one member from the US said: 'There is little incentive for a purely abstract discussion.' This comment emphasises the importance of making concrete progress on technical regulatory issues over the discussion of differences of approach or ways of understanding the problem. Another frustrated US official who participated in the March 2002 meeting stated: 'If they regard this sector as a good example of cooperation, then they must be pretty desperate.' However, when interviewed six months later, the same person saw more value in the TEP Biotechnology Working group despite the lack of concrete results:

> There seem to be two chains of thought. One is why get together and talk if nothing ever happens. Let's just forget it until there's something to talk about. There's another chain which is that we should be talking on a regular basis even if we don't make a lot of progress. We need to at least have a dialogue so that we know who the players are. Things change. People leave and others start. It is important that folks in the US and the EU know who the people are. So should we meet when there really isn't a lot of progress? I would say that both sides are fairly interested in just keeping the lines of communication open and therefore are

willing to meet every six months or so. A lot of time is spent at these meetings just giving an update.

(Interview, 10 September 2002)

Thus the relatively simple trade liberalisation agenda was replaced by more complex interactions in the agbiotech sector. For a period the TEP Biotechnology Working Group became one of the few places where the EU and the US could discuss differences of approach at a technical level in an effort to reach an understanding, even if agreement on a common approach was unlikely. Not surprisingly, the EU regularly emphasised the importance of discussions and argued that a formal complaint to the WTO would be unhelpful. However, interest in the TEP discussions declined over time, in parallel with TABD discussions around agricultural biotechnology being constrained by domestic pressures. In 2003 the US made a formal complaint to the WTO and thus ensured that EU–US interactions in relation to agricultural biotechnology would take place on an overtly antagonistic basis.

Conclusion

At the beginning of this chapter we outlined EU and US efforts to clarify the purpose of their relationship following the collapse of the USSR. The New Transatlantic Agenda, agreed in 1995, was central to this effort. Amongst other issues, the NTA identified trade liberalisation as a shared goal that could cement and redefine the transatlantic relationship for the new era. The Transatlantic Business Dialogue (TABD), which pre-dated and informed the NTA, was identified as the type of transatlantic network to be encouraged and as a key partner in the trade liberalisation agenda. The Transatlantic Economic Partnership (TEP), a network overseen and organised by trade officials in the EU and the US, was created in 1998 as an expert body to promote trade liberalisation, including in the agbiotech sector. Drawing on our description of these processes, we can begin to answer the four narrative questions raised in the introduction to this book.

How did policy actors try to advance particular policy agendas?

In these developments, we begin to see the role played by collective problems – or the definition of problems as collective ones. In the mid-1990s business leaders and politicians in the EU and the US identified two strategic problems. The first was the future basis of the US–EU relationship and the second was 'barriers to transatlantic trade'. These problems were brought together in the New Transatlantic Agenda, through complex processes which linked political and commercial agendas. Transatlantic trade liberalisation then became a basis for building a new special relationship between Europe and the US.

By linking policy problems in this way, a powerful transatlantic coalition, eventually including businesses, politicians, trade officials and regulatory officers, was created. The TABD and the TEP were institutional expressions of this coalition. Drawing on Chapter 1, we can say that these developments illustrate the role played by collective problems in governance. While uncritical accounts of governance focus on cooperation to deal with collective problems, a critical account focuses on how problems come to be identified as collective ones, especially as the basis on which a new policy coalition can form.

Approval and commercialisation of the first agbiotech products took place in this context. As our discussion shows, efforts to commercialise products in the EU and the US ran in parallel with efforts to create a harmonised regulatory regime between these markets. Issue-framing played a central role in these efforts. In Table 2.1 we analyse the TABD position on biotechnology products from an advocacy coalition perspective and in Table 2.2 we do the same from a discourse coalition perspective. Both illustrate how specific policy proposals were linked to beliefs or narratives, respectively, about wider issues – e.g. trade liberalisation, the role of technology in society and the regulation of risk.

For example, science is understood as an objective source of knowledge about risks and therefore as a basis for harmonised regulatory standards across the Atlantic. Through risk assessment, this policy agenda classified the first generation of agbiotech crops as similar to conventional ones. This was as a basis on which to gain access to a market that treats grain as a homogenous product. Such framing of agricultural biotechnology helped to cement the relationships between coalition members focused on this technology, which included the TEP. Issue-framing also informed specific policy proposals, such as the proposal for a TEP pilot project on simultaneous assessment of a GM product in the EU and the US.

How were expertise and knowledge used to influence policy making?

TABD members claimed authority to inform the regulation of agbiotech products by emphasising certain types of knowledge and expertise over others. In the area of risk, for example, biotechnology companies combined claims about objective risk assessment with claims about the precision of GM techniques. They dismissed other forms of knowledge, such as that possessed by consumers, as if they were irrational or at least needed to be educated about product benefits and safety. In practice TABD members also controlled knowledge that others required, such as data on safety experiments and on molecular composition; the latter was required for any procedure to identify GM corn varieties and thus overcome the corn ban. Beyond science, businesses were able to claim knowledge of what practices would be commercially viable and technically feasible in the food chain. This was particularly the case in the US, where grain traders emphasised the commercial and technical difficulties associated with any effort to segregate GM corn.

Table 2.1 TABD and Biotechnology Products: An Advocacy Coalition Analysis

Deep (Normative) Core Beliefs	Near (Policy) Core Beliefs	Secondary Aspects
Definition: Fundamental normative and ontological beliefs. These are very difficult to change. This would be akin to religious conversion.	Definition: Fundamental policy beliefs. Basic strategies for acting on deep core beliefs. Can change if experience reveals serious anomalies.	Definition: Instrumental decisions – legislative and administrative – necessary to implement core policy positions. Moderately easy to change.
The World View	*EU–US Trade and Biotechnology*	*The Regulation of GM Products*
New technologies improve the quality of life by solving problems and addressing needs.	'Sound science' can provide a common, objective basis for EU and US risk regulation.	Risk assessment is the only regulatory problem and it should be done on a case-by-case basis.
Society is comprised of self-interested competitive elements – people, businesses and countries.	Regulations based on 'sound science' should produce common standards in the EU and the US.	The EU and the US should adopt the same regulatory standards for risk assessment.
Competition is essential because it results in progress and economic growth.	Common standards for risk assessment will encourage trade between the EU and the US.	The EU and the US should move towards a single, centralised regulatory procedure.
Markets and trade are the primary mechanisms through which competition takes place.	Regulatory authority should pass from domestic institutions to transatlantic ones.	Traceability is unnecessary and impossible in practice because of the bulk handling of goods.
Demand means that the market will tend to deliver what consumers (and society) want.	Scientific experts and business people have the knowledge to make decisions about standards.	The costs of segregation also make traceability and identity preservation too expensive.
Businesses can expect a minimum of government interference in the market and their activities.	Biotechnology is a sunrise industry that will solve various social and environmental problems.	Labelling of GM products is not justified because they are not different from conventional products.
The main role of government is to ensure that the market operates efficiently.	The 'precautionary principle' facilitates politically motivated decisions and threatens trade.	Consumers will misunderstand GM labels as a 'skull and cross bones' and this is unfair.

Apparently the TEP was conceived as a technical body in a manner that is consistent with the TABD perspective on knowledge and expertise – not as a place where policy problems would be debated and perhaps redefined. TEP members adopted the view, promoted by TABD amongst others, that regulatory harmonisation is a largely technical exercise, which can be achieved by regulatory and trade officials alone. For agbiotech products, US officials had already undertaken successful technical interactions with Canadian officials, leading to an agreement on mutual recognition of safety assessments. Following the US–Canada model, it was proposed that the TEP

Table 2.2 TABD and Biotechnology Products: A Discourse Coalition Analysis

Storylines	*Discourses*
Definition: Narratives on reality through which elements from many different domains are combined. Provide actors with a set of symbolic references and suggest a common understanding.	Definition: Ensemble of ideas, concepts, and categorisations that are produced, reproduced, and transformed in a particular set of practices.
'…industry requires Government action… [on] a transparent and predictable science-based approval system on both sides of the Atlantic… cooperation between the authorities is necessary…'.	Sound science
'Arbitrary use of the precautionary principle will cause trade conflicts; add to the cost of doing business; stifle innovation; and drive away investment from those countries that use it arbitrarily'.	
Business needs a '…results oriented approach to the construction of the New Transatlantic Marketplace… and a new transatlantic model based on the principle of "approved once, accepted everywhere"'.	Trade liberalisation
'…the ultimate goal should be to arrive at compatible regulatory requirements leading to full consensus on and mutual recognition of safety assessments'.	
'…a barrier free transatlantic market which will serve as a catalyst for global trade liberalisation and prosperity… stimulate innovation and economic growth, more investment and create new jobs'.	Market benefits
'The transatlantic marketplace demonstrates that large, open markets are elements of stability… Increasingly, world peace and political stability are based on transatlantic and global interdependence'.	
'Industry is… committed to engage in a dialogue with society to address the concerns and needs of the population. The current debates in several countries in the transatlantic marketplace, demonstrate that the end-users of the products should be more actively informed about the potential benefits of the products as well as the rigor of the health and environmental safety assessments during the approval procedures'.	Uninformed public

Note: All quotes taken from TABD documents.

would involve face-to-face meetings between a range of technical experts and officials involved in agbiotech regulation. These meetings would allow participants to identify regulatory differences, as a first step towards overcoming them.

This technocratic view of regulatory harmonisation continued even after the European public backlash against GM products. For example, the TEP discussed technical means of overcoming the corn ban by using some form of identity preservation with associated monitoring. These cooperative efforts did not lead to a mutually agreeable solution, partly because the problem was more political-economic than technical. Techniques were devised to identify specific GM corn varieties, as a basis for segregating the one that lacked EU approval. But US farmers and grain traders generally declined to accept responsibility for solving this problem – which had been created by the EU, in their view.

How were regulatory standard-setting processes and trade conflict linked?

In this chapter we see a reversal of the stereotypical relationship, which assumes that trade liberalisation shapes regulatory standards, either upwards or downwards. Rather, regulatory standard-setting processes and trade conflict have shaped the terms for trade liberalisation in practice. In the mid- to late 1990s, for example, TABD promoted a view of regulation that focused entirely on pre-market safety assessment; no other regulatory issues were acknowledged. The TEP largely adopted this view. Together they sought to shape a standard-setting process that could achieve trade liberalisation, understood largely as the absence of any difference that would impede trade. This agenda rested on the assumption that the market tends to deliver what consumers want, thus adequately providing consumer choice (see Table 2.1).

Challenges to this view began to emerge in the late 1990s, when 'anti-globalisation' campaigners identified trade liberalisation as a threat to safety standards and consumer choice, amongst other things. Eventually the European backlash, regulatory delays and commercial blockages broke the original link between standard setting and trade liberalisation. In response TABD members sought to extend their original approach. For example, as the European backlash against biotechnology products gained momentum, and European politicians and policy makers began to accommodate public concerns, TABD requested an 'early warning system' to identify future trade barriers at an early stage. They also reiterated that regulation should be based on 'sound science' – rather than the 'precautionary principle', which threatened transatlantic trade.

Eventually the European regulatory standard-setting process began to reshape the terms for trade liberalisation in practice (see Chapter 3 for more). By accommodating the European backlash against the technology, regulatory procedures allowed greater scope for the scientific and cultural complexities of risk assessment. It also helped to place more regulatory issues on the policy agenda. Traceability and labelling are good examples, particularly disagreements about what is the threshold (percentage of material) to require GM labelling. With these regulatory changes and new issues, the transatlantic grain trade would depend on a different standard-setting process than before. These observations confirm that we should not assume that trade liberalisation shapes regulatory standards before considering that regulatory standard-setting processes might shape trade liberalisation in practice.

How were EU–US interactions and intra-jurisdictional conflicts linked?

As described in this chapter, many EU–US interactions had the opposite of their intended effect. Efforts to promote regulatory harmonisation and trade liberalisation led instead to contending coalitions, trade conflict and regulatory divergence (as discussed in subsequent chapters). These developments fractured the collective problem and issue-framing which underpinned TABD's engagement with agri-food biotechnology. Consequently, this transatlantic coalition was thrown into disarray. Indeed, transatlantic trade, rather than trade barriers, quickly became part of the problem for some European businesses, particularly food retailers. They began to view US agricultural exports as a threat to their markets. Moreover, the original basis for the TABD coalition was undermined in the USA by the emergence of new products, such as GM pharmaceutical crops and GM wheat. US food producers, who had previously accepted or even promoted agbiotech, feared these new products for commercial reasons – for example, pharmaceuticals ending up in cornflakes by mistake.

For all these reasons, by 2000 there was a much less coherent basis for a TABD policy coalition to advocate transatlantic trade liberalisation and regulatory harmonisation for biotechnology products. Likewise, the TEP Biotechnology Working Group reached an impasse and became dormant. It was unable to address fundamental policy differences on how to regulate a new and controversial technology. Over time a new US coalition formed, including US members of the former TABD–TEP coalition. This was focused on the AgBiotech Planning Committee and it redefined its members' interests and focused on the EU in a different way. Previously they had worked with European partners in an effort to promote biotechnology through trade liberalisation, but now they increasingly viewed the EU as a threat. The AgBiotech Planning Committee tried to persuade the US government to submit a formal complaint to the WTO, in order to isolate the EU and to discourage others from obstructing agbiotech products in the same way.

3 'Right to know, right to choose'

Biotechnology products and transatlantic civil society networks

Introduction

In Chapter 2 we discussed the Transatlantic Business Dialogue and the Transatlantic Economic Partnership. These networks were created in the mid- to late 1990s to encourage and facilitate transatlantic trade liberalisation. In the agbiotech sector, pre-market safety assessment was the only significant regulatory issue acknowledged by TABD. When the TEP was created, it took the same view. These networks therefore sought to ensure that the EU and the US adopted the same regulatory standards for safety assessment in an effort to avoid trade barriers. This exclusive focus on pre-market safety assessment continued until the regulatory debate was complicated by the backlash against biotechnology products in Europe.

In retrospect TABD–TEP framed the regulatory issues associated with GM crops and foods narrowly. Even in the mid- to late 1990s, critics were already painting a much more complex picture of the regulatory challenges. The following quote from a 1996 Consumers International publication illustrates this:

> The safety of GEFs [genetically engineered foods] is not the only issue of importance. Consumers also have the right to choose. This choice may be based on product characteristics such as taste, nutritional value and price, which can be affected by genetic engineering. It may also be based on concerns about how the food has been produced. Consumers have a growing interest in learning about the risks and benefits of the food production processes . . . Finally, the process of genetic engineering also raises moral and religious questions for some people who may want to choose not to buy foods produced in this way.
>
> (CI, 1996: 4)

This statement draws attention to issues that justify regulatory interventions that go beyond pre-market safety assessment.

In this chapter we examine the various ways that civil society groups acted through their own transatlantic networks to challenge and extend the regulatory framework for GM products from the late 1990s onwards. We also identify links between criticisms of agricultural biotechnology and criticisms of transatlantic trade liberalisation. In the first section we discuss criticisms of these two developments that began to emerge and converge in the late 1990s. The second section examines the creation of the Transatlantic Consumer Dialogue (TACD). The third section focuses on its arguments in relation to agricultural biotechnology. The fourth section discusses the short-lived Transatlantic Environmental Dialogue (TAED) and its position on agricultural biotechnology. The fifth section focuses on the EU–US Consultative Forum on Biotechnology, an expert group created by the EU and the US to find a consensus on agricultural biotechnology after the European backlash against GM products. For ease of reference, these networks, and the ones discussed in Chapter 2, are summarised in Table 3.1.

Criticisms of the TEP process

Critics of trade liberalisation have refined their arguments over the past decade, particularly following the creation of the World Trade Organization. At the most fundamental level they argue that trade theory, which informs trade liberalisation, is simplistic and ignores unacceptable outcomes. For example, trade theory emphasises comparative advantage, regional specialisation and efficient markets to promote economic growth. It says very little, however, about job losses, destruction of communities and the environment, even though these can be associated with trade liberalisation in practice. To those who say these are acceptable costs because trade liberalisation makes everyone richer in the end, the critics respond that in practice the wealth

Table 3.1 Transatlantic Networks and Biotechnology Products

Network	Description
Transatlantic Business Dialogue (TABD)	An EU–US business-to-business network which argues for trade liberalisation and regulatory convergence in various sectors.
Transatlantic Economic Partnership (TEP)	An EU–US government-to-government network run by trade officials but also involving regulatory officials and technical experts.
Transatlantic Consumer Dialogue (TACD)	An EU–US network of consumer groups which campaigns for consumer rights in the context of EU-US trade liberalisation.
Transatlantic Environmental Dialogue (TAED)	An EU–US network of environmental groups which campaigned for sustainable development in the context of EU–US trade liberalisation.
EU–US Consultative Forum on Biotechnology (Consultative Forum)	A time-limited expert group created to examine the EU–US conflict over GM products and to make recommendations.

accumulates in the hands of a lucky few. Critics have captured some of their concerns in the phrase 'all ships are NOT lifted on a rising tide'.

The New Transatlantic Agenda and the Transatlantic Economic Partnership were vulnerable to criticisms of this kind from the outset. Although the NTA–TEP involved more than just trade liberalisation, as the previous chapter showed, this was one of its central elements. For our purposes it is particularly significant that some critics, from the moment that the TEP Action Plan was published, focused specifically on agricultural biotechnology to illustrate the wider threat posed by EU–US trade liberalisation. A good example of this is found in a Corporate Europe Observatory publication of October 1998, which featured an article on 'EU–US trade deregulation: the TEP of the iceberg – how the New Transatlantic Marketplace Became the Transatlantic Economic Partnership' (CEO, 1998). This article discussed the emergence of the TEP and the work it intended to do in the area of agricultural biotechnology. Regarding the TEP in general it argues:

> Whereas the NTM [New Transatlantic Marketplace] – in fact a proposal for a transatlantic free trade zone – was politically too controversial, the TEP is far less likely to run into major public opposition. Although the aims are practically the same, the TEP agenda of step-by-step removal of barriers to trade and investment efficiently moves the process away from the political sphere and into the technical sphere. Controversial words like 'harmonization', not to mention 'common market' or 'free trade area', are carefully avoided. Nonetheless, although the process of creating joint regulation is avoided, the TEP will result in harmonization . . . the TEP builds on the approach and recommendations of the Transatlantic Business Dialogue, which since 1995 has operated to identify barriers to transatlantic trade and investment . . . Undoubtedly, the EU and US administrations have learned from their experience with the Multilateral Agreement on Investment (MAI), a typical 'big bang' treaty committing the signatory countries to the end goal of full-scale investment liberalization. The MAI ran into unprecedented opposition from a wide-ranging global coalition of social movements. The proposed NTM was also very vulnerable because of its ambitious 2010 deadline for the removal of all barriers to transatlantic trade and investment.
>
> (CEO, 1998)

In this analysis the TEP is linked to earlier controversial initiatives like the OECD-inspired Multilateral Agreement on Investment and Sir Leon Brittan's proposal for a New Transatlantic Marketplace or Transatlantic Free Trade Association (mentioned in the previous chapter). However, the article argues that the TEP shows how governments learned from these initiatives and created something that is basically the same but less likely to attract attention. Later the article discusses the work that the TEP intended to do in the area of agricultural biotechnology and concludes: 'This might sound benign, but a look at what biotechnology crusaders in both US industry and government hope to achieve from the TEP unveils a disturbing scenario.' This linking of criticisms of the trade liberalisation agenda with criticisms of agricultural biotechnology is an important theme in this book.

In addition to a number of general criticisms that can be levelled at any trade liberalisation project, critics of the TEP process drew attention to some specific problems associated with EU–US trade liberalisation. They pointed out, for example, that the TABD played a central role in the creation of the NTA and the TEP but no equivalent 'dialogue' represented the interests of consumers or the environment. They continue to argue that in practice it is hard to find out what is being negotiated, particularly by EU and US trade officials. Even though both the EU and the US are supposed to be advanced democracies, and trade officials are supposed to be representatives of governments and the public, there is a lack of transparency. For many the lack of involvement of elected officials in the TEP is a serious concern.

In the late 1990s criticisms of trade liberalisation were not restricted to the NTA–TEP. At this time a wide variety of groups were increasingly gathering around an 'anti-globalisation' banner and all mechanisms and institutions associated with trade liberalisation were being identified as problematic. Lack of transparency and a democratic deficit were common criticisms. A wide variety of groups identified trade liberalisation as the major threat to their core area of concern – jobs, environment, development or consumer rights. In 1998, out of this context, and in part in response to it, the US and the EU governments agreed to encourage additional transatlantic dialogues to form in an effort to engage civil society in the New Transatlantic Agenda.

Two of the most important civil society transatlantic dialogues to emerge in the late 1990s were the Transatlantic Consumer Dialogue (TACD) and the Transatlantic Environmental Dialogue (TAED). We discuss these in detail below. That discussion, however, can be placed in context by considering some of the explanations given for their creation. This happened three years after the EU and US governments had invited businesses to establish the Transatlantic Business Dialogue and after the New Transatlantic Agenda and the TEP Action Plan had already been agreed. When asked, government officials explain this action with reference to the NTA's stated goal of building bridges between the EU and the US (see Chapter 2). They also claim that there is no reason for the creation of additional dialogues other than the desire to promote interactions of various kinds between the EU and the US. However, other officials give more instrumental explanations and refer to the need for greater 'coordination' of civil society groups in the EU and the US so that they can contribute to the policy process more effectively.

Unfortunately, even some member organisations viewed the creation of TACD and TAED with scepticism. Critics pointed out that a business dialogue was created in 1995 and it enjoyed access to the highest level of decision makers. They wonder why it was only after the emergence of the NTA and agreement on the TEP Action Plan was reached that civil society was encouraged to contribute to policy making through the transatlantic dialogue process. Today they continually raise the problem of lack of access to high-level decision makers. Even those who are involved and are enthusiastic refer to the civil society dialogues as an 'afterthought', explained by the fact that the EU and the US administrations were embarrassed by the lack of civil society involvement in EU–US policy making. A central and troubling problem for civil society groups is captured as follows:

> If NGOs decide to participate in the TEP because of the possibility of presenting their concerns to the EU–US Summit, they risk contributing to the survival of a project which lacks a popular mandate and could be stopped . . . social movements have far more power than they tend to think when they dare to reject and organize against the illegitimate projects of the powers that be.
>
> (CEO, 1998)

The Transatlantic Consumer Dialogue

The Transatlantic Consumer Dialogue (TACD) was launched in September 1998. It is a network of approximately 60 consumer organisations from 16 countries sharing the common aim of influencing EU and US policy in the interests of consumers. These groups are supported directly by 10 million members but the TACD claims to represent the interests of 600 million consumers in total – the combined populations of the EU and the United States (TACD, 1999a). It encompasses well-known consumer groups like Public Citizen (US), Centre for Science in the Public Interest (US) and Consumers Union (UK), and Consumers International, based in London, acts as the secretariat.

It is relatively easy to identify the core of the TACD's agenda. Most members take consumer rights as their starting point and argue that these should inform all public policy which impacts on consumers (see CI, 2002). The existence of the TACD is partly explained by this shared belief in consumer rights, even if there are differences of opinion on interpretation and strategy. One member of TACD from a European consumer group explained in an interview:

> I've just been surprised at how we have reached agreement on lots of issues . . . where there have been things that people don't agree on, they have tended to be quite specific issues rather than the broader principles. People tend to agree on the principles . . . The basis of what we do is still, even though it is not done explicitly, the core consumer principles . . . That is where a lot of the issues come from – safety, choice, quality, redress, right to be heard. I think they are still at the heart of a lot of the way consumer organisations approach issues.
>
> (Interview, 11 October 2002)

Drawing on this shared belief in consumer rights and principles, TACD members began to engage in the EU–US policy-making process from 1999 onwards. Leaving aside proposals in specific areas, some of the most interesting (and for some troubling) aspects of their involvement have been associated with the process of formulating and prioritising policy positions. One member of TACD commented:

> In the first few years it was all about putting down resolutions in many different areas. So we had positions on all these different things. By 2000–2001 the governments were asking us to prioritise. And we realised we had to prioritise. So we drew up a list of eight priorities. We focused on these although the working groups were taking forward other issues as well. Then we thought let's have the dialogue with government and try to move the priority issues along. So rather than just jumping on new issues let's focus.
>
> (Interview, 15 November 2002)

Elsewhere the same person elaborated on the way in which the TACD acted to bring together consumer groups with different approaches, particularly in the US:

> In America the consumer movement is very divided . . . [Some] are very much of the old school. They are small 'c' conservative consumer organisations. They spend a lot of their time testing products and selling magazines and that's where their funding comes from. Lobbying governments is another one of their activities. On the other side you've got the Ralph Nader groups, the biggest one being Public Citizen. They are more into campaigning. They're more radical and more suspicious of governments. These groups didn't really work together but TACD has brought them together. So now the American consumer movement is much more unified.
>
> (Interview, 15 November 2002)

A US government official described this process as follows:

> In the early years the TACD discussions were more confrontational. The various NGOs put forward different views. But eventually the NGOs agreed on common approaches . . . the TACD forced them to put on a governance hat. The May 2001 meeting was more effective in developing common views and communicating with government reps.
>
> (Interview, 8 October 2001)

Such observations imply that TACD may act to co-opt consumer organisations into a policy process that is inconsistent with their aims. Some of the more radical US consumer groups have raised this concern. Critics point out that EU and US governments try to elicit a consensus policy position from consumer pressure groups on a range of complex and often controversial consumer issues. Policy makers and politicians are also keen to be able to say that they are listening to consumer groups. By extension, this allows them to claim that they are taking account of the public's concerns around EU–US trade liberalisation.

TACD concerns like this often surface in direct comparisons with TABD and its relationship to the TEP. For example, TACD members are concerned that TABD consistently gets access to a higher level of officials and politicians. They also know that the TABD has more resources and is better funded. And TACD members fear that the TEP's lack of transparency allows the TABD to shape the policy agenda without their knowledge. Such concerns have led to various proposals, some of which involve access to more information. For example, on some issues TACD has asked for joint meetings with TABD. TACD has also asked for the creation of an early warning system for any new measures that might lower regulatory standards. In this way they have taken a TABD proposal – an early warning system for trade barriers – and recast it in their own image. Public Citizen in particular promoted this initiative.

Why has the TACD continued to operate despite the reservations of some member organisations? This question can be answered in a number of ways. First, TACD is an opportunity to interact in a network. According to a representative of a European consumer organisation:

[It is a way of having] greater contact. We've always worked closely with European consumer groups, and with some of the US consumer groups that are members of Consumers International, but there is a wider range of consumer organisations involved in TACD ... it's an opportunity to discuss issues. On some issues the US is more advanced and on others the EU is ... it's partly the exchange and sharing of information ...

(Interview, 11 October 2002)

Another TACD member summarised the value of the TACD as follows:

It is a very good way for them to share information. It's a network. If we forget the governments it's a network. It's a way of finding out what is happening in other countries. The Europeans can find out how the Americans are doing something or vice versa. They can use that information when they're discussing with their own governments. It's another layer on which to build on a stronger consumer movement ... They know each other and they see each other. They put names to faces and have the opportunity to meet. The annual meetings are great for the consumer movement. They allow people to come together. So there are a lot of reasons why it is useful.

(Interview, 15 November 2002)

In practice, a lot of effort has been required before TACD discussions lead to consensus proposals on specific issues. Member organisations also continue to operate outside this arrangement, while trying to influence views within TACD.

Trade liberalisation had the potential to be a divisive issue from the start. At the first TACD meeting a representative of Public Citizen attacked trade liberalisation measures as 'corporate-managed trade', representing 'a giant step in the decline of democratic institutions'. She attacked the US government's role in the TEP: 'Given [that] the TEP negotiations have neither Congressional authorisation nor public legitimacy, it might be politically prudent for the government to take a sharply different approach to avoid another defeat with TEP.' She also proposed that limits be set on international standard-setting, especially given that the 'current global-isation model' regards diversity as inefficient (Claybrook, 1999). However, the TACD has been able to overcome significant differences of opinion on a range of issues such as trade liberalisation, consumption and develop-ment. When speakers attacked the General Agreement on Trade in Services (GATS) at the 2002 TACD meeting, on grounds that its trade liberalisation agenda would harm public services, not all TACD members accepted this view.

Based on this overview we can make some important observations about the TACD. First, this network was invited to form in relation to a transat-lantic trade liberalisation agenda that had already taken shape. Trade liberalisation, therefore, has been the context within which most of its discus-sions have taken place. Second, the member organisations share a commitment to consumer rights; this underpins the network and allows it to function. Third, there are diverse opinions on the purpose of the TACD. Some fear it is a mechanism designed to co-opt them into the policy-making process, whilst others draw attention to its networking benefits, regardless of how it relates to the official processes of transatlantic trade liberalisation.

The Transatlantic Consumer Dialogue and biotechnology products

The Transatlantic Consumer Dialogue was created at the moment when the backlash against GM products in Europe was gathering momentum. Not surprisingly, agricultural biotechnology, and GM food more specifically, became a priority issue. The first TACD position paper on transgenic foods and plants was released in 1999 (TACD, 1999b). A more comprehensive one – 'Consumer concerns about biotechnology and genetically modified organisms' – followed the next year (TACD, 2000). In these papers TACD members make it clear that they do not object to agricultural biotechnology and related products in principle. However, they do argue that the regulation of GMOs in the EU and the US is inadequate and that it has been shaped by business interests trade liberalisation.

TACD demands in relation to the regulation of GM products are derived from the core consumer rights mentioned above. The starting point is risk – mainly to human health but also to the environment because this is a consumer concern. In 1999 TACD argued that there must be clear consumer benefits associated with biotechnology products and that they should 'present no harm to human health or the environment' (TACD, 1999b: 1). Building on this in subsequent papers the TACD called for a rigorous and mandatory pre-market safety assessment procedure for all GM products. With respect to the safety of GM foods, TACD members raised concerns in a number of areas, such as allergenicity, antibiotic resistance, toxicity and nutritional changes. Although consumer groups have not argued that products already authorised and on the market are unsafe, they have argued that regulatory procedures are not robust enough to deal with these issues effectively.

From the outset TACD documents also raised the problem of unintended effects of genetic modification and associated unknown risks. The problem of unintended effects and unknown risks underpins the TACD demand for post-market monitoring:

> . . . the long term impact of GMOs on human and animal health and the environment should be carefully assessed before their commercial introduction and release into the environment, and monitored and assessed after their release . . . Long term monitoring of the use of GM foods should be a legal requirement and efforts are required to develop appropriate mechanisms for doing this.
>
> (TACD, 2000: 1–2)

Post-market monitoring was one of a number of regulatory issues which TACD and others were keen to put on the policy agenda in addition to mandatory pre-market safety assessment.

In Chapters 4 and 5 we discuss risks to the environment and human health in much more detail but it is worth noting here that TACD criticisms regarding safety have targeted the arguments and practices of regulators and businesses directly. For example, at the time of writing (March 2006), the US still has no mandatory pre-market safety assessment procedure for GM foods. Mandatory pre-market safety assessment is a basic TACD demand. In addition, biotechnology companies have argued that there are no unintended effects or unknown risks associated with genetic modification and therefore there is no need for post-market monitoring. As mentioned above, TACD members consider post-market monitoring to be essential. Therefore, from the late 1990s, TACD members, with others, were involved in introducing new arguments about risk into the policy-making process.

Beyond pre-market safety assessment and post-market monitoring, TACD members argue that the consumer has the 'right to know, right to choose'. On this basis TACD make an unambiguous demand for the labelling of all GM foods and foods derived from GM ingredients:

> TACD believes that consumers have a fundamental right to know what they are eating. Therefore, all GM food including food produced from GM ingredients which do not remain detectable in the final product should be labeled. Consumer concerns relate to the process of GM and not to the end product . . . consumers want information which includes the full disclosure of all aspects of the safety evaluation of GM foods, as well as the clear and truthful labeling of any approved products that come to market . . .
>
> (TACD, 2000: 3)

It is important to realise that in making this demand the TACD was arguing for two distinct and controversial regulatory developments. The first is the labelling of GM products where GM material is detectable. The second is the labelling of GM-derived products where it is not. From the TACD's perspective, however, this might simply be referred to as meaningful labelling:

> [the] right to choose is being undermined by the mixing of GM products (namely soya and maize) with conventional varieties . . . Consumers consider that labeling of the final product should depend on the presence of GMOs in the raw materials from which the product is made. Such an accurate and rigorous labeling requires complete traceability of GMOs throughout the entire production, processing and distribution chain.
>
> (TACD, 2000: 3)

The biotechnology and food industry fundamentally opposed such proposals for labelling and traceability for various reasons. They argue, for example, that if consumers want to choose they can select a product that is GM-free – for example, one labelled 'organic'. Concerning traceability, they argue that it is unnecessary, impossible to achieve, and that it would impose unacceptable costs on business because of the attendant need to segregate and preserve the identity of products (as outlined in Chapter 2).

Just as controversial as traceability and labelling are TACD demands that the EU and US governments should develop legislation on liability and mandatory insurance to cover situations where unforeseen problems emerge at some point in the future. Objections in this area focus on the economic implications of liability and insurance for the industry, and the knock-on impact on innovation, which businesses claim will be stopped in its tracks. Some objectors also argue that when a government authorises a product for commercial use, using the best knowledge available at the time, it takes on the responsibility for the costs of dealing with problems that emerge later, provided the business concerned has respected the conditions of approval.

In this section we have outlined TACD policy proposals in the area of agricultural biotechnology. It is clear that these are very different from those proposed by the TABD in the mid-1990s and taken up by the TEP in the late 1990s. Here there is no mention of a pilot project on simultaneous assessment of a biotechnology product in the EU and the US. Instead we see demands for mandatory pre-market safety assessment, post-market monitoring, traceability and labelling, and mandatory liability insurance. The TACD as such was not the source of these ideas. By the time the TACD formed, all of these proposals were circulating, particularly in the more critical debate in Europe. The TACD, however, provided additional opportunities to promote these ideas and to transfer them to the US. In an interview a member of the TACD reflected on the value of being able to make transatlantic arguments:

> . . . on an issue like GM, where it is often portrayed at a political level as though US consumers aren't concerned and EU consumers just get worked up about it, don't understand it, and are completely irrational, to be able to say, well actually, there is no difference whatsoever, US consumers and their representatives think exactly the same as EU ones, is useful. I think the development of consensus positions can be quite a useful way to influence government policy.
>
> (Interview, 11 October 2002)

For EU policy makers having to defend the different path that EU regulation started to take in the late 1990s, in the face of growing US hostility and threats, it was also useful to have arguments of this kind. They were evidence of a transatlantic consensus amongst consumer groups and, they could argue, consumers. TACD statements therefore became a resource for EU policy makers in different ways.

The Transatlantic Environmental Dialogue and biotechnology products

Consumer groups contested the introduction of GM crops and foods from the mid-1990s onwards. They are still vocal critics and they continue to argue that major changes need to be made to the regulatory frameworks of the EU and the US. On the whole, however, they do not campaign for a complete ban on agricultural biotechnology and related products. Instead, drawing on the idea of consumer rights, they campaign for legislation on such things as traceability, labelling, insurance and liability. This approach can be contrasted with that of environmental pressure groups, many of whom have demanded a complete ban on all uses of GMOs. In this section we focus on the creation of the Transatlantic Environment Dialogue (TAED) and the contribution it made to the EU–US debate on GM crops and foods in the late 1990s. The TAED provides us with a valuable counterpoint to the TABD and the TACD, both at the level of argumentation and at the level of engagement with the transatlantic dialogue process itself.

The EC invited environmental groups to organise a Transatlantic Environmental Dialogue in 1998. It was an invitation to contribute their perspective on a variety of policy issues in the context of transatlantic trade liberalisation. Some environmental groups accepted and the TAED was eventually launched on 3 May 1999. A press release issued by the European Environment Bureau at the time outlines the starting point:

> European and U.S. non-governmental organisations meeting here today established the Transatlantic Environment Dialogue (TAED) to protect and benefit the environment and to integrate environmental protection into all aspects of EU–US relations. The launching of the TAED is in response to bilateral governmental initiatives under the EU–US New Transatlantic Agenda, but it is in no way intended to legitimise these processes.
>
> (TAED, 1999)

This statement clearly shows that the TAED was problematic from the outset. Many of its members were unhappy with the idea of contributing to the transatlantic trade liberalisation process in any way because they believed that it should be abandoned altogether.

Sir Leon Brittan (Vice-President of the EC), one of the strongest advocates of transatlantic trade liberalisation, made a speech at the launch of TAED (CEC, 1999). In it he felt that it was necessary to defend the TEP process from the criticisms of those who were present. He argued that environment was already at the heart of TEP activities, regardless of what the critics might be saying, and that more generally there is no conflict between trade liberalisation and environmental protection. He went on to address one concern directly:

> It's natural that you should view the TransAtlantic Business Dialogue with a degree of envy: they are very much part of the process of co-operation. They weren't like that to begin with, but they were able to get together and come to conclusions which they shared, and these conclusions carried weight for two reasons: because they were shared, and because they were well argued and carried conviction.
>
> (CEC, 1999)

For the assembled the two reasons outlined by Brittan failed to cover what they perceived to be the real reasons why TABD is influential – resources, networks and the fact that TABD members share the same vision as the trade officials who oversee the TEP process.

Despite these reservations, however, TAED was launched. The members identified a number of core tasks (TAED, 1999): (1) monitor all EU–US negotiations and seek to make sustainable development their overall objective; (2) promote the highest environmental standards and regulations in the EU and the US; (3) campaign for transparency and accountability of EU–US negotiations and increase public participation in them; and (4) increase the amount of dialogue between environmental NGOs in the EU and the US. However, at the outset environmental groups explicitly stated their belief that trade liberalisation processes tended to lead to the downward harmonisation of environmental standards and regulations. To pursue their work the TAED established five working groups – agriculture, biodiversity, climate, industry and trade. The agriculture group developed the TAED's position on agricultural biotechnology.

The TAED working group on agriculture met on 2 May 1999 and agreed an outline of their concerns regarding agricultural biotechnology. sixteen NGOs from 10 countries participated in the meeting. Significantly, as we have seen before, as well as criticising agricultural biotechnology on its own terms, this technology was also used as a vehicle for criticising transatlantic trade liberalisation. The TAED working group on agriculture stated its concern that the governments were making 'trade-related interests the priority in how they develop policy for regulating and managing genetic engineering and GMOs'. They explained this by drawing attention to the impact of business on trade negotiations. They argued that a wider range of issues – social, environmental, health and ethical – should inform biotechnology policy and that the full participation of civil society was necessary to achieve this. The group also voiced concern about the concentration of corporate control over the food system and the need to ensure that countries had the power to decide how to regulate GM crops and foods according to their own choices.

A stated aim of the TAED agriculture working group in relation to agricultural biotechnology was also to 'prevent the use of GMOs in agriculture as long as there is no convincing evidence about its [sic] harmlessness to man and nature'. This statement can be contrasted with the TACD demand that GM products should bring benefits to consumers. By asking for evidence of 'harmlessness to man and nature' the environmental groups were seeking to change the burden of proof. They rejected the view that it was their role to prove that GM products are harmful. Instead, they argued that supporters of the technology should prove they are harmless. That said, this statement is ambiguous enough to accommodate environmental NGOs on both sides of the Atlantic. Environmental NGOs in Europe had campaigned for a complete ban on the use of GMOs in agriculture whereas their equivalents in the US placed more emphasis on creating conditions under which non-GM agriculture could flourish.

This view of agricultural biotechnology continues to be the one adopted by large numbers of environmental groups today but the TAED itself had a very limited lifespan. On 21 November 2000 the European Environmental Bureau issued a press release confirming the suspension of TAED activities.

John Hontelez, Secretary General of the EEB and a member of the TAED Steering Committee, explained the decision as follows:

> We have to stop our activities because the US government has not been able to provide its part of the necessary finances to run this dialogue. It has faced opposition in the Senate, and apparently it is not giving it enough priority. The US government has always pretended the TAED is of great importance to them. This failure does not confirm this.
>
> (TAED, 2000)

Although there were financial problems associated with the TAED it is worth pointing out that TACD was launched with the same support as TAED. TACD took it upon themselves to secure separate funding for the initiative which confirms the assessment that enough people believe it is a worthwhile initiative. TAED, however, did not make similar efforts to secure funding beyond the government contribution. The decision to suspend the TAED was linked at least in part to the underlying scepticism amongst environmental groups concerning the transatlantic dialogue process itself.

The Transatlantic Environmental Dialogue, therefore, existed for less than two years. Despite this, however, and perhaps because of it, it illustrates a number of important points. In broad terms the groups that formed the TAED were sceptical about the transatlantic dialogue process from the outset. Many of them viewed transatlantic trade liberalisation as something that should be abandoned altogether and not reformed from within. This points to a central tension facing civil society groups in this situation, and one that eventually contributed to the TAED's demise. In relation to agricultural biotechnology the TAED articulated a more critical position than the TACD. We must be careful, however, not to suggest that TAED argued for the abandonment of agricultural biotechnology altogether. European environmental groups would have supported this but US ones would not. As a result TAED identified very high standards that should be satisfied before agricultural biotechnology could be used. They cited concerns as diverse as unknown risks to the environment and corporate control of the food chain. It is also important to note that the TAED linked their critiques of trade liberalisation and their critiques of agricultural biotechnology.

The EU–US Consultative Forum on Biotechnology

As the new millennium approached there was no sign of progress on the EU–US conflict over biotechnology products. The moratorium in Europe was still in place and US maize was still excluded from the European market. The Transatlantic Business Dialogue was falling silent on agricultural biotechnology and the TEP was coming to terms with being unable to implement its Action Plan in this area. The TACD and the TAED had emerged as new transatlantic networks articulating critical perspectives with challenging regulatory implications. In this context, and in an effort to over-come the impasse or simply delay a formal case at the World Trade Organization, EU and US politicians decided to create a high-level transat-lantic expert advisory body. Its task was to establish an expert consensus on agricultural biotechnology.

The EU–US Consultative Forum on Biotechnology (also the Consultative Forum) was launched at the EU–US Summit on 31 May 2000 and it submitted its final report in December of that year (EU–US Biotechnology Consultative Forum, 2000). It was a joint initiative of President Prodi of the EC and President Clinton of the United States. It was co-chaired by Ruud Lubbers, the former Prime Minister of the Netherlands, and Cutberto Garza (US), a Cornell University Professor of Nutrition. Interestingly the Consultative Forum was made up of 20 distinguished members, including critics and advocates of the technology, from government, academia, busi-ness and civil society. It was therefore a multi-stakeholder group with a brief '[to] consider the full range of issues of concern in biotechnology in the United States and the European Union, most of which relate to . . . food and agriculture' (EU–US Biotechnology Consultative Forum, 2000: 4).

The first notable aspect of the Consultative Forum's final report is that it begins by placing agricultural biotechnology in context. The argument is made that GM crops and foods should not be burdened with the full weight of all the challenges facing society, but at the same time decisions should not be made in a way that is divorced from broader issues either. Three contem-porary concerns in particular are set out: the relationship between agricultural biotechnology and the costs and benefits of globalisation; the role of the citizen in decisions about agricultural biotechnology; and the relationship between agricultural biotechnology and sustainable development (EU-US Biotechnology Consultative Forum, 2000: 5–7). Not surprisingly, given that the report is the outcome of discussions between people with diverse perspectives, it does not offer definitive positions on these complex issues. It is, nevertheless, significant that the discussion is contextualised in this way. This is in sharp contrast to many government discussions in the early to mid-1990s.

Specific recommendations made by the Consultative Forum are of interest here, particularly in the area of regulation. The first recommendation is that all genetically modified food and animal feed products should be subject to a mandatory pre-market examination by the appropriate regulatory authori-ties to ensure they are safe (EU–US Biotechnology Consultative Forum, 2000: 8). The report also argues that one purpose of regulation is to produce public confidence and for this reason alone it argues that standards in the area of agricultural biotechnology may need to rise: ' . . . regulatory processes must be sufficiently strong to ensure public confidence. This may necessitate strengthening existing regulatory systems for agricultural biotechnology products in some respects' (EU–US Consultative Forum on Biotechnology, 2000: 8). When the argument for mandatory assessment was made the US did not have such a system for GM foods, although the US FDA was discussing a proposal.

The role of science and risk assessment is also covered in various places in the report. The third recommendation of the Consultative Forum is: 'More public funds should be invested in basic research that addresses safety concerns' (EU–US Consultative Forum on Biotechnology, 2000: 9). The fourth recommendation is: 'Consideration be given to changes in public policy regarding public funding for basic research that would ensure the existence of a vigorous and independent public scientific research enterprise' (EU–US Consultative Forum on Biotechnology, 2000: 10).

The report makes various arguments to justify the emphasis on public funding for research in both of these recommendations. First, there may be gaps in available scientific knowledge and testing methodologies, yet there is no incentive for private funding to address these. Second, the Forum expresses a concern that scientists are increasingly being seen as serving the goals of industry rather than the public at large. Also, in practice, the report acknowledges that fewer public funds increase the influence of the private sector over research priorities and findings.

Moving beyond pre-market safety assessment the report of the Consultative Forum addresses a range of other regulatory issues. For example, recommendation 8 endorses traceability and monitoring: 'Governments should undertake to develop and implement processes and mechanisms that will make it possible to trace all foods, derived from GMOs, containing novel ingredients or claiming novel benefits' (EU–US Consultative Forum on Biotechnology, 2000: 12). Underpinning this recommendation is the judgement, outlined in the report, that traceability and monitoring are necessary to assess claims made for the benefits associated with GM crops and foods. Such systems are also needed, it is pointed out, to detect and deal with unanticipated negative effects by establishing causes, arranging product recalls and establishing liability. In order to encourage effective monitoring of GM products under commercial use, the report also argues for the use of time-limited licences, with ongoing product approval based on the results of effective monitoring (recommendation 9).

The last specific regulatory issue dealt with in the Consultative Forum's report is consumer choice and labelling. It is clear from the treatment of this issue that agreement was difficult to reach. This is not surprising because above all other issues this is the one that illustrates how US and EU regulatory approaches were diverging at this time. The report endorses the idea that consumers should be 'informed truthfully and adequately' about GM foods. It also acknowledges that food labels are an important source of information. It is less clear, however, about just how labels should be used. The report states, for example, that ' . . . standardisation and harmonisation in this area are desirable, but flexibility should be maintained to enable higher standards to be introduced where necessary to meet consumer requirements' (EU–US Consultative Forum on Biotechnology, 2000: 15). Recommendation

15 argues: '... at the very least, the EU and the US should establish content-based mandatory labelling requirements for finished products containing novel genetic material' (EU–US Consultative Forum on Biotechnology, 2000: 16). The report therefore endorses mandatory labelling but not of products where GM genetically modified material is no longer detectable. It does indicate, however, that some regions may want to adopt higher or different standards than the minimum in the area of labelling.

The Consultative Forum: process and response

From the outline given in the previous section it is clear that the EU–US Consultative Forum on Biotechnology was a novel process and its final report was challenging in many ways. We focus on it here largely because it was a multi-stakeholder body, left relatively free to explore the definition of the policy problem, whilst at the same time attempting to formulate policy proposals. Before moving on to consider the EU and US responses to the Consultative Forum, we can usefully explore the process itself.

The following quote usefully captures the impressions of one participant involved in the Consultative Forum process. The person concerned can be described as a critic of agricultural biotechnology based in European NGO, although not against the technology in principle.

> It came out of the [1998] Birmingham summit where it was decided that because GM was causing such problems they would try new mechanisms to resolve some of the differences between the European and US approaches. So the idea was to have this forum, with people with a range of different interests, produce a consensus report. We started with a very broad range of issues to do with biotechnology but decided to focus on agricultural biotechnology ... It was a fascinating thing to be involved with. It was a really interesting way of doing it. You had very different views on the subject and I think it was quite amazing the report that came out of it and that people all agreed to it. Which I thought went a lot further on a lot of issues than I would have expected given some of the views that people had to start with. I think it just shows how useful it was to have people sitting down in a room and actually discussing issues. Working together and actually trying to understand each perspective. Rather than just making assumptions about what particular people thought. The US side and the EU side understanding each other but also the different interest groups ...
>
> At the time it was set up there was just a general feeling that most people have no confidence in these products and something different needs to happen because we can't just ignore the fact that people are so concerned about it. And that biotechnology raises so many different issues. I think the introduction of the report sets out the climate and the broader context quite well. And I think that was what surprised me.

That on the whole people recognise that people won't just accept something as OK because you say science says it is OK. The report needed to come up with some concrete recommendations about how it should be regulated. And so some things that surprised me, and that I was pleased about, were recommendations about mandatory approval, mandatory labelling, about long-term monitoring, getting a better grip of what was happening around the world.

(Interview, 11 October 2002)

Another participant, who was appointed from the Consumer Federation of America, explained the Forum's process as follows:

The Clinton–Prodi agreement gave us an assignment to finish our report by December 10th. We had no staff. We wrote every word ourselves. To deal with disagreements we shifted to more general language and so left open opportunities for different interpretations of that language . . . It was a useful process, showing that diverse interests could reach agreement, though we had only a few months . . . My appointment to the Forum was controversial because US NGOs wanted Michael Hansen [from the Consumers Union] to represent them. He is a good scientist, but I am more experienced in dealing with a group of people with widely divergent views.

(Interview, 15 October 2003)

As both these reflections illustrate, the nature of the process is central to understanding the outcome of the Consultative Forum's deliberations. In particular, Forum members were selected for their ability to deliberate and find consensus.

The US (US Dept of State, 2000) responded briefly to the Consultative Forum's report. The US response applauds the Consultative Forum for pointing out the potential of agricultural biotechnology and goes on to claim that existing approaches to regulation in the US in many areas are already consistent with what it recommends. However, in some areas, particularly labelling, the US appears to interpret the words in the report in a convenient way. In relation to labelling, the US response states:

The Forum's advice on labeling coincides with our view that any labeling should be based on content rather than on process. The FDA already follows a procedure for labeling of food. This process would apply to any bioengineered food product that contained a substantive change when compared to conventional food.

(US Dept of State, 2000: 2)

The Forum's own comment in this area focuses on content but does not refer to 'substantive change'. It also makes it clear that consumers should have 'the right of informed choice regarding the selection of what they want to consume'. US food labelling legislation emphasises novelty and changes with health implications, and does not necessarily result in GM foods being labelled. In other areas, perhaps where current US practice clearly does not match the recommendations of the Consultative Forum, the response from the US simply says, 'Further steps recommended in the Report are also under consideration.'

The report got a mixed response from some in business. The biotechnology coordinator of a major trade association involved in the US food chain reflected on it as follows:

> The US–EU Consultative Forum represented disparate interests across the food chain. In their report of December 2000, the wording was so vague as to allow both sides to claim victory. It could not be implemented in a common way across the Atlantic.
>
> (Interview, 14 October 2003)

This argument draws attention back to the regulatory harmonisation agenda which this person was familiar with from involvement in TABD.

European officials welcomed the report and focused on its recommendation to take into account a broad range of contextual issues (CEC, 2001a). This is somewhat different from the US government's emphasis on opportunities related to the technology. Elsewhere the response resembles that of the US in that the EC claims that European practice and future plans already incorporate many of the Forum's recommendations, for example science-based risk assessment, time-limited approvals (in some areas), monitoring and mandatory pre-market assessment. The European commentary also welcomes the Consultative Forum's endorsement of the precautionary principle and claims this is already part of established practice. Here the EC cites its Communication on the Precautionary Principle of February 2000. In the area of labelling, the EC, like the US, also sees the Consultative Forum's position as a validation of its approach. Concerning liability the Commission argues that it sees no need for a technology-specific regime but instead is seeking to develop general environmental liability rules.

By the time the report of the Consultative Forum was launched, the US political landscape was changing. The Forum had agreed several regulatory positions which were controversial in the US, and the new Bush Administration was moving policy even further from those positions. An NGO member of the Consultative Forum reflected on the fate of the Consultative Forum's report as follows:

> . . . it just disappeared because it came at the end of the Clinton administration. There was obviously a different emphasis with the Bush administration . . . The EU gave a progress report on the recommendations. The US acknowledged the recommendations but it's never been

clear what they did to follow them up . . . I think it is really disappointing. What made it so difficult was it falling between the two presidents. It was set up as a Clinton–Prodi initiative and it reported in that December. I think it was really useful considering the mix of people who were on it and their perspectives. I would have hoped that it would have been taken more seriously because I don't think anything has changed since it came out. The issues are still relevant now. And I think it was a really useful model more generally for these kinds of issues. I think it was probably the first time something like that had been tried really. Obviously you can only have a limited number of people participating in it, you can't blow it out of all proportion as to what you can do. But as one initiative as part of others I think it was quite useful.

(Interview, 11 October 2002)

In a separate interview a US official involved in the transatlantic conflict over agricultural biotechnology reflected on the Consultative Forum's report as follows:

It hasn't really gone anywhere. It's there. They put out recommendations but we haven't really followed up on it . . . My understanding is that the US wasn't sure what more could be done on that. I think if there were some great ideas then the US would be happy to look at those. But I don't think right now that they think that is the case . . . I think the EU would like to see the Consultative Forum discussed further. But where it is actually going to go who knows. I think the EU likes to discuss things more than the US. We tend only to discuss things if there is an endpoint that we want to reach. If there isn't we tend not to pretend to get together to talk about things. I think we feel that if we get together to talk about things we're going to have to commit to something. Why talk if the outcome is that we have to commit to something we don't necessarily think is in our interest. If that's the case we don't want to start the conversation.

(Interview, 10 September 2002)

Both of these quotes suggest that the Consultative Forum's report was forgotten because of its controversial conclusions and the change of administration in the US. In practice, however, the report played a more complex role at different levels. For example, it quickly emerged as a resource that EU officials, NGOs and others could use to criticise the US government. Later the EU also drew attention to the report in its evidence to the WTO in the formal dispute over biotechnology products.

Amid the transatlantic conflicts, the Consultative Forum's report became a reference point for domestic policy debates. In a meeting of the USDA's Outlook Forum in February 2001, US Political Science Professor Robert Paarlberg offered an interesting if somewhat biased account of the work of the Consultative Forum (AgraFood Biotech, 2001). He argued that given the choice the US would quickly forget the report. He went on, however, to locate the report amongst other recent developments. He argued that while USDA was strongly committed to open markets for biotechnology products other parts of the US government had 'conspicuously blinked on the issue' over the past year. Paarlberg identified the report of the Consultative Forum as the most recent example of this. He suggested that USDA had not been closely enough involved in the process of selecting or vetting US members. Paarlberg also gave what he believed were two other recent examples of the US 'blinking', or deviating from its firm resolve on biotechnology policy – the UN Biosafety Protocol and the US officials agreeing to the formation of a biotechnology working group in the Codex Alimentarius Commission (see Chapters 5 and 6 in this book).

Conclusion

In this chapter we have focused on transatlantic networks of consumer and environmental groups – TACD and TAED, respectively. These emerged in the late 1990s and they went on to pursue policy agendas antagonistic to the TABD and the TEP (as discussed in Chapter 2). Nevertheless, all of these contending coalitions were closely related. All emerged in relation to the transatlantic trade liberalisation agenda that gained momentum in the mid- to late 1990s. This underlying policy agenda presented NGOs with problems and opportunities, which we highlighted by focusing on the regulation of agricultural biotechnology. This conclusion will offer brief answers to the narrative questions raised in the Introduction to this book.

How did policy actors try to advance particular policy agendas?

Drawing on the above accounts of TACD and TAED, it is clear that they sought to redefine the transatlantic policy problem for EU and US policy makers from the late 1990s onwards. They also sought to reframe agricultural biotechnology as a policy issue. Consumer groups tried to shift the focus to new issues such as threats to consumer rights, risk assessment criteria and loss of public/consumer trust in regulatory procedures. Environmental groups attempted to frame trade liberalisation itself as a threat to the environment and sustainability. Using these problems, TACD and TAED member organisations tried to challenge the TABD–TEP definition of the transatlantic policy problem, which focused on barriers to transatlantic trade. In response to shocks like the failure to launch WTO talks in Seattle in 1999, TABD members began to engage with some of these issues, although they did so in their own way. They emphasised, for example, the need to educate the public about the value of trade liberalisation and the rigour of regulatory oversight procedures.

The TACD and TAED reframed agricultural biotechnology in a two-stage process. Each network first tried to frame agricultural biotechnology in a way that would create an internal consensus for the network across the Atlantic. This effort required them to put aside some differences of opinion, for example on the value of agricultural biotechnology to consumers in developing countries. With an agreed framing in place, TACD and TAED members then tried to use this to reframe agricultural biotechnology for EU and US policy makers.

In both of these steps the TACD was more successful than the TAED. For TACD consumer rights were a solid basis for a shared framing across the Atlantic. Consumer groups put disagreements on other issues to one side and thus, as noted by a US trade official, they put on a 'governance hat'. By contrast, TAED members were unable to establish such a common basis. They disagreed, for example, on whether they should oppose agricultural biotechnology or support alternatives which they regarded as more environmentally benign. TAED faced additional problems, such as funding, and all these resulted in a short-lived network.

We have analysed the TACD framing of agbiotech products in terms of beliefs and discourses (in the ACF Table 3.2 and the DCF Table 3.3, respectively). The ACF analysis shows how consumer groups developed their regulatory proposals by building on a set of core beliefs. The most obvious example of this is the proposal for legislation on traceability and labelling of GM foods, which emerged from the more foundational commitment to the consumer's right to know. The DCF analysis shows how this was expressed discursively in the phrase 'right to know, right to choose', and how different narrative elements were brought together. For example, uncertainty about risk was linked to a demand that consumer groups should be allowed to participate in decision making. More generally, the tables show how TACD reframed agbiotech products along different lines compared to TABD (as shown in Tables 2.1 and 2.2).

How were expertise and knowledge used to influence policy making?

In the late 1990s NGOs in the US and the EU cooperated to challenge the basis on which their governments were making regulatory decisions about biotechnology products. TACD and TAED members both attacked the scientific basis of decision making. They raised questions about scientific uncertainty, even if they lacked the expertise to answer them. TACD emphasised the need to apply the precautionary principle in regulation, but without suggesting that products already on the market placed consumers at risk. By contrast, TAED tried to reverse the burden of proof entirely. They wanted companies to be required to prove that GM products are safe, rather than critics having to prove they are unsafe. Although this united environmental groups, it was an awkward basis on which to engage governments.

Table 3.2 TACD and Biotechnology Products: An Advocacy Coalition Analysis

Deep (Normative) Core Beliefs	Near (Policy) Core Beliefs	Secondary Aspects
Definition: Fundamental normative and ontological beliefs. These are very difficult to change. This would be akin to religious conversion.	Definition: Fundamental policy beliefs. Basic strategies for acting on deep core beliefs. Can change if experience reveals serious anomalies.	Definition: Instrumental decisions – legislative and administrative – necessary to implement core policy positions. Moderately easy to change.
The World View	EU–US Trade and Biotechnology	The Regulation of GMOs
New technologies can benefit society but they can also have unexpected negative consequences.	Scientific uncertainty means that the 'precautionary principle' should be applied.	Risk assessment is a key regulatory problem. All GMOs should be subject to risk assessment.
Society is comprised of a diverse range of stakeholders involved in competition and cooperation.	Regulatory standards should be informed by consumer preferences and may differ across the Atlantic.	Standards of risk assessment may be different in the EU and the US for cultural and political reasons.
Both competition and co-operation have a part to play in delivering a desirable society.	A diverse range of stakeholders should be included in decision-making processes.	Sovereignty of risk assessment is important so that regulators can take account of cultural difference.
Government regulations are needed to ensure that there is competition and co-operation.	Biotechnology has the potential to produce beneficial products and negative/unforeseen consequences.	Post-market monitoring is needed to detect harm and to confirm the assumptions in the risk assessment.
Markets are imperfect and they will respond to consumer preferences on their own.	Biotechnology creates a new, inherently different category of products that should be regulated.	Traceability is essential to make product recall and process-based labelling possible.
Consumers have a number of rights which should be respected in all situations (see CI, 2002).	Regulatory standards in the US are too low to guarantee the safety of consumers and the environment.	Labelling of GMOs is needed to act on the consumer's 'right to know and the right to choose'.
Governments have a central role to play in ensuring that consumer rights are respected.	Consumer rights should be a central part of the regulation of biotechnology products.	Consumers want to make choices about biotechnology so labels should be process-based.

In arguments involving knowledge and expertise, the consumer groups could claim to know what consumers want. This was particularly important in Europe after the backlash against biotechnology products. Policy makers could easily portray their discussions with TACD as 'listening to the public'. The TACD claim to know what the consumer wants was analogous to the TABD claim to understand commercial realities and what is technically

Table 3.3 TACD and Biotechnology Products: A Discourse Coalition Analysis

Storylines	Discourses
Definition: Narratives on reality through which elements from many different domains are combined. Provide actors with a set of symbolic references and suggest a common understanding.	Definition: Ensemble of ideas, concepts, and categorisations that are produced, reproduced, and transformed in a particular set of practices.
'The precautionary principle should apply in cases when the scientific evidence is not conclusive ... [and] it is a necessary to take measures to protect public health, safety or the environment.'	Precautionary principle
'Judgements will have to be made about the precautionary principle when risk assessment highlights scientific uncertainty. It is essential that consumers are involved in this process.'	
'Long-term monitoring of the use of GM foods should be a legal requirement and efforts are required to develop appropriate mechanisms for doing this.'	Regulatory oversight
'TACD calls for mandatory safety assessment of all foods produced using genetic engineering... such a system should... enable effective public participation throughout the risk analysis process.'	
'Consumer participation at Codex is restricted by... limited financial resources, a lack of training and, in some cases, by limited access to documents and interpretation. Other fora lag further behind.'	Legitimate decision making
'The TACD comprises 65 consumer organizations from 16 countries, supported directly by roughly 10 million individual consumers and speaks for the interests of 600 million.'	
'TACD believes that consumers have a fundamental right to know what they are eating. Therefore, all GM food including food produced from GM ingredients... should be labeled.'	Consumer rights
'Consumers must have the right to choose, and therefore both governments must require mandatory labelling... For choice to be meaningful, alternatives to GM must also be ensured.'	

Note: All quotes taken from TACD documents.

possible, for example in relation to identity preservation and traceability of GM material.

The Consultative Forum is interesting from the perspective of expertise and knowledge. It was a multi-stakeholder group which was allowed to define to policy problem for itself to a large extent. Not surprisingly, therefore, it produced a final report that is sometimes vague and inconsistent but nevertheless challenging and thought-provoking. It argues that agricultural biotechnology raises a large number of complex questions. The outcome of this process is in sharp contrast to the work of the TEP, which was also a group involving a range of knowledge and expertise, but one which was conceived along technocratic rather than deliberative lines.

How were regulatory standard-setting processes and trade conflict linked?

This chapter also extends our understanding of the relationship between standard-setting processes and trade conflict. As we saw in the previous chapter, the TABD successfully promoted a narrow view of regulation until the late 1990s. Focusing on standards for pre-market safety assessment, the TABD emphasised the need for common (and perhaps centralised) approaches across the Atlantic. Through risk assessment, the TABD agenda sought to classify the first generation of agbiotech crops as similar to conventional ones. This in turn would be a basis on which to promote trade liberalisation and access a grain market that treated grain as a homogeneous product.

However, the 'anti-globalisation' movement framed trade liberalisation and agbiotech as dual threats, thus turning this sector into a political weakness for the regulatory harmonisation agenda more generally. Activists gained popular support for their warnings against industry 'homogenising consumer tastes, and harmonising civic standards downwards' (see Chapter 1). Trade conflict created a greater opportunity to challenge the TABD–TEP agenda through contending coalitions. Led by Public Citizen, for example, the TACD appropriated a TABD proposal – an early warning system for trade barriers – and recast it in their own image as an early warning system for any regulatory changes that could lower standards.

Moreover, the TACD promoted a more culturally informed view of standard-setting and trade liberalisation. They argued, for example, that GM products should be labelled even if GM material is no longer detectable. Such labelling would allow consumers in different jurisdictions to express their views, which would probably vary in different places. They sought to use standard-setting processes as a way of sensitising trade liberalisation to cultural values, thus stimulating a differentiated market dependent on diverse or more stringent standards. This demand challenged the TABD agenda, which saw no scientific justification for a GM label on all products derived from new biotechnology.

Since the mid-1990s, different views on the regulatory role of science have shaped trade liberalisation along different lines. As seen in the previous chapter, the TABD–TEP agenda regarded regulatory harmonisation as a technical exercise underpinned by science, thus assuming experts could readily agree objective regulatory standards across the Atlantic. Soon the European public backlash and the transatlantic trade conflict helped critics to challenge this assumption and thus undermine a particular form of trade liberalisation.

The TACD and TAED mounted their challenges in different ways. TACD members argued that risk assessment of GM foods involves many uncertainties so that scientific experts and policy makers in different jurisdictions could legitimately reach different conclusions, taking into account the preferences of consumers. Likewise, TAED members emphasised that GM crops would interact with diverse local environments in different and unpredictable ways. Such arguments challenged TABD–TEP assumptions about 'science-based regulation' guiding standard-setting for trade liberalisation.

How were EU–US interactions and intra-jurisdictional conflicts linked?

In the first section of this chapter we showed how some civil society groups linked concerns over agricultural biotechnology and concerns over transatlantic trade liberalisation, so that agricultural biotechnology was turned into a 'bridging issue' (see Chapter 1). EU–US trade in biotechnology products, and the efforts of the TEP to harmonise regulatory standards, became a focal point for various critics. In this way EU–US cooperation among businesses (TABD), politicians (NTA) and officials (TEP) created the context from which the trade conflict emerged. In particular the trade conflict around GM corn, which occupied much of the TEP's time after the public backlash, emerged because varieties of corn had been approved and used commercially in the US before they were authorised in Europe. US commercial interests were depending on, and perhaps expecting or anticipating, approval in the EU. As a result any regulatory delays had high stakes, both symbolically and commercially.

In their own ways, TACD and TAED sought to exploit the legitimacy crisis of transatlantic trade liberalisation. Meetings with policy makers made a greater difference for NGOs in the USA than in the EU, where they had relatively better access. For any particular issue that raised conflict between NGOs and their own government, the Transatlantic Dialogues provided more opportunity to challenge policy and sometimes to counterpose a better policy which existed across the Atlantic.

In the context of the European backlash against agbiotech in particular, the TACD quickly identified a basis on which to make acceptable policy proposals, some of which were being taken up in the EU system. For European officials, the TACD had the added advantage of being a group particularly critical of the US government, especially for its non-regulation of GM foods. Environmental groups were sceptical about the value of their transatlantic dialogue with the governments and ultimately abandoned the initiative.

The EU–US Consultative Forum on Biotechnology had a subtle and ambiguous role in the policy process. The EC welcomed its report and continues to cite it, while the US government largely ignored it and any proposals that conflicted with its own policy. Nevertheless, such proposals elicited US domestic criticism, for example when pro-biotech commentators cited the report as another example of the US government 'blinking' in the face of overly stringent approaches to biotechnology regulation. More generally, the Forum became a resource that EU officials and NGOs could use to criticise the US government. All these developments illustrate how transatlantic interactions and divergences were used strategically in inter- and intra-jurisdictional conflicts.

4   Environmental risks of GM crops

The case of *Bt* maize

Introduction

In Chapters 2 and 3 we examined a range of arguments made by different transatlantic networks in relation to agricultural biotechnology. These chapters show that members of TABD, TACD and TAED often promoted incompatible frames as they argued over 'approved once, accepted everywhere', 'right to know, right to choose' and threats to sustainable agriculture. Their frames converged thematically, however, on the role of science in regulation. The Transatlantic Business Dialogue, for example, argued for the use of 'sound science' in assessing risks, whilst the Transatlantic Consumer Dialogue campaigned for the use of the 'precautionary principle'. Members of the Transatlantic Environmental Dialogue went further and argued that producers of biotechnology products should be required to prove that they are safe. In Chapters 4 and 5 we focus on such links between science, risk assessment and regulation.

What role does (or should) science play in the regulation of GM crops and foods? We can begin to answer this question by contrasting EU and US positions. For example, one EU policy statement argues that 'science-based regulatory oversight' aims 'to enable Community business to exploit the potential of biotechnology while taking account of the precautionary principle and addressing ethical and social concerns' (CEC, 2003a: 6, 17). In a more focused account, the US government, through the USTR, has said that 'The U.S. regulatory process ensures that all biotech products . . . are as safe . . . as their conventional counterparts. Biotechnology in the United States is rigorously regulated under a risk-based system . . . based on sound science' (USTR, 2003a: 1). In the first example we see the role of science in regulation being linked to a range of actors and agendas whilst the second one suggests that the only role for science is the assessment of product safety.

Although these statements are different, both were in fact shaped by their context. In the first we see the efforts of the EC to retain science as a basis for decision making whilst at the same time accommodating the demands of diverse policy actors. This makes sense in relation to a technology that is highly controversial in Europe. The EC's statement suggests that commercial, ethical and social concerns can be balanced in a science-based regulatory system. The second statement gives a much narrower account of the role of science – simply establish the risks of a product, or its safety. This account was also shaped by context, however. When the US began to challenge EU agbiotech regulation at the WTO it also emphasised its view of how science and regulation should be linked. The US wanted to emphasise that its approach has put safe biotechnology products onto the US market.

Such accounts of 'science', and their strategic use in policy discourse, are an important feature of the US–EU conflict over agricultural biotechnology. But they do not help us to understand the role of science in practice. The following chapters show that quite different risks became prominent issues in different jurisdictions at different times; moreover, even 'the same' risks were debated along different lines, and different conclusions were drawn by different regulators. These observations raise doubts about science providing an objective basis for common standards that apply across all jurisdictions at all times. In the case of herbicide-tolerant crops, for example, the effects on farmland biodiversity quickly became a high-profile issue in the UK and other EU member states took this issue up later, but it remained irrelevant in the US regulatory debate.

In this chapter we unpack the relationship between science and regulation in practice, using the case of *Bt* maize and its environmental risks. For this product various risk issues gained a high profile on both sides of the Atlantic, though they did so at different times and with different emphases. As a result this product category gives us an opportunity to analyse transatlantic conflicts and interactions. In the first section we provide a brief description of *Bt* maize and the related regulatory challenges. In the second section we focus on the risk assessment and regulation of *Bt* maize in the US, and in the third section we do the same for the EU. For both jurisdictions we discuss the treatment of two environmental risks, the problem of insect resistance and the problem of risks to non-target organisms. In the fourth section we discuss transatlantic interactions, and in doing so develop a key theme of this book further. In the final section we provide an overview of regulatory standards and how they have changed.

Bt maize and its regulatory issues

The genus *Bacillus* includes over 20 species of bacteria (see Nester et al., 2002 for an overview). We use many of these today for a diverse range of purposes. *Bacillus subtilis*, for example, is a source of industrial enzymes. *Bacillus anthracis* is an agent in anthrax. *Bacillus thuringiensis* (*Bt*), however, is particularly important in agriculture. It was first identified and named in the early 1900s and for over 40 years it has been applied to crops in a spray as an insecticide. Today it is used to control insects like bollworms, stem borers and bud worms which affect field crops. *Bt* sprays are regarded as an important method of insect pest management in agriculture alongside other methods like insect parasites or fungal pathogens, crop rotation, changes to the date of planting, poly culture and conventional chemical sprays.

Bt sprays include a mixture of spores and associated protein crystals. The *Bt* does not act on contact with an insect in the same way as a chemical spray but as an ingested toxin in the gut. The death of an insect which has ingested *Bt* can occur many days later. In agriculture the use of *Bt* sprays increased as insects became resistant to chemical sprays and as people became more concerned about their negative side effects. And in recent years a new market for *Bt* sprays was created with the emergence of organic agriculture where they can be used because *Bt* is a natural product. *Bt* sprays represent 1–2 per cent of the global insect spray market but this is approximately half what it was before the development of *Bt* crops. *Bt* sprays are also used to protect stored commodities (foodstuffs) from infestation.

A major development in the history of *Bt* occurred in 1987 when research was published showing that genes from the microbe could be introduced into tobacco and tomato plants. By doing this it was possible for an insecticidal protein to be expressed in the tissue of the plant. In the language of the industry the plant became 'pest-protected'. The potential for plants with built-in pest resistance was immediately clear. Since this date biotechnology companies have invested considerable amounts of money in *Bt* crop research. Hundreds of different subspecies of *Bt* have been described and although only a small number of genes have been engineered into commercial *Bt* crops so far this diversity means that a wide range of insect species can be targeted.

In the future it is likely that more targeted products will emerge, possibly also involving expression in particular parts of a plant. In practice, however, the future use of *Bt* crops will be determined at least in part by their environmental impacts. So far critics have focused on two problems in particular and we examine these in detail in this chapter. First, they have pointed out that constant exposure to the *Bt* toxin could generate insect resistance in the target pest population. Second, they argue that the *Bt* toxin could also harm non-target insects, including beneficial predator insects. We focus on insect resistance and non-target harm in the rest of this chapter.

Supporters and critics of *Bt* crop technology have framed both of these risks in different ways at different times. For example, some proponents have argued that these risks are acceptable because they are no worse than those already associated with the use of chemical insecticides in conventional agriculture. Critics, however, have challenged this. They argue that it is wrong to simply assume that chemical insecticide-based agriculture is the right comparator. They point to other agricultural regimes that could also be used for the purpose of comparison. We argue below that the choice of comparator – a normative judgement – is an implicit regulatory standard, which frames science and risk assessment in particular ways.

More specifically there have been scientific disagreements about the detection and assessment of impacts. For example, non-target harm was originally examined using direct toxicity tests drawing on the model of toxicity that underpins the testing of agricultural chemicals. This model assumes that a toxin kills when it is ingested directly by a non-target insect. However, critics challenged the use of this model in relation to *Bt* crops and pointed instead to research on indirect causal pathways of harm. Critical scientists tested whether non-target insects might be harmed if they ate target insects that had previously ingested the *Bt* toxin. In this chapter we analyse conflicts around test methods such as this.

Much of the evidence that shows how companies and regulators have dealt with these issues can be found in company submissions to regulators and the responses to them. In both the US and the EU, the regulatory process for a *Bt* crop begins with the submission of a dossier to the regulator. The dossier includes basic information about the product and information on safety tests that have been carried out. The regulator then evaluates the submission and makes a judgement. Explicit and implicit regulatory standards are involved (devised and agreed) in this exchange and they can be uncovered through interviews with participants and analysis of the relevant documents.

US regulation of *Bt* maize

The starting point for the regulation of GMOs in the US was the Coordinated Framework for Regulation of Biotechnology (OSTP, 1986). In this document the US government made it clear that GMOs would be regulated under existing legislation, such as regulations for food and agricultural chemicals. No new legislation was planned. Various judgements underpinned this decision: GM techniques produce precise genetic changes; GMOs pose 'no unique risks'; and risks associated with GMOs are predictable. In general it was judged that agricultural biotechnology would not produce a novel category of organism or be a source of unique risks (Levidow and Carr, 2000).

Under the Federal Insecticide, Fungicide and Rodenticide Act (FIFRA), the US Environmental Protection Agency (EPA) was required to conduct a risk–benefit analysis of all new pesticides. This act required the EPA to balance any 'unreasonable adverse effect' against environmental benefits. Initially, however, it was unclear whether this requirement extended to *Bt* toxins *in* plants – eventually called Plant Incorporated Protectants (PIPs). However, in the early 1990s, the EPA claimed the authority to regulate PIPs. It assumed that *Bt* crops would mainly replace chemical insecticides, thus leading to a 'significant reduction in risk' with additional environmental benefits. In the mid-1990s, using similar arguments, the EPA approved several types of *Bt* maize.

Insect resistance to Bt

Insect resistance to *Bt* crops emerged slowly as an issue in the US during the 1990s. In the early part of the decade some biotechnology companies argued that it was not a risk-regulation issue or even a significant problem. They argued that if insect resistance developed they could identify and insert alternative *Bt* toxins into crop plants. The President of one US company stated: 'We have many bullets in the gun which we call *Bt*' (cited in Cutler, 1991). In the mid-1990s, however, the issue began to attract more attention and interested individuals and groups began to attend conferences to discuss Insect Resistance Management (IRM). The consensus was that IRM strategies would have two key elements: (1) *Bt* crops designed to express the *Bt* toxin in a sufficiently high dose to kill nearly all insect pests; (2) refuges of non-*Bt* crops planted nearby so that susceptible insects could interbreed with resistant ones. Not surprisingly, there were differences of opinion on what a sufficiently high dose might be and how close and how large non-*Bt* crop refuges should be.

Insect resistance also became a more public issue in the US in the mid-1990s. The EPA's unconditional registration of a *Bt* potato in 1995 was one of the main triggers for this. The EPA placed no obligation on the company involved to prevent insect resistance. In response, a network of environmental groups, organic farmers and entomologists began to protest. They argued that 'natural' *Bt* is a public good and should be protected as an option for organic farmers and that widespread commercial planting could generate insect resistance. This growing concern produced a commercial response. Significantly, biotechnology companies began to ask farmers to plant non-*Bt* maize refuges on a voluntary basis. However, refuge guidelines and their implementation remained a contentious issue. Refuge sizes in the US corn belt varied from 0–20 per cent of the planted area (Hutchison and Andow, 2000; US EPA, 2001). In 1998 one company regulatory manager argued that a 5 per cent refuge level might be enough to delay resistance. He added that farmers might ignore more stringent guidelines anyway (Head, 2000).

In the late 1990s critical entomologists and environmental groups mounted a more sustained challenge to the EPA's hands-off approach. New scientific research played a central role. For example, evidence from laboratory studies suggested that insects could develop resistance more quickly than originally thought. Research also showed that some insects had a gene that conferred resistance to several *Bt* toxins. This cast doubt on the possibility of substituting one *Bt* toxin for another to deal with insect resistance as it emerged (Andow and Hutchison, 1998).

At this time, the EPA's approach was also challenged by agronomic developments. The EPA had argued that conventional maize fields would delay insect resistance by providing 'unstructured refuges'. However, *Bt* maize cultivation had increased rapidly to approximately one-third of all fields. This raised doubts about the efficacy of unstructured refuges. In addition this level of cultivation was high in comparison to the 5–10 per cent of maize fields that had previously been sprayed with insecticides against the European Corn Borer. This indicated that *Bt* maize was not simply replacing conventional maize in areas where agricultural chemicals had been used to control specific pests, thus raising doubts about the EPA's belief in wider environmental benefits associated with *Bt* maize.[1]

In the late 1990s the EPA's own Scientific Advisory Panel (SAP) recommended that it should embrace the idea of mandatory refuges to control insect resistance to *Bt* maize (SAP, 1998). In doing so they drew on the work of critical scientists published by the Union of Concerned Scientists (UCS, 1998). Eventually an expert body representing biotechnology companies and academic scientists reached a consensus on refuges. This group made recommendations on refuge sizes whilst at the same time acknowledging ongoing scientific uncertainties (ILSI, 1999).[2] Building on some existing requirements, the EPA then put in place mandatory refuge requirements for all *Bt* field corn products for the 2000 growing season (US EPA, 1998; US EPA, 2001). The target pests were European Corn Borer, Corn Earworm and Southwestern Corn Borer. For any area sown with *Bt* maize, a refuge area of one-fifth its size was required to be planted with conventional (non-*Bt*) maize within half a mile, or within a quarter of a mile in areas where insecticides had historically been used to treat corn borers. For areas where most cotton was grown, the EPA required a refuge of half the size to be planted with conventional maize for certain types of *Bt* maize. This larger refuge was deemed necessary to delay resistance in Corn Earworm populations that feed on both maize and cotton.

Risks to non-target insects

Environmental groups were concerned about the impact of *Bt* crops on non-target insects from the outset, but this did not become a public issue in the US until the late 1990s. Drawing on the results of direct toxicity tests – of the kind used to test agricultural chemicals – applicants and the EPA had judged that *Bt* crops did not represent a risk. The significant development in 1999, however, was a Cornell University laboratory study showing that pollen from *Bt* maize could harm the larvae of the Monarch butterfly (Losey et al., 1999). This was followed by further research that linked harm to pollen deposits on milkweed plants, an important food plant of the Monarch caterpillar (Hansen-Jesse and Obrycki, 2000).[3] For several reasons environmental groups were able to use this research to launch a national debate in the US. Significantly, the Monarch butterfly is a wildlife symbol so NGOs were able to use it to undermine the cultural distinction between areas where industrial agriculture is practised and areas where nature conservation takes place. Also, the Monarch butterfly migrates internationally, has special aesthetic qualities and butterfly fanciers are an organised constituency. In addition, they could argue that 'toxic pollen' contradicted the claim that GMOs posed no unique or unpredictable risks.

Responses to the Monarch research were defensive at first. Critics argued that the methodology involved an unrealistically high dose of *Bt* pollen, so that it was impossible to draw conclusions about exposure in the field. As a result, they argued, the regulatory implications were at best unclear (see, for example, Hodgson, 1999). Such criticisms circulated at Cornell University and more widely on a pro-biotech website linking scientists across the Atlantic (BioScope), where articles questioned the research methods and raised concerns about exaggerated risks as a political use of science (Rautenberg, 1999a, 1999b).

Despite the efforts to ignore or discredit the research, however, it was used to criticise the EPA. Critics claimed it showed that EPA risk–benefit assessments had been based on inadequate science. At a meeting in 1999 the EPA's Scientific Advisory Panel stated: 'It is disappointing and perplexing that the Agency failed to follow through and address the questions its personnel identified in the 1980s. These same questions now appear to be emerging issues, i.e. monarch butterfly and *Bt* corn' (SAP, 2000: 16). At the same time environmental groups argued that the EPA should require farmers to plant buffer zones to protect Monarch larvae.

In the late 1990s the stakes were high because the EPA was approaching a deadline by which it must decide whether or not to re-register *Bt* toxins in maize. This decision was expected in 2000. At this time the US was also already embroiled in the trade conflict with the EU with potential implications for the worldwide regulation of GMOs. There was, therefore, considerable pressure on the regulatory oversight system for GM crops in the US and perhaps not surprisingly there were significant institutional changes in the area of expert advice. The US Department of Agriculture asked the National Research Council to evaluate existing regulatory procedures and capacities in the area of GM crops. The panels that were set up for this purpose included sceptics of safety claims, whose input was reflected in the final reports (NRC, 2000, 2002). As one NRC expert member stated: 'The NRC have got more sophisticated about who they put on committees in order to represent the diversity of opinions. That is one of the ways in which change internationally has affected US policy' (interview, 7 September 2003). Similarly, more critical scientists were included in the EPA's own advisory bodies (SAP, 2000, 2001).

In December 1999 the EPA issued a Data Call-In in relation to the re-registration of *Bt*-toxins in maize. Companies had to submit more evidence on causal pathways of potential harm, drawing particularly on *Bt* pollen field studies. Industry supplied evidence that non-target harm would not occur in practice. This evidence related mainly to three butterfly species. Industry admitted that harm might result from one *Bt* maize variety, *Bt*-176 from Novartis, because it had relatively greater expression of *Bt* in pollen (ABSTC, 2001). However, this variety was being phased out anyway, partly because its *Bt* levels declined during the growing season. The research results were published by the National Academy of Science and pre-publication copies were made available to inform the re-registration debate (see, for example, Hellmich et al., 2001).

US NGOs commissioned a group of European entomologists to prepare a report (EcoStrat, 2001) and then used its arguments to oppose re-registration

(UCS, 2001). In addition, the NGOs argued that the industry submission evaded further questions about research methods. For example, although the new research showed that pollen from *Bt* maize would not harm non-target insects, it did not examine the role of maize anthers. Industry-funded research had used purified pollen with anthers screened out, as if they were irrelevant (ABSTC, 2001; cited in EcoStrat, 2001). This was despite the fact that earlier field tests had indicated that anthers could spread to milkweed and be ingested by Monarch larvae (Hansen-Jesse and Obrycki, 2000; see also Hellmich et al., 2001). Several prominent US entomologists also criticised the research in the industry submission to EPA (Obrycki et al., 2001b). In their view, optimistic assumptions about causal pathways were again limiting research design and the available information about real-world risks.

The EPA eventually made a judgement on the re-registration of *Bt* maize based on the new safety data in 2001 – the *Bt* re-registration decision had been delayed by a year because of the various difficulties. The EPA decided in favour of *Bt* maize, registration was not limited to one year and they did not impose any buffer zone requirements. The EPA argued that *Bt* pollen poses no significant risk (US EPA, 2001).

Monsanto's anti-CRW Bt *maize*

A more recent case from the US, which led to further conflicts, helps to extend our narrative. In 2002 Monsanto sought approval for a *Bt* maize product that offers protection against Corn Root Worm. Insect resistance was particularly controversial in this case because the variety produces a relatively low dose of the *Bt* toxin – giving it greater potential to encourage insect resistance. Environmental NGOs argued for a 30 per cent refuge requirement (UCS, 2002). The EPA's advisors concluded that the evidence on which to base a decision was lacking and that a more stringent 50 per cent refuge would be appropriate (SAP, 2002).

When the EPA came to its decision it accepted Monsanto's proposal of a 20 per cent refuge. The agency noted that 'there are no registered microbial or PIP products for the control of this organism'. With this comment it implied a relatively less stringent norm for the acceptability of resistance in this case. However, Monsanto was asked to revise its IRM plan in consultation with its critics and the product was approved on a time-limited basis with a 'further research' requirement (US EPA, 2003).

Non-target harm was also contentious in this case. Industry-funded tests found no evidence of harm to non-target insects and an initial evaluation by the EPA found that the product 'results in less impact on non-target invertebrates than conventional pest management practices'. In response, however, NGOs argued that there was a need for caution (UCS, 2002). The EPA's advisors also systematically questioned the evidence for safety and made several recommendations (SAP, 2002). Once again their arguments drew upon the work of EcoStrat and UCS. As a condition of registration the EPA required Monsanto to undertake 'appropriately designed field monitoring during the initial years', in order to test long-term effects (US EPA, 2003).

In sum, the EPA basically accepted Monsanto's data as adequate enough to register anti-CRW *Bt* maize. However, at the same time it tried to accommodate critics by imposing extra requirements on commercial use. Environmental NGOs opposed registration, but they also acknowledged that the data requirements in this case were more stringent than had been the case for earlier high-dose *Bt* crops. Some of the EPA's advisors responded to the decision with sarcastic characterizations of the EPA's approach as 'register now, test later'. One SAP member argued: 'The EPA called for science-based regulation, but here that does not appear to be the case . . . ' (cited in Powell, 2003).

EU regulation of *Bt* maize

From the outset the EU took a very different approach to regulating GMOs. As outlined above, in the mid-1980s the US government judged that GMOs were not a novel category of organism and that they would not be a source of unique risks. On this basis they declared that existing legislation was sufficient. EU policy makers reached the opposite conclusion and decided that GMOs created a need for new regulations. Starting in 1990, GMOs in the EU were regulated under the Deliberate Release Directive 90/220 (the Directive). This legislation required member states to ensure that GMOs would not cause 'adverse effects'. It also established an EU-wide approval procedure for commercial use.

In the EU, also unlike the US, there was well-organised opposition to GM products as early as 1997. As mentioned in the introduction, in 1996 the EC approved a Monsanto GM soybean for use in animal feed and processed products. US soybean shipments then provided a target for organised opposition to the technology. Opponents in Europe accused governments of 'force-feeding us GM food'. NGOs successfully encouraged, and to some extent coordinated, a widespread public backlash and consumer boycott. In the late 1990s major supermarket chains in Europe decided to exclude GM ingredients from their own-brand products (Levidow and Bijman, 2002). Then, in June 1999, the EU Environment Council imposed its unofficial *de facto* moratorium on the approval of new GM products (FoEE, 1999).

Insect resistance to Bt

In 1997, despite objections from most member states, the EC approved the first *Bt* maize product for commercial cultivation in the EU. At this time, largely because of ongoing debates in the United States, insect resistance was already recognised as a potential problem and companies were developing IRM strategies for use in Europe for commercial reasons. When they applied for product approval, however, the same companies argued that insect resistance was an 'agronomic problem' and not an 'adverse effect' on the environment. Using this argument they were able to claim that insect resistance was not covered by the Deliberate Release Directive. The EC agreed and on this basis approved Ciba-Geigy's *Bt*-176 maize in early 1997 (CEC, 1997a) (see this book's Introduction).

Despite this apparent success, however, companies became more cautious about insect resistance as they faced widespread protests against GM crops and more focused criticism of their IRM strategies. For example, in a subsequent application Monsanto included a plan to monitor its *Bt* maize for insect resistance during commercial use. The EC's approval decision for this product mentioned this plan even though it had previously judged that insect resistance was not covered by the Directive (CEC, 1998b). Companies also planned further research on the high-dose/refuge strategy. For example, Novartis (formerly Ciba-Geigy) commissioned entomologists at the University of Milan to establish a baseline of prior susceptibility to *Bt* in insect populations.

Even though there was generally more criticism in Europe of the scientific and normative basis for approving products, insect resistance remained a minor issue there compared to the US. There were are a number of reasons for this difference. First, few European farmers bought *Bt* maize seeds, except in Spain, where there was limited protest against GMOs. Other European farmers were deterred by the widespread anti-GM feeling and by the retailers' boycott of GM grain. Second, opponents of agri-biotechnology did not focus on the insect resistance issue, partly because it might be seen as a manageable risk. Instead they emphasised other issues, such as non-target harm and 'GM contamination' of conventional products.

Risks to non-target insects

When companies applied for *Bt* crop approval in the EU, their safety claims in relation to non-target harm were based on two types of evidence. They argued that laboratory studies revealed no harm to various insect species and that field monitoring had found no fewer beneficial insects in *Bt* maize fields compared with conventional maize fields. However, these claims were undermined in 1997 when Swiss scientists reported laboratory results showing harm to lacewing, a beneficial predator insect (Hilbeck et al., 1998a, 1998b). This research involved a 'tritrophic' experiment (one involving three levels of the food chain). It suggested that lacewing were harmed when they ate corn borers which had themselves ingested a *Bt* toxin. The researchers argued that more research should be done on indirect causes of non-target harm. They also argued that tritrophic research raised doubts about the value of the direct toxicity tests that the industry were using to test *Bt* toxins in plants.

As had occurred with the Monarch studies in the US, a debate over the relevance and adequacy of the lacewing experiments followed. Industry representatives questioned whether the results had any implications for commercial field cultivation. The EU's Scientific Committee for Plants (SCP) also criticised the research, and in doing so scrutinised research that produced evidence of risk more stringently than research that did not. For example, questions were raised about the high mortality rate of control insects in the lacewing research, but not about even higher mortality rates in other studies, particularly when the researchers reported no evidence of non-target harm (Riddick and Barbosa, 1998). The SCP therefore appeared to single out the lacewing research for criticism and ignore the weaknesses of other studies (SCP, 2000).

As it had in the US, the non-target harm issue also led to a wider debate about the baseline of acceptable harm. From the outset regulators assumed the comparator of conventional agriculture. According to the EU's Scientific Committee on Plants, any harm to non-target arthropod insects 'will be less than that from the use of conventional insecticides' (SCP, 1998). One member portrayed this as a purely scientific issue: 'We have to evaluate potential effects on the basis of existing agricultural practices. A comparison with chemical insecticides makes the potential harm acceptable . . . This is a scientific issue . . . We are asked only scientific questions' (interview, 18 June 1998). Not surprisingly critics targeted this assumption. When the same issue was raised a few years later, the same respondent implied that a more stringent norm might be appropriate: 'Safety should be understood as a relative absence of harm, which in turn depends upon a definition of acceptable effects. This requires an extra judgement – i.e. beyond our advice. . . . In the future we could compare *Bt* maize to any non-target harm from pesticide and non-pesticide regimes' (interview, 18 June 2002).

Throughout the late 1990s, to accommodate the wider public controversy, regulators in EU member states delayed the regulatory process by citing results from experiments that indicated potential risks. These experiments were no less realistic than those that showed no evidence of harm. At the same time regulators moved away from simply accepting conventional crops as an obvious norm against which to compare *Bt* crops. The EC also funded more ecologically informed research on non-target harm (Kessler and Economidis, 2001; DG Research, 2003). To some extent these delays and changes anticipated more stringent regulatory criteria.

Bt *maize cultivation under the revised directive*

Significant changes were made to the EU's regulatory regime in 2001 when the Deliberate Release Directive was revised. The 'adverse effects' provision was broadened to include 'risk to human health and the environment, whether direct or indirect, immediate or delayed'. Companies were required to submit case-specific monitoring plans to confirm any assumptions made in their risk assessments (CEC, 2001b). More detailed risk assessment guidelines were provided and these mentioned insect resistance (CEC, 2002), a risk for which industry generally proposed market-stage monitoring (EuropaBio, 2002).

As the EU system began to consider products under the revised directive, conflicts ensued over the prospect of non-target harm and the appropriate form of market-stage measures. For two different types of *Bt* maize (*Bt* 11 and *Bt* 1507), safety testing had originally been done for applications to the US EPA. When the companies submitted similar data under the Deliberate Release Directive, some EU member states argued that the tests did not adequately encompass European species and environments, and they raised numerous scientific questions (FoEE, 2005).

Disagreements and uncertainties were translated into conflicts over the appropriate form of market-stage measures, and especially the general requirement for case-specific monitoring. EU guidelines allow exceptions in cases where no risks are identified (CEC, 2002b). Citing the results of safety tests, the companies argued that case-specific monitoring should not be required. Similar views came from the EU-wide rapporteur countries, France and Spain, and likewise eventually from the EU-level expert body. The latter argued that 'maize is not a significant food source for endemic Lepidoptera', that is butterfly species (EFSA GMO Panel, 2005).

In contrast to these views, some member states demanded a requirement for case-specific monitoring. In addition, Denmark proposed mandatory buffer zones to protect non-target species, just as US environmental NGOs had proposed *Bt* maize cultivation in 2000. Few Competent Authorities indicated a willingness to support approval of the products, at least on the basis proposed by the Commission. In sum, conflicts continued over the standards of evidence and the measures necessary to manage uncertainties about risk.

Transatlantic interactions and networks

In this chapter so far we have described conflicts within the US and the EU associated with the regulation of *Bt* maize. In relation to insect resistance and non-target harm, in both jurisdictions, there was pressure for higher standards of risk assessment and regulatory oversight. Having analysed each jurisdiction in turn, in this section we focus on transatlantic interactions and networks involved in the standard-setting processes.

F2 screen and insect resistance

Detection at an early stage is one of the main problems associated with assessment (and management) of insect resistance. Using conventional methods, by the time any resistant insects are found, resistance genes can be widespread in an insect population. To overcome this problem some US entomologists developed a more sensitive test called the F2 screen. This involves interbreeding insects over two generations and testing their progeny for rare resistance alleles (Andow and Alstad, 1998). This new test was a potential replacement for the discriminating-dose test, which is widely used by companies. Significantly, the F2 screen emerged at the same time as some EU member states began to demand earlier detection of possible insect resistance through 'active monitoring'. In response to this demand, scientists based at INRA (National Institute for Agricultural Research) in France adapted the test. It was also recommended by a working group of EU regulatory officials and then by the relevant EU scientific committee (SCP, 1999). Although they had no direct means to implement or enforce this recommendation, this illustrates how a US development was taken up in the EU.

From 2003 onwards an EU-funded research project used the F2 screen to test insects from maize fields on both sides of the Atlantic. No resistance was found and the researchers concluded that it 'is probably rare enough in France and the northern US corn belt for the high-dose plus refuge strategy to delay resistance to Bt maize' (Bourguet et al., 2003). Likewise, some US university projects took up the new technique. In one example lab tests were used to induce increases in resistance in corn borers. This occurred but not enough for corn borers to survive on *Bt* maize (Huang et al., 2002; for other related research see Tabashnik et al., 2003).

In practice companies have continued to use the discriminating-dose test despite the SCP (1999) recommendation to adopt the F2 screen test. This is partly because the latter is more laborious and expensive, but some critics, such as a SAP member, argue further: 'I think the deeper reason is that they don't really want to find resistance because in their minds it will automatically mean that failure is around the corner . . . If you use cheap methods, you'll never find it, and it [any greater resistance] becomes a customer satisfaction problem' (interview, 7 September 2003). Regardless of whether or not companies have such motives, the F2 screen is an example of a more sensitive test, originally developed by US scientists, which was taken up by scientists and expert advisors in Europe. It illustrates both the pressure for higher standards and transatlantic dynamics.

EcoStrat and non-target harm

As outlined earlier, non-target harm became a dynamic area of debate in the late 1990s with new research and an emerging US–EU network of critical entomologists playing an important part. A European entomologist, temporarily based in the US, developed the tritrophic test that eventually identified harm to the lacewing (Hilbeck et al., 1998a, 1998b) – her project was funded by the Organization for Economic Cooperation and Development and the Swiss National Science Foundation. As the validity of the lacewing results was being debated, the project leader set up the EcoStrat consultancy. European pressure groups then contracted EcoStrat to identify weaknesses in the evidence for the safety of *Bt* maize (EcoStrat, 2000). These developments then had implications in the US. On the basis of EcoStrat's European work, Greenpeace contracted further studies which criticised regulatory oversight by the US EPA (EcoStrat, 2001). It was this EcoStrat critique, more so than the lacewing research, which was taken up in the US. In particular, the EPA's own Scientific Advisory Panel criticised the EPA for applying a double standard to evidence of safety and risk: 'The Hilbeck data was dismissed by the agency, based on standards that were not applied to all the work reviewed by the agency, and the Hilbeck work was singled out for an excessively critical analysis . . . ' (SAP, 2001: 54).

Transatlantic links were particularly important for US environmental groups at this time because few US scientists were willing to be critical in public. As a result US environmentalists looked to European scientists. One US NGO scientist commented:

> We need someone like Angelika Hilbeck because most agricultural scientists in the US are unwilling to write reports for NGOs. We operate in a socially different environment here, where US academics are unwilling to be seen as NGO consultants. Their colleagues fear that strong criticism of safety claims could lead regulators to restrict GM crops.
> (Interview, US NGO scientist, 15 April 2002)

Following the intervention by EcoStrat, however, more critical US scientists began to engage with the non-target harm issue. Some extended the critique and argued that risk research on *Bt* crops must 'consider the ecological complexity of agroecosystems'. They drew an analogy to past mistakes and the rapid adoption of agrochemicals in the 1950s. They argued that at that time ecologically based management practices had suffered, and adverse effects were ignored, thus limiting the management options for farmers. They also warned against 'the acceptance of yet another silver bullet for pest management' (Obrycki et al., 2001a: 359).

In an interview, and speaking in relation to risk in general rather than any specific risk, a representative of the Union of Concerned Scientists tried to clarify the practical meaning of 'more stringent' regulatory standards:

> More stringent standards pertain to a wider range of risks evaluated, more than to the quality of evidence submitted. . . . Over seven years the EPA has learned more about what questions to ask, but it hasn't clarified the data requirements, nor criticised the data which it receives. There is no improvement in the quality of studies being done . . .
> (Interview, 28 October 2002)

At the same time, such NGOs saw public funds as a means to improve the quality of regulatory science. The UCS interviewee commented later: 'Scientists who receive risk-assessment grants from government agencies want to publish journal papers, so they will have higher standards . . . Scientists on the SAP could also push the agency to raise standards. But this would be a slow, slow process' (email, 20 August 2003).

Regulatory standards: types, changes and pressures

Drawing on the above examples, we can identify three types of regulatory standards for *Bt* maize. These are summarised in Table 4.1. First, there are regulatory standards implicit in normative judgements, which can favour some agricultural cultivation methods over others. A good example is the initial decision to compare the non-target impacts of *Bt* crops with conventional (chemical) agriculture rather than less intensive forms. Second, there are regulatory standards associated with risk assessment, such as the testing methodologies that have been accepted as adequate or judged as inadequate for identifying potential harm. These in turn have depended on models of causal pathways. Such standards are also implicit if regulators simply regard particular tests as acceptable, though they become explicit if they are written down in guidance. Third, there are regulatory standards associated with risk management measures. These more clearly assign responsibility for detecting or preventing potential effects; such standards are usually made explicit as a statutory condition of product approval. This category includes the spatial specification of non-*Bt* refuges used to delay insect resistance, for example.

Table 4.1 Regulatory Standards for *Bt* Maize: Types and Changes

	Insect Resistance	*Non-Target Harm*
Normative Judgements	*Early:* Insect resistance to *Bt* is an 'agronomic problem' and not an 'adverse effect' on the environment.	*Early:* The impacts of *Bt* should be compared against the impacts of using chemical insecticides.
	More stringent: Bt is a public good and should be protected as such. Insect resistance threatens this.	*More stringent:* The impact of *Bt* is unacceptable if it causes more harm than non-chemical control methods.
Risk Assessment	*Early:* The discriminating-dose test can be used to test for insect resistance.	*Early:* Direct toxicity tests can be used to test the impact of plant *Bt* on non-target insects.
	More stringent: The F2 screen should be used to test for insect resistance because it is more sensitive than other methods.	*More stringent:* Tritrophic tests should also be used to test for more subtle impacts of plant *Bt* on non-target insects.
	Other issues: Recessive or dominant trait? Baseline of susceptibility? Changes in susceptibility?	*Other issues:* How to conduct field monitoring? The role of toxic pollen and anthers?
Risk Management	*Example:* Non-*Bt* maize refuges (specifying area and distance from the crop) as part of a strategy to manage insect resistance.	*Example:* Planting buffer zones to limit the flow of pollen to milkweed plants where it might impact on non-target insects.
	Other issues: Engineering high-dose *Bt* gene expression in the maize stalk. What contexts require a refuge?	*Other issues:* Engineering low-dose *Bt* gene expression in maize pollen.

Source: This table was originally produced in Murphy et al.. (2006).

Based on the material discussed in this chapter we can see that there have been many changes in regulatory standards over time. In the area of normative judgements, for example, in the US it was argued initially that insect resistance is acceptable because individual *Bt* toxins can be replaced and are therefore dispensable. Over time this argument was undermined by the argument that insect resistance must be avoided because *Bt* toxins are a public good. Similarly, in the EU it was argued initially that insect resistance was acceptable because it was only an 'agronomic problem'. Although companies did not officially change their view, they began to submit insect resistance monitoring plans under EU legislation, and in this way began to act as if insect resistance is an 'adverse effect' on the environment.

There have been similar changes to normative judgements in relation to non-target harm. In both the US and the EU, it was initially argued that non-target harm is acceptable if it is no greater than that which is associated with chemical insecticides. By making this argument its proponents were assuming that the use of chemical insecticides is the appropriate comparator against which to assess the impacts of *Bt* maize. This basis for comparison assumed that *Bt* maize would only replace conventional maize in areas previously sprayed with insecticides. However, this assumption was contradicted by surveys, which showed that in practice farmers extended *Bt* maize cultivation far beyond fields previously sprayed against the relevant pest. Thus the original comparator became less acceptable; potential harm from *Bt* maize was increasingly compared with those of other agricultural regimes, particularly non-chemical ones.

In the area of risk assessment, changes in regulatory standards are seen in the emergence of new research questions and methodologies. In many cases the optimistic assumptions of regulators and others were recast as issues that require further research and in some cases the development of new test methods. For example, in relation to non-target harm, the tritrophic lacewing experiments contributed specific data and highlighted the limits of direct toxicity tests. The direct toxicity test had been appropriated from the testing of agricultural chemicals and it was not designed to examine biological pathways. In relation to insect resistance, the F2 screen emerged as a more sensitive test method, as compared to the discriminating-dose test. Developed originally in the USA, the F2 screen was adapted in Europe and it was then used for testing insect resistance on both sides of the Atlantic. More generally, US and EU regulators scrutinised research that indicated harm more rigorously than research that indicated safety, but later they were put on the defensive in relation to this double standard.

Finally, there were also some changes in regulatory standards in the area of risk management. The insect resistance problem, for example, led to a debate over refuge requirements and specifications. Over time the EPA moved towards actually specifying refuge sizes, thus going beyond reliance on 'unstructured refuges', which it had previously regarded as adequate to delay insect resistance. Changes in risk management standards in relation to non-target insects are less clear. Although buffer zones were proposed in the US by environmental NGOs in 1999, the EPA did not make them mandatory. When the EU-wide regulatory procedure began to evaluate new applications for *Bt* maize cultivation after 2002, some EU member states proposed mandatory monitoring and buffer zones for non-target harm, contrary to the safety assumptions of the EU-level expert body; arguments were continuing in 2005.

This discussion shows that many regulatory standards became more stringent over a relatively short period. This trend can be seen in the US more clearly than in the EU, where regulatory decision procedures were suspended between 1999 and 2002. It also shows how regulatory standards of different kinds are linked. For example, as normative judgements about unacceptable effects became more stringent, this in turn led to criticism of existing risk assessment assumptions and test methods. This criticism highlighted methods that were not sensitive enough or did not adequately simulate realistic exposure or causal pathways. This in turn led to demands for more sensitive tests whilst at the same time creating a context more favourable to ecological perspectives. In this process we see regulators increasingly applying more stringent judgements across a range of regulatory standards as a way of managing uncertainty and controversy. At the same time, more public funds were invested in risk research.

In broad terms, therefore, we can say that public controversy, transatlantic conflict and expert criticism created pressures for more stringent regulatory standards of different kinds; moreover, changes in different types of standards were linked. More specifically, however, we can ask, where did pressure for higher standards come from? The following quotes give an indication of some of the sources:

> NGOs here tried to use the US failure to persuade the rest of the world as an argument for why we need to harmonise upwards.
>
> (Interview, UCS, 28 October 2002)

> ... the US is aiming to spread US oversight [regulatory] systems as rapidly and as extensively as possible around the world. They see as one possible challenge the incipient oversight system that has to be formed out of the EU Directives, even though it isn't there yet ...
>
> (Interview, SAP member, 8 September 2003)

> In the US, industry will routinely seek academic support and advice about whether they're doing the right sort of things ... There will always be efforts to improve the science ... At the same time there is also an effort to anticipate regulatory trends. Realistically speaking, if a large portion of the world is going to move in step with Europe, it makes sense to anticipate where they are going.
>
> (Interview, company regulatory officer, 8 September 2003)

These comments are important because they draw our attention to strategies that have helped to shape regulatory standards in the US. In each comment the EU plays an indirect but central role – as a source of higher standards to be adopted, influenced or anticipated by various policy actors. Such transatlantic influences differ from the formal negotiations over regulatory standards that accompany negotiation of an international agreement, for example.

Conclusion

In this chapter we have described the risk assessment and regulation of *Bt* maize in the EU and US. To develop the case study we focused on how regulatory authorities and others have dealt with two environmental risks – insect resistance and non-target harm. In the final section we identified three types of regulatory standards – normative judgements, standards associated with risk assessment and standards associated with risk management. We showed how standards in these areas were tightened over a relatively short period, particularly in the US. We also showed how changes in normative judgments help to shape more concrete regulatory standards, and how the emerging EU regulatory system created pressure for higher standards in the US in various ways. To conclude this chapter we will briefly explore how this case study helps us to answer the narrative questions in the introduction to this book.

How did policy actors try to advance particular policy agendas?

From this chapter it is clear that advocates and critics of *Bt* maize (and we can say GM crops more generally) tried to build support for their policy agendas by framing the issues in different ways. Advocates emphasised the precision of the genetic modification process, the economic gains to be reaped by using GM crops and the reduction in the use of agrichemicals that would become possible. If insects developed resistance to the *Bt* toxin, then this would be an 'agronomic problem' and not an 'adverse effect' on the environment, and alternative *Bt* toxins would be available anyway if they were needed.

Critics challenged this favourable framing in various ways. They raised an analogy to the pesticide treadmill: that insects would acquire resistance to different *Bt* toxins. Some also argued that there were unknown risks, such as the potential harm to non-target insects through indirect causal pathways. When new research indicated potential harm to the Monarch butterfly, US environmental groups used this to launch a national debate about threats to wildlife. They also emphasised the need to ensure that other production methods, such as less intensive or organic agriculture, continued to be an option. European environmental groups, in contrast, campaigned for a complete ban on GM agriculture. All such critics cast *Bt* maize as a threat to sustainable agriculture.

These framings underlay contending coalitions of policy actors promoting different regulatory standards. In the US in particular the pro-biotech framing of *Bt* crops underpinned a coalition that included biotechnology companies, the environmental regulators and a farmers' organisation (see Chapter 6). In the mid-1990s, however, a new US coalition demanded that *Bt* toxins be preserved as a public good, and on this basis they demanded Insect-Resistance Management strategies or more stringent versions of them; this coalition included organic farmers, critical entomologists and environmental NGOs. Their challenge eventually led to more stringent regulatory standards, such as larger and/or mandatory refuges to manage insect resistance.

As GM crops became more controversial in Europe in the late 1990s, and some evidence of non-target harm emerged, agbiotech critics used this to challenge regulatory assumptions on both sides of the Atlantic. Normative judgements about acceptable harm had rested on the assumption that *Bt* maize would only substitute for a previous use of agricultural chemicals, and would therefore lead to environmental benefits through less use of insecticide sprays. This assumption was eventually challenged and this in turn raised the question of whether any non-target harm would be acceptable. In this way regulatory norms became more stringent.

As they intervened in these arguments, scientists coordinated their activities through two transatlantic networks. A pro-biotech website published articles challenging new evidence of risk. In parallel, ecologically oriented scientists and environmental NGOs exchanged critical perspectives in an effort to gain more rigorous regulatory standards in relation to evidence of safety.

How were expertise and knowledge used to influence policy making?

Scientific knowledge and expertise have played a changing role in the regulation of *Bt* maize, on both sides of the Atlantic. When the first *Bt* maize varieties were approved, their supporters emphasised the scientific basis on which decisions were made. Questions soon emerged, however, regarding implicit normative judgements, risk assessment assumptions and test methods. These doubts eventually influenced risk management decisions.

In the disputes that followed, policy actors on both sides sought to discredit any empirical results that might undermine their policy agenda. They challenged evidence of risk or safety particularly on methodological grounds. When experiments yielded evidence of risk, for example, their design was criticised for failing to simulate realistic field conditions. Those who were more critical of safety assumptions, however, were able to point out that evidence of safety was not scrutinised in an equally rigorous way. Such dynamics ultimately led the EPA to adopt more stringent normative judgements, test methods and scientific criteria, partly as a way of managing the conflict. The transatlantic transfer of test methodologies, empirical results and critical arguments was important, as were changes in expert advice to regulatory agencies.

The case of *Bt* maize therefore illustrates what can happen when the relatively 'private' world of regulatory science is opened up to greater public scrutiny. In this case critical scientists and NGOs, with a different framing of the issues, and deploying alternative scientific tests, were able to turn various optimistic safety assumptions into issues that required further research or deliberation. Many of these were industry assumptions which had been accepted by regulators. As regulators came under challenge they promoted additional risk research and new control measures.

On both sides of the Atlantic, public funding also increased, improving the breadth and quality of scientific research. For example, US companies and regulatory agencies jointly funded research on novel hazards of toxic pollen, with experimental design overseen by a group including environmental NGOs. The content of regulatory science was self-consciously changed in response to contextual factors that included the EU–US conflict over biotechnology products, the public backlash in Europe, the commercial boycott and various transatlantic networks. This case therefore draws attention to other important influences on regulatory science, particularly the source of research funding and the composition of expert advisory bodies as a peer-review procedure.

Transatlantic interactions are an important feature of the *Bt* maize example. In particular we see critical arguments and more stringent or sensitive test methodologies moving across the Atlantic with the help of expert networks. The F2 screen, for example, was developed in the US before it was taken up in the EU. In the EU it was adapted in the context of recent member-state demands for more rigorous monitoring of insect resistance. European researchers also applied it back in the US as part of a research project funded by the EU. In the reverse direction, after EcoStrat made critical arguments regarding the test methods linked to *Bt* maize, these were taken up by a US environmental NGO to critique the basis of EPA product approvals, and in turn they were taken up by the EPA's own expert advisors. This case therefore draws our attention to transatlantic networks of critical scientists and NGOs working together in an effort to shape regulatory standards.

How were regulatory standard-setting processes and trade conflict linked?

The conflict over the regulation of *Bt* maize involved a diverse range of arguments. Advocates of the technology emphasised economic competitiveness and environmental benefits, while critics focused on environmental risks and threats to other forms of agriculture. Critics initially found it difficult to create a regulatory debate in the US, apart from the need to protect *Bt* toxins as a public good. They gained more opportunities, however, with conflicts over trade liberalisation, which were followed by an actual trade conflict and diverging regulatory frameworks across the Atlantic.

As discussed in Chapter 2, efforts to harmonise regulatory standards across the Atlantic exposed policy makers to the criticism that they were favouring commercial objectives over other concerns. The EU and transatlantic conflicts helped US NGOs and critical scientists who were trying to influence standard-setting processes there. They played upon the doubts that US agencies had regarding whether their regulatory criteria were scientifically robust and defensible at the international level. The EU played various indirect roles – as a source of higher standards to be adopted, influenced or anticipated by US policy actors. This case therefore illustrates how standard setting in the US was shaped by trade conflict in various ways.

Because there was a tightening of regulatory standards over time, rather than a levelling down, the concept of 'trading up' might be useful in this case. The dynamics in this case, however, were more complex than the concept suggests. First, a trade liberalisation agenda provoked trade conflict and it was the latter which became a resource for NGOs. Second, the transatlantic networks and interactions discussed in this chapter, which help to explain changes in regulatory standards, were informal; they differ from the formal rules and processes emphasised in most accounts of trading up. Finally, this case involves normative judgements and testing methodologies. Such regulatory standards are unlike those that are normally the focus of a trading-up analysis. With these caveats in place, Chapter 7 shows how trading up nevertheless illuminates aspects of this case.

How were EU–US interactions and intra-jurisdictional conflicts linked?

In the case of *Bt* maize there was a mutual shaping of transatlantic interactions and intra-jurisdictional conflicts. Taking advantage of transatlantic regulatory divergences, US NGOs helped to bring more critical scientists into the regulatory debate there, while also playing upon regulators' doubts about whether they could defend their standards on the international stage. US government threats against the EU in relation to a potential WTO dispute therefore resonated domestically as well as across the Atlantic. Such concerns led eventually to more critical scientists being included on US expert advisory bodies, for example the NRC and the SAP. These in turn questioned the optimistic assumptions of US regulatory agencies.

Meanwhile, after new EU rules were finalised in 2003, public antagonism towards agricultural biotechnology continued. It was aggravated by the suspicion that any EU approval decisions would accommodate US political pressure (see Chapter 6). In this context, when EU regulatory procedures evaluated specific files for *Bt* maize cultivation, many regulatory authorities and expert advisors demanded more stringent risk management for non-target harm. Others simply opposed approval. Conflicts continued over standards of evidence and measures to manage uncertainties about risk. These examples illustrate complex links between transatlantic interactions and intra-jurisdictional dynamics.

5 Health risks of GM foods

The concept of 'substantial equivalence'

Introduction

As we outlined in the Introduction to this book, agricultural biotechnology led to a legitimacy crisis for politicians and policy makers in Europe in the late 1990s. A consumer boycott of GM foods was accompanied by NGO direct action against GM crops in fields. These developments led to delays in the approval of new GM products, blockages of US maize exports, and a commercial boycott by food retailers. This context created more opportunities for critics to challenge the claim that GM products were safe, and as a result expert-regulatory debates and procedures became much more sensitive to critical perspectives. In Chapter 4 we outlined how the treatment of environmental risks associated with *Bt* maize changed in this context.

This chapter examines analogous changes in the regulation of GM foods – regarding their risks to human health. We focus on the controversial concept of 'substantial equivalence', the regulatory concept that guides the risk assessment of GM food. The first section of this chapter describes the emergence and wider adoption of this concept in the mid-1990s. The second section outlines how it underwent various challenges, particularly in Europe. The third section describes the process of recasting the concept along more stringent lines, particularly through the international negotiations of the Codex Alimentarius Commission. This was one of the ways of dealing with the conflict. The fourth section outlines recent developments in EU regulatory practice, while the fifth section discusses the policy impasse around the US non-regulation of GM food.

The chapter focuses on interactions between the EU and the US in relation to GM foods. From the early 1990s onwards the EU and the US interacted almost constantly in relation to risk assessment of GM food, particularly in international fora. Anticipating an international trade in GM foods, policy makers and regulatory officials sought to establish a harmonised regulatory framework. The focus initially was on the Organization for Economic Cooperation and Development, but later and much more importantly a range of issues were negotiated through the Codex Alimentarius Commission. It is worth noting that with regards to the environmental risks of GM crops, there were no analogous international negotiations on regulatory standards, although there were important informal interactions across the Atlantic.

Agreeing and implementing 'substantial equivalence'

Food regulators in the US and the EU faced new practical questions in the early 1990s. How should the safety of GM foods be evaluated? What type of regulatory framework should be put in place? The answers to these questions were not obvious because novel food products are not normally subjected to a statutory risk assessment and pre-market approval. It is assumed that new foods are safe if producers use ingredients with a history of safe use. However, given the possibility of novel risks from GM foods, it was not clear that this approach was appropriate. In this section we outline the solution that emerged in OECD (Organization for Economic Cooperation and Development) negotiations and how this was implemented in the US and the EU.

OECD negotiations in the early 1990s

In the early 1990s the Codex Alimentarius Commission sought advice on risk assessment of GM foods from an FAO/WHO expert consultation. According to the report that emerged, a GM food could be compared with a conventional counterpart, although the report also warned that adequate baseline information might not be available: 'Comparative data on the closest conventional counterpart are critically important in the evaluation of a new food, including data on chemical composition and nutritional value. The Consultation believed that such data are not widely available at the present time' (FAO/WHO, 1991: 24). Moreover, argued the expert report, safety assessment should be based on 'scientific principles' (FAO/WHO, 1991).

Also in the early 1990s, although slightly later, the OECD organised a series of expert meetings on the risk assessment of GM foods. Government officials and food safety experts appointed by OECD countries attended the meetings. In a way consistent with its broader commitment to regulatory harmonisation, the OECD sought to facilitate a consensus on the risk assessment of GM foods in order to avoid any future barriers to trade. At these meetings, by going beyond the cautious approach of the 1991 FAO/WHO consultation, a consensus emerged around the concept of 'substantial equivalence'. In the landmark publication *Safety Evaluation of Foods Derived by Modern Biotechnology*, government officials announced the following conclusion:

> . . . if a new food or food component is found to be substantially equivalent to an existing food or food component, it can be treated in the same manner with respect to safety. No additional safety concerns would be expected. Where substantial equivalence is more difficult to establish because the food or food component is either less well-known or totally

new, then the identified differences, or the new characteristics, should be the focus of further safety considerations.

(OECD, 1993: 13)

This document omitted the earlier FAO/WHO warning that comparative data may not be available to underpin such an approach.

In the years that followed, the concept of substantial equivalence became increasingly controversial. By the end of the 1990s OECD staff came under pressure to defend the concept. Some did so by defending the process from which it emerged:

> The concept of substantial equivalence was developed proactively before any new genetically modified GM foods came to the market . . . [the 1993 report was] produced by about 60 experts from 19 OECD countries, who spent more than two years discussing how to assess the safety of GM foods. Most of these experts, all nominated by governments, were regulatory scientists from government agencies and ministries responsible for consumer safety.
>
> (Kearns and Mayers, 1999: 640)

In this way they retrospectively sought to reinforce the legitimacy of substantial equivalence by emphasising the multi-government and scientific nature of the discussions. Perhaps in a way that they did not intend, however, this statement draws attention to the assumption that such a concept could be developed based solely on the involvement of government-appointed scientists.

US practice: 'substantially similar' products

In the early 1990s the US had a significant lead in the commercialisation of GM products. It was the first jurisdiction to market GM crops and foods, and, as is still the case today, it was the home market for many important biotechnology companies. In addition, the US government identified biotechnology as essential for the future of US agriculture and its competitiveness. For all these reasons, the US played a prominent role in the OECD's discussions, partly because it was an opportunity to establish regulatory precedents that other countries might then adopt.

For its domestic policy, the US had already set out important regulatory arguments in its 1986 *Coordinated Framework for the Regulation of the Products of Biotechnology* (see also Chapter 4) (OSTP, 1986). This document was constructed around four key principles or assumptions: the products of recombinant DNA technology will not differ fundamentally from unmodified organisms or from conventional products; existing laws are adequate to regulate the products of this technology; product, not process, should be regulated, and regulation should be risk-based; regulation should be directed toward the intended end use for products, and should be conducted on a case-by-case basis.

Several years later, and building on the *Coordinated Framework*, the US Food and Drug Administration published guidance on the assessment of foods from new plant varieties, including GM crops (US FDA, 1992). This guidance was consistent with the broader principles given above. It made no *a priori* distinction between GM foods and conventional foods and made it clear that no special legislation to regulate them was planned because existing legislation was sufficient. In general the FDA expected genetic modification of plants to result in components 'substantially similar' to those commonly found in food and 'generally recognised as safe', known by the abbreviation GRAS.

At this time the FDA also indicated how it would be appropriate to establish the similarity between a conventional food and a GM food – mainly by testing physical-chemical composition. In cases where this approach could not resolve safety concerns, 'feeding studies or other toxicological tests may be warranted'. However, it was also acknowledged that 'feeding studies on whole foods have limited sensitivity because of the inability to administer exaggerated doses'. According to the FDA, its guidelines were 'consistent with the concept of substantial equivalence' which was being discussed by OECD experts at that time (US FDA, 1992).

In practice, although there was no statutory obligation to do so at this time, companies began to seek FDA review of their safety claims before placing GM foods on the market in the US.[1] To do this they submitted data on the physical/chemical composition of the GM foods, as suggested by the FDA. This data, they claimed, established the similarity between a GM food and its conventional counterpart, and therefore meant that no risk assessment was warranted. Sometimes companies also submitted data from toxicological tests on the novel protein and/or the whole food. In response, the FDA began to send each company a letter noting the safety claim and stating: 'It is our understanding that [the developer] has concluded that [the food product] does not raise issues that would require pre-market review or approval of FDA.' It is clear from this wording that in practice the FDA takes no responsibility for any company judgements relating to safety.

In this way, as the 1990s progressed, physical-chemical composition was placed at the centre of GM food safety assessment in the US and the implementation of the concept of substantial equivalence. This emphasis can be explained in relation to a number of influences, such as the methodological difficulties associated with testing the toxicity of whole foods or complex mixtures. However, at the same time, it was also US government policy to support agricultural biotechnology as both safe and an economic necessity. According to the President's Council on Competitiveness in 1991, the government must maintain 'risk-based regulation', and thus 'avoid excessive restrictions that would curtail the benefits of biotechnology to society' (BWG/CoC, 1991). In this policy context, FDA guidelines and practice in the 1990s facilitated safety claims, particularly through the use of compositional tests.

EU practice: simplified procedure

In contrast to the US, EU policy makers in the late 1980s judged that GM products were associated with new uncertainties about risk and therefore required special legislation. Directive 90/220, on the deliberate release of GMOs, aimed to prevent 'adverse effects on human health or the environment', and was the first significant piece of European legislation in the area (EEC, 1990). It placed a legal duty on producers to seek prior approval before release of any GMO in the EU. As part of the approval process, producers had to submit a dossier providing information that could be used to evaluate any risks. Directive 90/220 briefly served as the EU's regulatory framework for assessing GM foods and two companies used it to obtain commercial approval for GM foods in 1996–97.

A dedicated regulatory framework for GM foods in the EU emerged in 1997 with Regulation 258/97 on novel foods (CEC, 1997b). It established a legal requirement on producers to seek approval before commercialisation of any GM food. However, unlike Directive 90/220, the new law also included a simplified procedure. In cases where a GM food was judged to be 'substantially equivalent' to an existing food, a company was required only to provide a scientific justification for this claim, and not a risk assessment of the product itself. This procedure was used to authorise several GM foods in the late 1990s. With this legislation, therefore, the EU applied the OECD concept.

At this point it is worth highlighting connections between these developments and related ones outlined earlier in this book. In Chapter 2 we discussed the Transatlantic Economic Partnership, which sought regulatory harmonisation and trade liberalisation, including the area of agricultural biotechnology. This aim was advanced when the EU incorporated the concept of substantial equivalence into Regulation 258/97, following the adoption of a similar concept by the FDA in the US. It also created conditions that would facilitate the TEP's proposed pilot project on simultaneous assessment of a GMO in the EU and the US.

Challenging 'substantial equivalence'

GM food became controversial in the EU in the late 1990s. In this section we outline how various critics raised concerns about GM food safety and risk assessment. In response to the emerging controversy, regulators became more dependent on expert claims about science. However, at the same time, risk assessment and expert claims became increasingly vulnerable to challenge as more uncertainties and conflicts emerged. Problems included weaknesses in available methodologies and inconvenient empirical results.

Disagreements amongst experts became more important. Ultimately, in the context of the public backlash, critics of safety claims gained a stronger basis from which to gain more stringent approaches.

Early criticisms of GM food regulation

An early challenge to the concept of substantial equivalence came from the umbrella NGO Consumers International. In a 1996 publication they emphasised various uncertainties, particularly around genetic novelty and available laboratory tests, which they argued had implications for the concept in practice:

> ... consumer experts are concerned that this concept has only limited value. First of all, it is very difficult to assess substantial equivalence ... Too much importance is attached to digestibility tests for assessing safety. Finally, there is a lack of available scientific data on safety of traditional foodstuffs used for comparison with GEFs [genetically engineered foods].
>
> (CI, 1996: 1)

Later in the same document CI went on to say: 'In a field of science in which many of the mechanisms are still a mystery, great caution is needed. Therefore consumer experts believe that the precautionary principle should be applied' (CI, 1996: 3). As a practical contribution the report recommended that GM food safety assessment should involve a wide range of additional tests, partly as a way of dealing with scientific unknowns and methodological weaknesses (CI, 1996: 4–11; see later citations).

NGOs and critics hostile to agricultural biotechnology attacked the concept of substantial equivalence in much stronger terms. For example, Monsanto was criticised for evaluating glyphosate-tolerant soybeans without using any tests to assess how their composition may be affected by the use of glyphosate sprays (Tappeser and von Weizsacker, 1996). More generally some critics argued that the genetic modification process itself is associated with novel risks, which substantial equivalence plays down. In the mid-1990s they argued that the concept is 'unscientific and arbitrary. . . . intentionally vague and ill-defined to be as flexible, malleable and open to interpretation as possible'. Furthermore, 'Genetic engineering carries its own inherent hazards which are unique to it', such as a general hazard from lab techniques which incorporate viral DNA into the new organism (Ho and Steinbrecher, 1997). Some critics argued more generally that there were doubts about the ability of science to reduce and clarify risks through more knowledge.

When US grain traders sent shipments containing GM maize and soybeans to European ports in 1996–97, activists exploited their arrival as an opportunity to encourage public protest and undermine safety claims. Supermarket chains were picketed and leafleted (Levidow and Bijman, 2002). In the broadest terms GM products were turned into a conflict over different agri-technological futures and democratic accountability for them. The term 'GM food' came to denote an entire agri-food system being driven by commercial-industrial forces. Especially in Europe, environmental NGOs opposed agricultural biotechnology altogether. They linked GM food with past food crises and attempts to industrialise agriculture. Drawing on the BSE experience, Greenpeace referred to 'untestable' risks of GM food (Greenpeace, 1997a: 5, 11), and in a direct attack on substantial equivalence, they stated: 'Sheep offal contained the scrapie prion but would not have been picked up by the conventional chemical analysis or short-term testing required to determine "substantial equivalence"' (Greenpeace, 1997b: 27).

Although there was a tendency at this time to try to reduce the GM issue to a technical problem, for many opponents GM 'Frankenstein' food was indicative of a particularly ominous form of globalisation. Related processes were understood to be undermining safety regulation and democracy more generally. For example, the UK Consumers Association criticised the agri-food industry for its 'unshakeable belief in whizz-bang techniques to conjure up the impossible – food that is safe and nutritious but also cheap enough to beat the global competition' (McKechnie, 1999). In this way arguments made by industry and government linking biotechnology, agricultural effi-ciency and international competitiveness were turned upside-down. When this happened the same arguments cast doubt on safety claims for GM food. In addition to demanding a more rigorous risk assessment procedure, consumer NGOs also began to demand segregation and labelling to ensure that consumers could choose non-GM products.

To understand this backlash against GM foods and its implications for substantial equivalence it is worth noting a broader cultural dimension. In Europe GM foods were widely understood to be inherently different from their conventional counterparts. As a result substantial equivalence was easy to ridicule as a careless and deceptive concept that plays down the novelty of GM foods and thereby serves the interests of biotechnology companies. Critics were therefore able to turn the concept itself into a problem for consumer confidence in regulation. Interestingly, in some ways this view of inherent difference, which emerged publicly in the late 1990s, was an echo of the assumption that underpinned the *a priori* decision by EU policy makers to develop GM specific legislation from the late 1980s onwards.

Tighter regulatory criteria in the UK and the EU

In response to this growing criticism of the treatment of GM food risks, various European expert bodies modified and extended risk assessment criteria. This happened particularly in the UK. For example, in 1997 the UK's expert body (the Advisory Committee on Novel Foods and Processes (ACNFP)) proposed restrictions on the use of antibiotic-resistance marker genes (ACNFP, 1997). This advice accommodated the concern that such a gene could spread to pathogenic organisms and thus undermine the corresponding antibiotic, an issue associated with scientific uncertainty and consumer concern. Some argued such a change was necessary for scientific reasons whilst others linked it more to the need to accommodate public concerns and thus maintain consumer confidence. In practice the boundary between these was very blurred and different groups drew it differently for various reasons. According to one chairman of ACNFP: 'Eventually the scientists learned how to ask questions which would concern consumers' (interview, 28 May 1998).

Other significant changes also had their origins in the UK. As outlined above, under the 1997 Novel Food Regulation, products could be authorised using a simplified substantial equivalence procedure. To use this procedure applicants had to establish substantial equivalence between the GM food and a conventional counterpart, rather than conduct a dedicated risk assessment. With this possibility in mind UK experts discussed whether substantial equivalence would adequately address all risks. After deliberating the ACNFP concluded that the simplified procedure was only suitable for fully processed foods, which were therefore not genetically modified in the strictest sense (ACNFP, 1998). This tightened the practical meaning of the concept. Similarly, they indicated that it was necessary to check the stability of the transgenic insert in the crop. In an interview in 1998 one ACNFP member commented as follows on substantial equivalence:

> If we must use that criterion alone, then we will tighten its definition . . . a food cannot be regarded as substantially equivalent if it contains any intact GM DNA, so the product must be highly refined to ensure that all the DNA has been denatured. Moreover, we will specify what tests are required; the company must monitor generations of the crop over two years at six sites.
>
> (Interview, 11 May 1998)

A similar requirement to test genetic stability had recently been proposed by NGO-associated scientists (e.g. Ho and Steinbrecher, 1997).

Developments of this kind in the UK soon had implications for the EU as a whole. In 1998 the Standing Committee on Foodstuffs, a body which represents the regulatory authorities of all EU member states, adopted one of the UK's proposals mentioned above: that the simplified procedure could only be used for products which contain no intact GM DNA/protein. Through this institutional mechanism, therefore, a national change, shaped by public protest and civil society, and involving the adoption of more stringent regulatory criteria, became an EU-wide standard which limited the statutory role of substantial equivalence. Through developments like this we see that at this time substantial equivalence was being defined more tightly and it was being given a more modest role. One outcome of this was that EU practice was beginning to diverge from US practice in relation to this concept, despite the fact that it was intended to function as part of a harmonised regulatory framework.

The politics of expert advice

In the late 1990s the situation described above was complicated further by a high-profile controversy involving expert scientific advice. At this time, as the public backlash against GM foods in Europe intensified, the UK government funded additional research. An important part of this was a major project to improve and standardise whole-food tests on animals. This project was based in the Rowett Research Institute (RRI) and led by Arpad Pusztai, an internationally renowned expert on lectins – naturally occurring toxins that protect plants from insects. The project used GM potatoes containing a transgene for a lectin that was understood to be harmless to mammals. However, unexpected experimental results, which were announced on a UK television programme in 1998, added fuel to the GM food controversy. After ingesting the GM potato, rats apparently suffered damage to their immune systems and organ development. The transgene itself was not a plausible cause but Pusztai raised the possibility that the process of genetic modification had led to an unknown change in the potato. This was controversial because it raised doubts about the safety of GM foods already on the market.

In the aftermath of this announcement the institutional response to Pusztai's results became as important as the research results themselves. Through its actions the Rowett Research Institute gave the impression that biotechnology enthusiasts were attempting to silence critics. The RRI ended its support for the research group's work, terminated Pusztai's employment and denied him access to his research data. Such actions led to speculation about the RRI's motives. According to some critics, the RRI were more interested in research contracts than in independent science (sources cited in Levidow, 2002).

Pusztai's work then led to a wider debate about the politics of scientific research and expert advice. The Royal Society convened a special committee, which concluded, 'there is no convincing evidence of adverse effects from the GM potatoes in question' (Royal Society, 1999). In response, however, *The Lancet* criticised the Royal Society for a 'breathtakingly arrogant' approach to risk research on GM safety ('Editorial', 1999). It also published a paper based on the GM lectin research, with various commentaries. International networks of scientists then took sides for and against the validity of Pusztai's work and the controversy was widely cited in debates beyond the UK.

The Pusztai controversy fed directly into further high-profile criticism of the concept of substantial equivalence. In an article in *Nature*, which referred to Pusztai's work, Millstone et al. (1999) attacked substantial equivalence as an inadequate way to judge the safety of GM food. The authors identified three problems: (1) it emphasises chemical composition at the expense of biological, toxicological and immunological tests; (2) there is no definition of the point at which a substance is no longer substantially equivalent; and (3) the concept itself acts as a barrier to risk research. More generally they asked why the concept of substantial equivalence was favoured over other regulatory approaches, such as treating GM foods like novel chemicals, which would have led to much more rigorous safety testing.

Although the *Nature* article focused on the scientific and regulatory value of substantial equivalence, the authors also offered some critical thoughts on where it had come from and why. They focused specifically on the business influence on policy making and the political agenda associated with agricultural biotechnology and GM foods:

> The adoption of the concept of substantial equivalence . . . signalled to the GM food industry that, as long as companies did not try to market GM foods that had a grossly different chemical composition from those of foods already on the market, their new GM products would be permitted without any safety or toxicological tests.
>
> (Millstone et al., 1999: 525)

> Substantial equivalence is a pseudo-scientific concept because it is a commercial and political judgement masquerading as if it were scientific. It is, moreover, inherently anti-scientific because it was created primarily to provide an excuse for not requiring biochemical or toxicological tests. It therefore serves to discourage and inhibit potentially informative scientific research.
>
> (Millstone et al., 1999: 526)

In a response to this article, also published in *Nature*, OECD staff defended substantial equivalence as an appropriate basis for risk assessment:

> Substantial equivalence is not a substitute for a safety assessment. It is a guiding principle which is a useful tool for regulatory scientists engaged in safety assessment . . . In this approach differences may be identified for further scrutiny, which can involve nutritional, toxicological and immunological testing. The approach allows regulators to focus on the differences in a new variety and therefore on safety concerns of critical importance. Biochemical and toxicological tests are certainly not precluded.
>
> (Kearns and Mayers, 1999: 640)

This account emphasises that through substantial equivalence a broad range of uncertainties can be identified and investigated. By 2002 some experts were suggesting that the concept might usefully be abandoned altogether, in favour of a 'comparative approach' (e.g. interview, OECD, 9 January 2003). This phrase suggested a more humble approach and onerous task to establish similarity.

Recasting 'substantial equivalence'

EU regulation of GMOs was in crisis by the late 1990s and the unofficial *de facto* moratorium on approvals was put in place. As outlined in the

Introduction, related regulatory delays then led to a high-profile trade conflict with the US and this raised the political stakes associated with regulatory differences across the Atlantic. In this section we focus on how the concept of substantial equivalence was recast in international negotiations in this context. Representatives from the US and the EU played leading roles in the meetings we discuss. In practice the concept was redefined to accommodate diverse views about scientific uncertainty and risk. In addition, efforts were made to accommodate diverse policy agendas, such as the 'regulatory efficiency' and 'consumer rights' agendas.

Transatlantic Consumer Dialogue

We discussed the Transatlantic Consumer Dialogue at length in Chapter 3 but it is worth noting here that at the end of 1990s this network became a place where US and EU consumer NGOs could formulate a common position on approval of GM foods in general and substantial equivalence specifically. TACD's first policy statement on GMOs demanded a mandatory approval process covering human health, safety and environmental protection (TACD, 1999b). This demand was aimed largely at the US, which had no mandatory approval process for GM foods (this is still the case). Soon after a more comprehensive statement raised doubts about the concept of substantial equivalence:

> It is important to consider the limitations of an approach based on 'substantial equivalence' and consider whether more robust methods for assessing the unintended consequences of genetic modification are available or could be developed. . . . TACD calls for the development of methods for assessing GM foods, which unlike 'substantial equivalence' can help to give a clearer idea of the potential unintended consequences of genetic modification.
>
> (TACD, 2000: 2/4)

Along similar lines, although outside the TACD structure, European consumer NGOs extended their long-standing criticisms of regulatory practice. In their view, regulators had a weak basis from which to identify any differences between a GM food and a non-GM counterpart. On behalf of all European consumer groups, a report by a biotechnology consultancy emphasised the inadequate baseline information available on conventional foods and therefore the problems associated with assessing GM foods against them. It also argued that only patchy data was being submitted on GM foods, saying that 'it is hardly plausible that compositional data have been analysed in a statistically sound way' (SBC, 2001).

In this context European consumer organisations reiterated earlier demands:

> More resources need to be made available for independent, unbiased scientific research, e.g. for further nutritional, toxicological and

> immunological evaluation where there are differences in the composition
> of a GM crop and its non-GM reference, whether intended or unintended
> (BEUC, 2001)

Using arguments like this, therefore, consumer NGOs presented uncertainties in ways that suggested they could be clarified by better data and new
test methods, whilst also arguing that achieving this would not be easy and
would require changes of approach and additional resources. Consumer
NGOs were using the TACD at this time to advocate their proposals directly
to policy makers in the US and EU administrations.

EU–US Consultative Forum

In Chapter 3 we also discussed the EU–US Consultative Forum on
Biotechnology (the Consultative Forum) so we will restrict our comments
here to its treatment of substantial equivalence. The final report of the
Forum, published in 2000, describes substantial equivalence in a relatively
modest way and allocates it a restricted role in regulatory oversight. At the
same time the report implies that this account does not involve a change to
its long-standing meaning:

> . . . the concept of substantial equivalence is often misunderstood as
> being a safety assessment in itself or as a means for characterising hazard.
> It is neither of these.
>   The concept of substantial equivalence should only be used to struc-
> ture a safety assessment. The fact that a biotechnology food is held to be
> substantially equivalent to a conventional food should not be taken auto-
> matically to mean that it needs less testing or less regulatory oversight
> than 'non-substantially' equivalent biotechnology foods. The concept of
> substantial equivalence should be improved by the development and
> application of new techniques, which can help to identify unintended
> and potentially harmful changes.
> (EU–US Biotechnology Consultative Forum, 2000: 10; Recommendation 5)

In this way the Forum gave its qualified support to the concept, but at the
same time suggested that more scientific tests were needed to make it
robust.

In response to the Forum's final report, both administrations sent written
comments and dealt with the concept of substantial equivalence explicitly.
Both accommodated the Forum's language. From the EU side:

> The Commission Services agree that the concept of substantial equiva-
> lence is a useful starting point, but not the end point, in safety
> assessments of novel foods, and is supporting the development of Codex
> guidance in this respect. In addition the EU's research programme is

funding a number of projects on development of new techniques for substantial equivalence.

(CEC, 2001a)

At this time the Commission was funding research into new test methods (Kessler and Economidis, 2001). An example is research into ways of more sensitively detecting compositional changes in novel foods.

Likewise the US side made a positive response to the Forum's report:

> We appreciate the Forum's effort to define what substantial equivalence is and is not. This concept is applied when structuring a safety assessment. Substantial equivalence is sometimes wrongly characterized as an attempt to avoid applying approval procedures to bioengineered food products. This is not the case. In the U.S., we use this concept as a starting point in our risk assessment process.

(US Dept of State, 2000)

In practice the US response was more difficult given that there is no mandatory pre-market approval procedure for GM foods. With this fact in mind this statement appears to imply a level of scrutiny that did not exist.

Codex Alimentarius Commission

Ultimately many of the supporters and critics of substantial equivalence engaged with each other directly at the WHO/FAO Codex Alimentarius Commission. The Codex sets global food standards which are assumed to be based on science and can be used by the WTO to judge trade disputes. In the late 1990s, with the commercialisation of GM food blocked in the EU, some members of the Codex suggested that there should be Codex standards in this area. This led to the creation of a Codex Ad Hoc Intergovernmental Task Force on Foods Derived from Biotechnology (the Task Force). As discussed in Chapter 3, some in the US criticised the US government for agreeing to this, giving it as an example of US officials 'blinking' in the face of pressure. In this section we focus on the Codex's deliberations as far as they relate directly to substantial equivalence.

The meetings of the Task Force took place in a context of considerable conflict around the regulation of GMOs and GM foods specifically. Critics argued that many of the problems were associated with a failure to involve civil society groups in regulatory debates at an early stage, for example the OECD discussions of the early 1990s. In this context, and particularly because of consumer concerns in Europe, consumer organisations were able to demand a significant role in the Codex discussions (CI, 2000a). Consumers International was admitted officially as an 'observer', along with other interests such as the Biotechnology Industry Organization, but in practice they took an active part in the meetings of the Task Force. Before its first meeting, a representative of the host set the stage by trying to define the problem the Task Force should solve:

> We are required to promote biotechnology based on consumer understanding about the safety of the technology. We have to reach an international consensus on the safety of foods derived from biotechnology.
>
> (Shingo Haketa, Vice-Minister for Health and Welfare, Japan Reuters, 2000)

In this statement we see consumer concerns, and therefore consumer confidence, being identified as a central issue.

Amongst other things this first meeting established the mandate for a new expert consultation to consider a range of issues that would occupy the Task Force, including 'What is the role, and what are the limitations, of substantial equivalence in the safety and nutritional assessment? Are there alternative strategies to substantial equivalence that should be used for the safety and nutritional assessment?' (CAC, 2000). The expert group included scientists, some of whom had been discussing the risk issues with consumer NGOs. Consumers International initially proposed that 'substantial equivalence' should be deleted from the expert report, on grounds that 'it is no longer a helpful concept' (CI, 2000b). However, they soon realised that this was not possible, given that governments were committed to the concept. As an alternative CI representatives supported moves to redefine the concept in ways that weakened the original emphasis on similarity with conventional food.

The report that emerged from the expert consultation emphasised that substantial equivalence has an important role to play but at the same time redefined the concept to some extent. Along lines that were already familiar it argued that 'increased precision of genetic modification' allows easier prediction of any unintended effects. It claimed that new profiling techniques could be used to detect such effects, given that 'substantial equivalence is a concept used to identify similarities and differences . . . '. It also stated that compositional changes were 'not the sole basis for determining safety'. Along lines that were less familiar the report stated that when a comparison is made, 'If the differences exceed natural variations, a nutritional and toxicological assessment is required.' In general it sought to avoid 'the mistaken impression that the determination of substantial equivalence was the end point of a safety assessment . . . ' (FAO/WHO, 2000: 7, 20).

The Task Force accepted the emphasis the expert consultation placed on identifying differences between a GM food and a conventional counterpart. It re-affirmed the concept of substantial equivalence, 'in the sense that this concept was a starting point for the safety assessment and not an end-point of the assessment'. It stated that a step-by-step evaluation process included toxicity, allergenicity and nutritional considerations. Its document also acknowledged 'unintended effects', which may be either predictable or unexpected (CAC, 2001; also CAC, 2002). It is also worth noting that during the deliberations of the Task Force some illuminating differences of opinion arose. For example, the US government initially proposed that when it came to analysing a GM food it should be possible for the 'conventional counter-part' itself to be a GM food. This proposal was not accepted and will not be for the foreseeable future (CAC, 2001).

Despite various disagreements, the Task Force did eventually agree final guidelines (CAC, 2003). Many viewed the explicit treatment of a range of risk issues, including unintended effects, as a particularly important development (see Haslberger, 2003 on unintended effects). According to consumer NGOs, the guidelines effectively changed the meaning of substantial equivalence, by focusing on differences and their significance for safety. According to one representative, the changes were a face-saving way to keep the phrase. Moreover:

> In many passages we wanted to say that the authorities 'should' require something, but instead it says 'could'. Nevertheless this wording is a protective shield for any strong risk assessment system which may be challenged at the WTO.
>
> (Interview, consumer representative, 30 October 2002)

Thus the concept was recast in a way that creates more opportunities to turn safety assumptions into uncertainties that require more information. Consumer NGOs understood the redefinition as helpful for the protection of consumer rights, particularly in relation to food safety, on a global scale. They also believed that the Codex criteria could provide a defence for more stringent regulation of GM food in countries around the world.

Re-interpreting 'substantial equivalence' in EU practice

From the late 1990s onwards, European regulatory agencies tried to regain control of the GM food debate by responding to concerns being articulated in the public debate. In this section we discuss related changes in European regulatory practice. Initially we focus on the demotion of 'substantial equivalence' as a regulatory concept in the EU's regulatory framework. After this we focus more specifically on changes in regulatory criteria associated with risk assessment. In general regulatory criteria became more stringent and were understood to be provisional and subject to further research and revision. These changes happened particularly as critics found more opportunities to highlight gaps and weaknesses in the available knowledge.

Changes at the EU level

August 2000 was a turning point for European regulation of GM food. In this month the Italian government invoked Article 12 of the Novel Food Regulation – a safeguard clause – and suspended the sale of products derived from four varieties of GM maize. These products had already been given EU-wide approval under the Novel Food Regulation via the simplified procedure discussed above. However, according to the Italian government, the notifiers had not shown that the GM maize was substantially equivalent to conventional maize, and therefore, they argued, the products should undergo a full risk assessment.

In response the European Commission attempted to lift the ban. The Directorate General of Consumer Affairs requested advice from the relevant EU-level expert body, the Scientific Committee on Food (SCF), regarding the safety of the disputed products. The SCF advised that the Italian authorities had not provided evidence that the GM maize posed a risk to human health. The European Commission then used this advice to demand that Italy remove the ban. It also requested support from the Standing Committee on Foodstuffs (StCF), which represented EU member states. However, instead of supporting the Commission's position, the Standing Committee sided with Italy. It stated: 'it was unacceptable that GMO-derived products were placed on the EU market under the simplified procedure, without undergoing a full safety assessment' (StCF, 2000).

Not surprisingly, conflicts like this within the EU had a major impact on new EU legislation that was drawn up to replace the 1997 Novel Food Regulation. Regulation 1829/2003, which was agreed in September 2003, does not include a simplified procedure or reference to substantial equivalence. In a footnote to a draft of the new legislation the European Commission explained why:

> In order to ensure clarity, transparency and a harmonised framework for authorisation of genetically modified food, this proposal does not include a notification (simplified) procedure as laid down in Regulation EC No 258/97 on novel foods and novel food ingredients for genetically modified foods which are substantially equivalent to existing foods. The use of this regulatory short-cut for so-called 'substantially equivalent' GM foods has been very controversial in the Community in recent years . . . and there is consensus at the international level . . . that whilst substantial equivalence is a key step in the safety assessment process of genetically modified foods, it is not a safety assessment in itself.
> (CEC, 2001c; cf. CEC, 2003b: 1)

This statement links the decision taken on substantial equivalence to the need to ensure a harmonised framework for authorisation of GM foods within the EU. In practice, a concept with its origins in an OECD-facilitated international consensus, which was introduced into EU legislation in part as a step toward a harmonised regulatory regime between the EU and the US, had produced considerable disharmony within the EU. The Commission recognised that harmonisation within the EU can be more important than, and indeed is a prerequisite for, harmonisation beyond it. It also recognised that EU-wide harmonisation might be difficult to achieve in relation to such a 'dynamic concept', the meaning of which is still developing (Pettauer, 2002: 23). The 'consensus at the international level' that the Commission refers to in this passage is found in the reports of institutions like the EU–US Consultative Forum on Agricultural Biotechnology and the Codex Alimentarius Commission.

The EU's Scientific Steering Committee, which takes an overarching view of risk assessment, eventually issued guidelines for the evaluation of food, feed and cultivation uses of GM crops. The logical and empirical burden of evidence was placed upon the applicant: 'the notifier must state the reasons for not submitting the required studies' or for carrying out other studies instead. For food safety assessment it outlined tests of nutritional content, toxicology and allergenicity. In cases of any uncertainty about the equivalence of the GM food and a non-GM counterpart, they required toxicological tests, for example a 28-day test for acute effects of the purified novel protein, and a 90-day test of the whole food (SSC, 2002, 2003). Welcoming the guidelines, European consumer groups proposed further work towards 'validated techniques' and 'the development of reliable tests' for the safety of GM food (BEUC, 2003).

These more recent developments illustrate a number of points. In general European procedures began to involve more explicit and stringent scrutiny of claims regarding the similarity of a GM food and its non-GM counterpart and the implications of this for risk. As critics raised methodological uncertainties and weaknesses, EU experts have proposed clearer standards and more rigorous test methods. Consumer groups played an important role in this process. Some of the proposals that became more acceptable at this time echoed those made by NGO scientists in the mid-1990s (CI, 1996; Ho and Steinbrecher, 1997; Tappeser and von Weizsacker, 1996).

Developments in the UK and the Netherlands

The demotion of substantial equivalence as a policy concept in the EU happened in parallel with further critical discussions about its role in risk assessment, particularly in the UK and the Netherlands. Until 1999 the UK was one of the EU countries that received the most applications for commercial approval of GM foods. In the late 1990s, when the UK received applications to approve fresh food products from new GM maize crops, its advisory body requested more evidence of safety. The company's dossier already went beyond compositional equivalence – by including toxicology and allergenicity data – but the advisory committee regarded it as inadequate (ACNFP, 2001: 7–8). More rigorous data were eventually submitted to satisfy the committee's concerns.

Having published a report on GM food in 1998, the UK's Royal Society faced criticism for simply endorsing 'substantial equivalence', so later it established a working group to re-examine GM food safety issues. The working group, which acknowledged weaknesses of available test methods, included a consumer representative. Their report emphasised the need to define the 'normal' composition of conventional plants, as a basis for any comparison with GM plants, as well as the need to develop more sensitive tests.

> It will be important to define the choice of growing conditions of the comparative plants, the scope of the comparisons, and the acceptable margins of measured differences in composition.
>
> (Royal Society, 2002)

The involvement of the consumer representative perhaps reflected a more cautious attitude by the Royal Society, particularly following its intervention in the Pusztai controversy.

From the late 1990s onwards, the Netherlands became a centre of critical work on risk assessment of GM foods. Specific scientists took the lead in arguing for and proposing more sensitive techniques (Kuiper et al., 1999). In their view, 'new profiling methods are of interest and should be further developed and validated', for example for detecting secondary effects due to the genetic modification of plants that have been extensively modified (Kuiper et al., 2001: 523). Other critics emphasised the limitations of existing methods for gathering useful information that might form the basis of a comparison, for example from animal tests on whole foods, and from compositional tests (Schenkelaars, 2002: 62).

In 1999, despite this critical activity, and indeed perhaps because of it, companies started submitting requests for GM food authorisation to the Netherlands. In two cases, Monsanto's maize GA21 and Syngenta's *Bt* 11 sweet maize, the authorities asked the companies to supply additional information, for example about the content of secondary metabolites in the GM crop compared to that of the non-GM control (SBC, 2001). Industry supplied this information, as part of its overall effort to harmonise data requests across the EU (EuropaBio, 2001; Amijee, 2002: 50). In 2001–2 the Netherlands received five more requests to authorise the food uses of GM crops. In the authorisation process, then, biotech companies opted for a relatively stringent national authority.

Policy impasse in the US: the regulation of GM food

In 2000, as outlined above, the US government bypassed the recommendation from the EU–US Consultative Forum on Biotechnology that there should be mandatory pre-market risk assessment of GM food. To do this it implied a greater level of scrutiny of GM foods in the US than was actually the case (see above and US Dept of State, 2000). US officials defended the existing approach – voluntary submission of safety claims by industry with no independent FDA assessment – in a variety of ways. They argued, for example, that the FDA enjoys high levels of public trust in their ability to put safe food on the market, unlike their European counterparts. In this section we will explore key aspects of US regulation of GM foods from the late 1990s onwards, focusing particularly on the FDA proposal for mandatory pre-market notification, the Pew stakeholder forum and responses to the GM food safety guidelines agreed by the Codex Alimentarius Commission.

Pre-market notification proposal

In the late 1990s the USA's voluntary review procedure for GM foods was put on the defensive by at least two legal challenges. In 1998 the Centre for Food Safety filed a lawsuit against the FDA for its failure to require safety testing of GM food. The complaint was dismissed on the grounds that the FDA had no rule that could be legally challenged. In a 1999 lawsuit, complainants obtained FDA documents indicating that some FDA staff were concerned about inadequate information for safety assessments of GM food products. On that basis they argued that 'There is more than enough evidence to convince a reasonable man or woman that current FDA policy is unscientific, unwise, irresponsible, and illegal' (cited in Nestle, 2003: 209). This case was also unsuccessful, but US consumer groups and others became more vocal in their demands for a mandatory risk assessment procedure (e.g. CCC, 1999).

At around this time there was also criticism of the claim that the US public were not concerned about GM food and that the FDA enjoyed a high level of public trust in the area. According to one US focus-group study, for example, people were worried about unknown long-term health consequences that might be linked to GM technology (Levy and Derby, 2000). This suggested that there were similarities between consumers in the US and the EU, a line of reasoning that was explored in the context of the Transatlantic Consumer Dialogue. The evidence of concern also raised the possibility that the US public's trust in the FDA in relation to the regulation of GM foods might be based on false assumptions about an FDA 'review' of data and 'approval' of products; there is still a low level of awareness that there is no mandatory risk assessment of GM foods in the US.

In this context the Clinton administration began to consider regulatory changes. In the administration's final month, the FDA published a proposal for mandatory pre-market notification (PMN) of all GM-derived foods. PMN meant that developers would have to submit a risk assessment of a GM food 120 days before it was marketed (US FDA, 2001). The proposal gained support from the food industry and US Biotechnology Industry Organization (Pollack, 2001). This is explained by the desire of industry to have a stronger safety imprimatur from the FDA; likewise they had advocated EPA regulatory authority over *Bt* insecticidal genes in GM crops in the mid-1990s.

As its official rationale for PMN, the FDA emphasised scientific uncertainties associated with transferring foreign genes into conventional crops. If compositional changes resulted in substances no longer 'generally recognised as safe' (GRAS), they argued, then those substances might warrant regulation as food additives. Pre-market notification was needed in practice so that the FDA could make that judgement on each GM product.

In addition, while its 1992 policy had acknowledged possible unintended effects from novel foods in general, now the FDA made specific arguments about GM techniques and their effects. For example, the phenotypes of bioengineered crops might be different to those of their parental strains, and unanticipated effects might be more prevalent as a result. And more specifically:

> . . . because bioengineering enables developers to introduce genetic material from a wider range of sources than has traditionally been possible, there is a greater likelihood that a developer using bioengineering to modify a food plant may introduce genetic material whose expression results in a substance that is significantly different from substances historically consumed in food . . . it is also possible with bioengineering that the newly introduced genetic material may be inserted into the chromosome of a food plant in a location that causes the food derived from the plant to have higher levels of toxins than normal, or lower levels of a significant nutrient. In the former case the food may not be safe to eat, or may require special preparation to reduce or eliminate the toxic substance. In the latter case, the food may require special labeling, so that consumers would know that they were not receiving the level of nutrients they would ordinarily expect from consuming comparable food.
>
> (USFDA, 2001: 4728)

Drawing on such arguments, the FDA now specified the information that should be submitted as part of a pre-market notification (USFDA, 2001: 4733).

The mandatory pre-market notification proposal, however, did not become a statutory rule. At this time there were divisions within the FDA regarding the PMN proposal. In addition, according to its chief legal officer, the FDA had no statutory basis to require a PMN procedure under the 1986 Coordinated Framework; such a requirement would contradict the original policy, which was built on the assumption that GM products present 'no unique safety concerns'. After the new Bush administration took office in January 2001, the FDA effectively abandoned its PMN proposal. The proposal does show, however, that the FDA had concerns about its regulatory oversight of GM foods at this time, at least as a problem of public credibility.

The Pew stakeholder forum

During the Bush administration there was an attempt to overcome the US domestic impasse through a multi-stakeholder dialogue. In May 2003 the

Pew Initiative – an independent research and facilitation organisation – launched a biotechnology stakeholder forum, 'conducted as a non-public opportunity to develop a common understanding' of the complex issues, in a manner 'that promotes joint problem-solving and collaboration'. The stakeholder forum took up 'questions regarding the credibility and effectiveness of the systems of oversight, both public and private, for the governance of agricultural biotechnology products' (Pew, 2003b: 6, 8). It was a multistakeholder initiative including members from the biotechnology industry and civil society. All these groups accepted the ground rules: 'nothing was agreed until everything was agreed'.

Ultimately the Pew stakeholder forum failed to create a concrete consensus or a tangible outcome, but the process gives us important insights. After some time participants agreed on the various components of a regulatory system but they could not reach a consensus on the 'full range of issues in sufficient detail', particularly at the level needed to propose a package of regulatory reforms (Pew, 2003c). Not surprisingly, GM food was one of the main obstacles. Some NGOs demanded mandatory pre-market safety approval of GM foods by the FDA, as an essential element of any overall consensus. For complex reasons, however, the group as a whole could not agree on this. The following quotes from Pew staff involved explain why:

INTERVIEWEE A: There was an awful lot of agreement on what the system should look like . . . But one of the big issues was, if the only way to get a mandatory pre-market approval process at the FDA is through a legislative fix, then the risks of going to Congress are just too high. From the industry perspective . . . the things that made it difficult to come to an agreement were the risks of going to Congress, the risks of how that action would be viewed in the international community and domestically, as an admission that products aren't safe.
INTERVIEWEE B: I think there's a lot of concern about how products on the market, currently on the market, would be viewed because they went through an old system.
INTERVIEWEE A: We spent a lot of time trying to work out some language on what we would say about products that are on the market now.
INTERVIEWEE B: People were really trying to make the distinction. Saying we need these changes for the future because the future products are going to be different. That's the kind of rationale they were adopting.
(Interview, 15 October 2003)

These contributions draw attention to domestic and international reasons why the Pew's stakeholder forum found it impossible to reach a consensus on FDA mandatory assessment of GM foods. Domestic concerns included the implications of such a move for products already on the market as a result of an 'old' system, and concerns that mandatory assessment would only be possible through new federal legislation – which could be unpredictable and would undermine the assumptions on which US biotechnology policy is based. Drawing on the stakeholder forum discussions, the representative of a consumer group offered the following perspective on industry reluctance in this area:

> [One company] saw no political need to concede anything – i.e. to accept regulation of GM food. Some biotech companies were sitting on the fence . . . People's reputations have been tied to a convoluted regulatory structure. So a proposal for change challenges their past work under the Coordinated Framework. They cannot separate feelings about food from science; but sometimes it is politically better to do regulation 'irrationally', in order to sell food. In many other sectors, the FDA finds a way to interpret the law to accommodate public concerns.
>
> (Interview, Consumer Federation of America, 22 October 2003)

The impasse also had an international aspect, particularly in the context of the trade conflict with the EU. A representative from Pew described this dilemma, based on his observations of the stakeholder forum, as follows:

> There was some agreement about what the outcome should look like but there was some disagreement about how you get there. And there was some concern about managing that message for the international marketplace. This is something we've heard not only from stakeholders but from members of the administration. How do you manage to say, 'Yes, we need to change, but everything up till now has been fine'? . . . That's a broader issue because many of the things that people talked about in the stakeholder group were an acknowledgement of the importance of the regulatory system, not only on a science basis to protect the food safety and environment, but also . . . to help ensure consumer safety and also provide a clear pathway to market for the industry.
>
> (Interview, 15 October 2003)

When it reached this impasse, the stakeholder forum had run its course and the Pew Initiative had no plans for further meetings. With the US government's decision in May 2003 to initiate a WTO case against the EU, it became even more difficult to find a route beyond the impasse. Some industry representatives apparently feared that the US case could be undermined by any suggestion that its own regulatory system was inadequate (Reuters, 2003).

The Codex Alimentarius and beyond

Given the impasse in the US, the negotiations of the Codex Alimentarius Commission (discussed above) were a particularly important and perhaps troubling development. We have already shown how some parts of the US government were criticised for 'blinking' when they agreed to these negotiations taking place. Not surprisingly, when the Codex actually reached a final agreement, the US government interpreted the outcome somewhat differently. They argued that there was no need to change US practice. This response echoed the one that had followed the publication of the report of the EU–US Consultative Forum on Biotechnology. According to one FDA officer:

> The final documents represent a consensus reached among member states, industry and consumer groups. There is no controversy about risk assessment principles, which are the same across countries . . .
> Codex documents reflect FDA practice on GM food. No new tests would be needed as a result of those documents. Having the documents on paper helps to clarify the standard, though this can be interpreted in different ways. The guidelines will be more useful to developing countries, which may not have the infrastructure to do adequate testing. Knowing that a product has been evaluated according to an international standard may give confidence to the authorities there.
>
> (Interview, 4 August 2003)

Thus the FDA interpreted the new standards as requiring no significant change for FDA practice.

In 2003 US NGOs continued to criticise the non-regulation of GM foods in the US, especially by contrasting this with EU practice. Some of this criticism was made at the level of food safety tests. In a detailed report, the Center for Science in the Public Interest emphasised weaknesses of the existing system, especially by linking the problems of scientific rigour and public credibility. The CSPI report proposed some solutions to the problems. For example, 'feeding studies should be considered because they might detect problems and they would add public confidence to safety determinations of a new technology with less-than-perfect testing protocols'. Likewise, if the FDA were to conduct and publish a detailed analysis of test data, such an explanation 'should increase the public's confidence in FDA's decisions' (CSPI, 2003). In this way the wider controversy and public concerns were translated into specific demands for better evidence of safety. In an interview, this report's author said he had seen no clear improvement in the safety data submitted for GM food products in recent years. In proposing improvements, he described CSPI as an 'honest broker' regarding the risks and benefits of GM foods (interview, 20 February 2003).

In sum we can say that the transatlantic conflict had contradictory outcomes for US regulation of GM food and perhaps for agricultural biotechnology in general. Using the conflict, US NGOs highlighted the non-regulation of GM food in the US and the poor quality of data being submitted to the FDA, especially in contrast to the EU system. Echoing arguments made by European TACD representatives, they emphasised the need for industry to gain consumer confidence through a more rigorous approach to safety testing and risk assessment. Some FDA staff also advocated more formal procedures for GM food. Policy brokers, such as the Pew Initiative, persuaded US industry to discuss a wide range of regulatory proposals with civil society organisations. However, no overall consensus could be reached. To a large extent this was because industry and people in government believed that regulatory changes could undermine the US case in the WTO dispute and confidence in products already on the market.

Conclusion

The risk assessment of GM foods has been a contentious issue. At the broadest level there are ongoing arguments about the need for mandatory approval of all GM foods. More specifically there are disagreements regarding the value of specific tests that might inform risk assessment. Disputes at both levels have stimulated changes in the concept of substantial equivalence. By drawing on the developments described in this chapter, the conclusion answers the four narrative questions from the Introduction to this book.

How did policy actors try to advance particular policy agendas?

In the debate over GM food safety, stakeholder coalitions framed the scientific uncertainties in three different ways. First, particularly in the early 1990s, the dominant frame (OECD, FDA and commercial interests) argued that GM techniques were more precise, and that compared with conventional products, any risks associated with GM foods were more predictable. This pro-biotech frame also suggested that any risks could be readily identified, especially by using compositional tests, which could be standardised across countries.

In the mid-1990s, however, this view was challenged by two alternative framings. Anti-agbiotech groups argued that GM techniques generate unique and unpredictable risks, which might go undetected in GM foods. Environmental groups such as Greenpeace, for example, argued that substantial equivalence would not have led regulators to detect the scrapie prion that was responsible for 'mad cow' disease transferring to humans. In contrast, consumer groups framed uncertainties in a way that suggested they could be clarified through more rigorous methods and new tests. They did not argue that products already on the market were unsafe, but they did argue that more rigorous methods were needed for the future.

These two alternative frames – from anti-agbiotech and consumer groups – emphasised irreducible and reducible risks, respectively. The latter frame then converged with the efforts of European food scientists who were proposing more stringent, sensitive or new test methods. The problem of European 'public/consumer confidence' provided a general basis for cooperative efforts to develop more stringent standards for GM food. It also allowed discussions to bypass expert disagreements about exactly what data requirements were scientifically justified.

This new problem-definition also informed international efforts to broaden the concept of substantial equivalence, for example in the EU–US Consultative Forum and at the Codex Alimentarius Commission. The three risk-framings therefore provided a basis for contending coalitions to shape risk-assessment criteria and on which to form a new coalition that might go beyond the original conflict. Through related processes European regulatory changes accommodated concerns about reducible uncertainties, while marginalising claims about irreducible uncertainties.

From the late 1990s onwards, US NGOs also warned their government that public confidence could be undermined by its non-regulation of GM food. The Pew's biotechnology stakeholder forum was a governance initiative designed to address all agbiotech regulatory issues. Participants were able to agree on a new common problem – public trust in regulation and products – and this could have formed the basis of an agreement and recommendations. But any new consensus faced numerous obstacles, particularly in relation to GM food. Any US requirement for pre-market notification would undermine existing assumptions about how to regulate biotechnology and might even raise doubts about the safety of GM foods already approved under a previous system. In these ways, a hegemonic frame from a previous period hampered a governance solution, even when a new coalition was prepared to form around a new collective problem.

How were expertise and knowledge used to influence policy making?

Shortly before GM foods were expected on the market, food regulators posed the question: what evidence is required to establish substantial equivalence between a conventional food and a GM food, and therefore GM food safety? In the early 1990s official experts answered this question by emphasising tests of physical-chemical composition, even though rigorous data on conventional products (for comparison) was not available. Other tests, such as animal feeding studies with whole foods, were largely dismissed as unnecessary or unreliable.

In the late 1990s, public controversy over GM food re-opened the question of the appropriate basis for comparison with conventional foods. As the conflict intensified, critics emphasised the limitations of existing tests and proposed new standards or changes to existing ones. For example, the incomplete data on non-GM counterparts became a more significant issue, and one which warranted more systematic collection of data. Such arguments, which largely had their origins in Europe, were also taken up in the US (see Table 5.1).

Table 5.1 Safety Tests for Novel Foods: Methodological Uncertainties and Changes

Problems and Tests	Limitations Identified	Proposed Standards or Changes
Physical–chemical composition:		
Establishing a 'normal' baseline before comparing conventional and novel foods.	The data available on conventional foods is incomplete (CI, 1996; Schenkelaars, 2002). The 'normal' baseline varies with cultivation conditions (Haslberger, 2002; Schenkelaars, 2002).	Collect more systematic data on conventional foods to establish a reliable baseline. Use standard and/or varied cultivation conditions to test a range of contexts (SSC, 2002).
Comparing a conventional food and a novel food to establish equivalence and safety.	Specifying acceptable difference between conventional and novel food (Kuiper et al., 1999).	Get data on secondary metabolites. Using new techniques like proteomics (Noteborn et al., 2000).
Toxicity and/or nutritional quality:		
Testing a novel protein for acute toxicity using feeding studies and laboratory animals.	It can be difficult to obtain a large amount of the novel protein from the plant. It is possible to test a novel protein only if it is known. This will not help to identify any pleiotropic effects.	Use a protein produced by microbes, but the equivalence of any microbial substitute must be demonstrated. Use 28-day repeated-dose test (SSC, 2002). (This contrasts with industry proposal that a 14-day test is as an adequate method.)
Testing a whole food for toxicity and/or nutritional quality using laboratory animals.	It can be difficult to feed laboratory animals large quantities of a whole food. It can be difficult to achieve nutritional equivalence in novel and control foods (US FDA, 1992).	Use a 90-day test avoiding any nutritional imbalance (FAO/WHO, 2000; SSC, 2002). Use new techniques such as metabolomics (Noteborn et al., 2000).
Allergenicity:		
Searching for sequence homology or structural similarity with known allergen.	Small differences can be significant for allergenicity (Donabauer and Valenta, 2002).	Methods used to search for allergens must be scientifically justified (SSC, 2002).
Conducting digestibility-degradation tests to establish protein stability in the gut.	Digestibility-degradation tests can falsely indicate that a protein is not an allergen (CI, 1996). Results depend on experimental design, e.g. duration and pepsin exposure (CSPI, 2003).	Digestibility-degradation tests must be well validated (SSC, 2002).

Like the *Bt* maize case discussed in Chapter 4, GM food illustrates dynamic relations between science and policy. Substantial equivalence initially served to depoliticise the risk assessment of GM food through science, by focusing on biophysical risk and mainly tests of physical-chemical composition. An expansive boundary was drawn around science, almost as if substantial equivalence was the 'scientific principle' that FAO/WHO experts had sought in 1991.

The initial effort to depoliticise GM food, however, was not entirely successful, and criticism of substantial equivalence stimulated a scientification process instead. To justify their risk-assessment procedures, European governments in particular became dependent upon more scientific information, which remained vulnerable to different expert interpretations and thus could reveal further uncertainties. Key actors engaged in a competition for the latest test results, new test methods and authoritative claims. This scientification process went hand-in-hand with the politicisation of science. Through these dynamics, the public-scientific controversy around GM food broke the science-policy link that was built during the early 1990s, especially in the OECD.

How were regulatory standard-setting processes and trade conflict linked?

Trade liberalisation and trade conflict have played important roles in the regulation of GM food. Substantial equivalence was devised in the early 1990s to link science and a particular policy agenda. In essence it provided a technocratic basis for standardising risk assessment within and across countries, while avoiding 'unnecessary' duplication of safety tests. Substantial equivalence thereby served the OECD's general remit of facilitating regulatory harmonisation and trade liberalisation.

By the mid-1990s both the EU and the US had included 'substantial equivalence' in their regulatory frameworks, thus creating the foundations for a harmonised regulatory system across the Atlantic. The Transatlantic Economic Partnership intended to organise a pilot project on simultaneous assessment of a GM product, involving EU and US regulators, in the late 1990s (Chapter 2). The scene was therefore set for the widespread adoption of GM food, as Buttel (2000) has suggested.

However, substantial equivalence soon became a useful target for critics of GM food, agricultural biotechnology and economic globalisation more broadly. In the late 1990s European NGOs accused the US of force-feeding GM foods to Europeans. They linked the agbiotech commercialisation and trade liberalisation agendas as dual threats to the environment and consumers. GM food was particularly vulnerable to this criticism, in part because it was easy to ridicule 'substantial equivalence' as a careless and deceptive concept.

These arguments gave momentum to the European public backlash and the trade conflict. After the trade conflict had emerged, many groups engaged with each other directly at the Codex Alimentarius Commission discussions which lead to global standards for the risk assessment of GM foods. Participation there was notably much broader than it had been at the OECD discussions in the early 1990s. Underlying the Codex meeting was a new collective problem – 'consumer/public confidence in GM food' – to supplement the earlier one of 'barriers to trade in GM food'. This new problem implied the need for more stringent regulatory standards. Thus standards, and the conflicts around them, can shape the terms for trade liberalisation in practice. This also illustrates how global governance is a response to the legitimacy problems provoked by a particular form of economic globalisation.

How were EU–US interactions and intra-jurisdictional conflicts linked?

The trade liberalisation agenda shaped the concept of substantial equivalence but trade conflict created opportunities to challenge it on both sides of the Atlantic, particularly because transatlantic trade conflicts contributed to intra-jurisdictional conflicts. For example, the transatlantic conflict over GM products created a context in which EU and US consumer groups in particular were able to cooperate more effectively in order to criticise regulatory assumptions. These interactions took place particularly through the Transatlantic Consumer Dialogue. As summarised above, EU consumer groups used this context to press for EU-wide regulatory changes along more stringent lines.

In this transatlantic context, US consumer groups could also more readily question the assumption that the US public is not concerned about GM food and that the FDA enjoys high levels of public trust. They warned that any public trust in the FDA might be based on false assumptions – for example, that the FDA actually reviews and approves GM foods. In this way, some US consumer groups have used transatlantic interactions to strengthen their interventions at the domestic level. They asked why Europeans deserve better regulatory protection than US consumers from GM foods.

However, the transatlantic trade conflict was appropriated in contradictory ways in the US. When Codex adopted guidelines including more rigorous tests for GM foods, with wordings that had been accepted by US representatives, this complemented FDA efforts towards pre-market notification of GM foods. The FDA had justified such efforts because of special uncertainties associated with GM techniques. However, it has been difficult for pro-agbiotech stakeholders in the US to accept moves towards regulation of GM food because they fear that such changes might imply flaws in the US regulatory procedure. In all of these ways, therefore, we see how transatlantic interactions have helped to shape government policy on GM foods in the EU and the US.

6 The WTO agbiotech dispute as a global contest

Introduction

In the early to mid-1990s, the EU and the US cooperated to achieve regulatory convergence for GM products. In the late 1990s, however, their regulatory approaches diverged; in previous chapters we have explored some reasons why. With this divergence, EU and US practices began to offer different regulatory models to countries around the world. The most recent EU procedures take a more cautious approach to the technology, compared with previous EU practice and the US approach. Many other jurisdictions are likely to consider drawing on one of these models. This is particularly the case because the EU and the US play important roles in the global marketplace for agricultural products, in addition to their expert roles in international fora where standards are discussed.

Thus EU–US interactions matter for the global governance of agricultural biotechnology, including the form and legitimacy of regulatory regimes, as well as global standard setting. We explore the global level further in this chapter. The first section below examines the origins and roles of the international agreements that provide a context for the EU–US dispute over biotechnology products at the World Trade Organization. The second section looks at US and EU strategies in other arenas in the run-up to that dispute, and how their relationship deteriorated with the conflict over GM food aid to southern Africa. The rest of this chapter discusses the WTO dispute in detail, focusing on the role of experts.

Learning from experience: anticipating future conflict

Learning from experience and anticipating future developments have been important features of the EU–US conflict over agricultural biotechnology. Previous WTO disputes and judgements have informed EU and US strategies in relation to their current conflict of biotechnology products. Similarly, from the late 1990s onwards, the EU and the US acted in other international fora in ways that they hoped would strengthen their position in any future WTO dispute. Both sides tried to anticipate the case that they might have to make at the WTO and acted accordingly. In this section we discuss past WTO judgements that have played a central role in the learning process for both sides. We then move on to discuss the negotiation of a Biosafety Protocol to the United Nations Convention on Biological Diversity.

SPS agreement and dispute over hormone-treated beef

It is often claimed that trade liberalisation endangers the environment and human health because trade law makes it difficult to exclude risky products from markets. The WTO Agreement on the Application of Sanitary and Phytosanitary Measures (SPS Agreement) is held up as an example of this problem because it imposes a heavy burden on countries to demonstrate the risks of imported agri-food products. The EU and the US understood that if their conflict over GM crops and foods led to a formal dispute at the WTO, then the interpretation of this agreement would play a central role in the legal process. To set the scene here, we will briefly outline elements of the SPS Agreement and how it has been interpreted in the past.

The SPS Agreement defines the legitimate grounds for restricting trade in agricultural products. For products that pose a threat to human or animal health, the SPS Agreement emphasises the need for scientific evidence in order to avoid politically motivated trade restrictions. For example, Article 2.2 refers to trade restrictions 'based on scientific principles and . . . not maintained without sufficient scientific evidence . . . '. The SPS Agreement therefore treats science as an objective and apolitical basis on which to make decisions about the risks associated with trade in agricultural products. Implicitly it rests upon the so-called 'sound science' model of knowledge: 'It is crucial to an understanding of this Agreement to appreciate the emphasis which it places upon science and scientific reason. Measures . . . in order to be compatible with the Agreement, must be susceptible to justification in the language of science' (Scott, 2000: 148–9). However, the precise meaning of key terms like 'sufficient scientific evidence' is unclear, so the SPS Agreement potentially addresses uncertainty and ignorance about risk. To some extent, these issues can be accommodated in Article 5.7, which uses somewhat precautionary language:

> In cases where relevant scientific evidence is insufficient, a Member may provisionally adopt sanitary or phytosanitary measures on the basis of available pertinent information, including that from the relevant international organizations as well as from sanitary or phytosanitary measures applied by other Members. In such circumstances, Members shall seek to obtain the additional information necessary for a more objective assessment of risk and review the sanitary or phytosanitary measure accordingly within a reasonable period of time.

This Article acknowledges uncertainty in a way that implies it will be a short-lived problem, readily clarified by further research. This raises some difficult questions: How long can a 'provisional measure' be in place? What is a 'reasonable period of time'?

The SPS agreement has been tested and interpreted several times in WTO cases, especially in the transatlantic dispute over hormone-treated beef. The dispute began in 1981, when the EC imposed a ban on hormone-treated beef with its origins mainly in the US. The EC justified the ban on the grounds that the hormones involved posed a threat to human health; the regime was extended further in 1988 and 1996. The US argued that the action was illegal and imposed retaliatory trade sanctions. The dispute ran for a long time, partly because the parties could not agree on how the scientific issues involved should be dealt with under the GATT system that existed before the Uruguay Round of trade negotiations was completed. During the Uruguay Round, however, the US government pursued the negotiation of the SPS Agreement to clarify how the WTO should deal with this kind of science-based trade dispute. The final wording provided a strong basis on which to challenge the EC's ban.

The US brought the conflict over hormone-treated beef to the WTO and the Dispute Panel ruled against the EC. The EC appealed and the Appellate Body ruling is seen as the definitive judgement. According to this ruling, the ban was incompatible with the SPS Agreement, even though it did not discriminate against US beef or represent a disguised barrier to trade. In coming to its conclusion the Appellate Body focused on Article 2.2 of the SPS Agreement, which allows countries to implement SPS measures, but only if 'not maintained without sufficient scientific evidence' (see above). In its view the EU ban was based on theoretical or hypothetical risks and not informed by a focused risk assessment. More specifically, the Appellate Body pointed out that EU experts had cited general evidence of risk from direct hormone exposure, but no risk assessment had extrapolated to realistic exposure levels from eating beef:

> ... articles and opinions of individual scientists submitted by the European Communities constitute general studies which do indeed show the existence of a general risk of cancer; but they do not focus on and do not address the particular kind of risk here at stake – the carcinogenic or genotoxic potential of the residues of those hormones found in meat derived from cattle to which the hormones had been administered for growth promotion purposes.
>
> (WTO AB, 1998: para. 200)

This criticism may appear to be a judgement on science, but the Appellate Body was actually making a procedural argument; the absence of a focused risk assessment. By emphasising a procedural weakness, the WTO did not have to present itself as the authority that should judge the state of scientific knowledge.

At the same time, however, the Appellate Body did identify some scope for trade restrictions based on scientific uncertainty in a risk assessment:

> In some cases, the very existence of divergent views presented by qualified scientists who have investigated the particular issue at hand may indicate a state of scientific uncertainty. Sometimes the divergence may indicate a roughly equal balance of scientific opinion, which may itself be a form of scientific uncertainty. In most cases, responsible and representative governments tend to base their legislative and administrative measures on 'mainstream' scientific opinion. In other cases, equally responsible and representative governments may act in good faith on the basis of what, at a given time, may be a divergent opinion coming from qualified and respected sources.
>
> (WTO AB, 1998: para. 194)

This part of the ruling suggests that a cautious government can impose trade-restrictive measures based on the divergent opinions of relevant experts. The judgment therefore implied that a defendant might highlight such expert disagreements. Using that scope, the EC funded more research to obtain more direct evidence of risk from consuming hormone-treated beef, and then presented a minority expert view as a plausible basis for the EU ban. In later stages of the case, therefore, the Disputes Panel had to make its own judgements on expert disagreements about scientific evidence.

This necessarily brief exploration of WTO law and judgements has highlighted important issues with implications for the EU–US dispute over biotechnology products (see final section).

The Cartagena Protocol on Biosafety

As concerns about trade liberalisation and the WTO grew during the 1990s, various groups began to emphasise the importance of international agreements outside the WTO system. Some went further, for example, and raised the possibility of a World Environment Organization, which would oversee all international environmental agreements. In the late 1990s, in this context, various governments and civil society groups met to negotiate a Biosafety Protocol to the United Nations Convention on Biological Diversity (UNCBD). Some viewed such a Protocol as a counter-balance to trade law in the event of a formal dispute over agricultural biotechnology at the WTO, although the precise relationship between international trade and environmental law was unclear. The Cartagena Protocol on Biosafety was finalised in January 2000. One academic analysis anticipated that because the Protocol is 'Neither a pure environmental nor a pure trade law', it will likely serve to highlight national differences in regulatory approaches (Falkner, 2000: 312). Indeed, the negotiation process did involve conflicts over such approaches.

The Cartagena Protocol establishes a framework for regulating trade in living modified organisms (LMOs) (see particularly Bail et al., 2002). Its most important feature is the 'advance informed agreement' (AIA) procedure. AIA requires exporters of LMOs that will be released into the environment to provide a description of them to the importing country in advance of the first shipment. The importer must acknowledge receipt of this information within 90 days and then authorise the shipment within 270 days or state the reasons for rejecting it. The purpose of AIA is to allow a risk assessment to be reviewed or carried out to the satisfaction of the importing country. During the negotiations, all parties agreed that risk assessment should be central to the Protocol and this is covered in Article 15 and Annex III.

Risk assessment was negotiated with relative ease, in sharp contrast to the controversy around where and how to include the 'Precautionary Principle' in the Protocol. Its final version contains two explicit references to precaution as Rio Principle 15 – in the Preamble and in Article 1 (Objective). Initially the EU and others argued that such framing references alone were insufficient, and that precaution should be explicit in Articles dealing with decision making. In response, the Miami Group (including the US) argued that such inclusion was unnecessary. Nevertheless EU Environment Ministers successfully pressed the case to include precautionary wording in Article 10. Although not mentioning the Precautionary Principle, the compromise wording allows countries to act on it:

> Lack of scientific certainty due to insufficient relevant scientific information and knowledge regarding the extent of the potential adverse effects of a living modified organism on the conservation and sustainable use of biological diversity in the Party of import, taking also into account risks to human health, shall not prevent that Party from taking a decision, as appropriate, with regard to the import of the living modified organism in question . . . in order to avoid or minimize such potential adverse effects.
>
> (Article 10: para. 6)

An almost identical paragraph is included in Article 11 on the procedure for LMOs intended for food, feed or processing (Bail et al., 2002: 336).

Developments elsewhere (see below) help to explain the way the text deals with the precautionary principle. Towards the end of the negotiations, after the penultimate meeting in Cartagena, supporters of the precautionary principle gained additional support from events at the 1999 WTO meeting in Seattle. A participant commented as follows:

> The readiness in Cartagena of all the negotiating groups to give up their positions on the Precautionary Principle for the sake of getting a final agreement could have weakened considerably the chance of getting the

principle firmly anchored in the protocol at the next negotiating session. Surprisingly, this did not happen in Montreal. On the contrary, the inclusion of specific language on the Precautionary Principle became a more important issue, in part because of the continuous insistence by the Miami Group on the 'savings clause' [see below] and because of the attempt to start a parallel process in the WTO on a market access regime for biotechnology products . . . Governments therefore became increasingly aware of the fact that precautionary measures in the area of LMOs could be subject to challenge through the WTO dispute settlement mechanism.

(Graff, 2002: 414)

This account draws attention to the change in political context between the 1999 collapse of the Biosafety Protocol negotiations in Cartagena and the successful agreement of the Protocol in Montreal a year later. In 1999 the developing countries around the G77 joined the USA, Canada and Australia in opposing inclusion of the precautionary principle. It was viewed as a potential cover for trade-protectionist measures. But political alignments had changed by the time of the 2000 Montreal meeting, where the G77 largely supported the precautionary principle, as proposed by the EU.

As mentioned above, the 'savings clause' tries to clarify the relationship between trade rules and the Biosafety Protocol, though arguably the final wording remains ambiguous. The EU preferred not to address this problem at all because principles of international law tend to emphasise more recent and more specific agreements rather than older and more general ones. However, the US argued in favour of greater clarity, as a way to maintain the authority of WTO agreements; likewise many other leading countries made a 'savings clause' a condition of any agreement. The result is an uncomfortable compromise at the end of the Biosafety Protocol's Preamble, which states:

> Recognizing that trade and environment agreements should be mutually supportive with a view to achieving sustainable development,
>
> Emphasizing that this Protocol shall not be interpreted as implying a change in the rights and obligations of a Party under any existing international agreements,
>
> Understanding that the above recital is not intended to subordinate this Protocol to other international agreements . . .

This compromise wording is explained largely by the desire of the US and others to make sure that WTO rules are respected, while the EU and developing countries were keen to establish the Protocol as not subordinate to WTO rules (Afonso, 2002). At this time, some countries were anticipating a future WTO dispute in which the Biosafety Protocol would be invoked.

Momentum towards a WTO dispute over biotechnology products

As the conflict over agricultural biotechnology developed from the late 1990s onwards, the EU and the US interacted in high-profile and sometimes acrimonious ways. This political competition attracted mass-media attention and comment around the world. We discuss two examples in this section. The first is the 1999 proposal that the WTO should have a working party on agricultural biotechnology. The second is the public fall-out in relation to GM food aid to southern Africa in 2002/2003. These examples are somewhat different from those outlined in the previous section. They illustrate problems associated with a high-profile conflict rather than formal negotiations. This section concludes with a discussion of the growing domestic pressure in the US for a formal complaint to the WTO.

A working party on biotechnology at the WTO?

In 1999 the WTO made an ambitious attempt to launch a new round of trade negotiations at its Seattle meeting. Ultimately this was unsuccessful and the meeting is remembered for other reasons. At this meeting the governments failed to reach agreement on a negotiating agenda. The US was accused of trying to finalise an agenda with a small group of countries without consulting the majority. The bad-tempered interactions between governments took place against a backdrop of public demonstrations in the streets of Seattle, which made it more difficult for delegates to attend meetings. The protestors were a mixture of labour, environment, consumer, religious, anarchist and development groups. Agricultural biotechnology was one of the issues being raised by protestors outside the conference, at the same time as some countries were trying to get it on the agenda in the meeting.

In the months and weeks running up to the Seattle meeting, some governments proposed that the WTO should establish a working party on agricultural biotechnology. The reasons behind the proposal were complex, contradictory and not entirely explicit in public documents. Those in favour included major agricultural exporters such as the US, Canada and Argentina. Japan also supported the initiative. The US proposed new disciplines for trade in GM products (Falkner, 2000: 305); apparently USTR (Office of the US Trade Representative) wanted to criticise the EU for its failure to comply with its trade-rule obligations in this sector. At the same time, the US had concerns that the EU would suggest re-opening discussions on the SPS Agreement – for example, in order to renegotiate its terms and/or to delay EU regulatory decisions on biotechnology products. On the other hand, some countries saw a Biotechnology Working Party as a way of avoiding such delays. Other countries were less focused on EU–US interactions and thought that such a group could discuss a range of issues, such as the relationship between multilateral environmental rules and trade rules, and problems facing developing countries (BRIDGES Weekly, 1999a, 1999b).

The Commission implicitly supported the proposal for its own reasons. It anticipated that the US government might reject the Biosafety Protocol, just as it had rejected the 1992 Biodiversity Convention. If this happened, a Biotechnology Working Party at the WTO would provide an alternative venue to discuss contentious issues. The US feared that the EU was seeking an opportunity to renegotiate the entire SPS Agreement, given their disagreements about whether it covered GM products in general. The Commission generally regarded such products as marginal to the SPS Agreement, given that its Annex specifies agents such as toxins, additives, etc. By contrast, the US argued that the SPS Agreement encompasses broad risk categories, not just specific product categories (von Schomberg, 2000: 125). In discussing whether or how to establish a Biotechnology Working Party in the WTO, then, the parties were anticipating arguments that would arise in the WTO biotechnology products case in 2004 (see next section).

Several countries were against the proposal for a WTO working party on biotechnology, largely because they expected it to weaken the ability of countries to regulate this sector in the way they preferred. Asian countries, led by Malaysia, and joined by Bolivia, Egypt, Nigeria, Norway, Peru and Switzerland, were against the idea of discussing biotechnology inside the WTO. Civil society groups were also publicly antagonistic. In a letter of 18 November to US Trade Representative Charlene Barshefsky, a group of NGOs expressed their concern about the US proposal. They argued the proposal could undermine 'the development of new national and international safeguards for trade in agricultural biotechnology products' and further 'could place excessive constraints on the rights of governments to regulate, hampering their ability to respond to scientifically uncertain threats on the basis of the precautionary principle' (BRIDGES Weekly, 1999b). The letter also warned that bringing biotechnology into the WTO could undermine the Biosafety Protocol. The sharp controversy can be seen from the following quote from Vandana Shiva, a well-known Indian activist. After criticising the initiative, she wrote (1999):

> The challenge at Seattle is to stop the further deregulation of G.M. trade which is already characterised by political and environmental unaccountability, and stop the trend of transforming environmental problems which need environmental solutions into trade problems having further trade liberalisation and deregulation as the solution.

Given this context, and a US agenda that appeared to target the EU, many were surprised to learn on 1 December that the Trade Commissioner Pascal Lamy had voiced EU support for the working group. He did this without asking individual EU country delegations. Unfortunately for European cohesion and credibility, five European environment ministers quickly issued press statements against the proposal. Various civil society groups also lashed out. Later the same night trade ministers of 15 EU countries joined the chorus of criticism. Lamy was accused of going beyond his remit to make an unexpected, unacceptable concession to the US. National ministers argued that the United Nations, not the WTO, should deal with biosafety issues.

The proposal for a WTO working party on biotechnology therefore highlighted conflicts and distrust within EU institutions as well as beyond them. Lamy defended the move by arguing that negotiations require trade-offs and that European politicians should defer judgement until they saw the whole negotiating agenda (Dawkins, 2000). This self-defence, however, should be viewed in the light of ongoing cooperation between EU and US trade officials to harmonise regulations for GM products in the context of the TEP (see Chapter 2). A European trade official commented in retrospect as follows:

> Against the background of the Biosafety Protocol talks being stalled, the Americans proposed at Seattle that as part of the launch of the round a working group, although not a negotiating process, be established on biotech in the WTO context. DG Environment, DG Trade and Mr Lamy all agreed that if we could, in return for that, also get environment on the agenda of the Seattle round, [then] that would be a price worth paying. That was not the position of the Environment Ministers . . . They were all extremely vocal and critical . . . They made a big fuss about it. My own view remains that if we'd had a deal to launch a round in Seattle, that would have been agreed and their vocal opposition wouldn't have changed that. The Council as a whole would have endorsed it. Would it have been useful in any substantive way? I don't know . . . I think if we had a working group on biotechnology in the WTO today, there wouldn't be the threats there are.
>
> (Interview, 2 April 2003)

As this quote indicates, the disagreements surrounding the WTO Working Group on Biotechnology were ultimately put to one side for other reasons – because the WTO failed to launch a new round of trade negotiations anyway. This was achieved only after a more private meeting in Doha in 2001 and with some rebranding as a 'development' round. That said, the biotechnology conflicts did have repercussions. Most immediately they gave further momentum to the Biosafety Protocol negotiations. Even countries antagonistic to those negotiations now accepted that a Biosafety Protocol might be the only option available to move the biotechnology issue forward. Those in favour redoubled their efforts because they now saw the political risk of not completing negotiations successfully (see quote in earlier section). In the medium term, as mentioned by the trade official above, it meant that agricultural biotechnology had no WTO process that could act as a buffer to absorb US threats regarding a formal dispute at the WTO.

US food aid to southern Africa

The US–EU conflict intensified in 2002 when food shortages and famine in southern Africa were drawn into the agbiotech dispute. The problem emerged when the US offered GM maize to the region as part of its food aid programme. Critics then accused the US of exploiting food shortages to achieve its political and economic goals in the area of agri-food biotechnology. They pointed to a long history of 'conditionality' associated with US food aid, as evidence that the US uses aid to achieve its wider political and economic objectives. Critics also pointed out that US food aid subsidises US agriculture and that this type of relief aid is bad practice because it disrupts local markets (e.g. Zerbe, 2004). In return, advocates of biotechnology and some US officials and politicians accused Europe of consigning Africans to death when food which Americans eat everyday was available cost-free. This issue erupted at the October 2002 TACD meeting and would soon become more public.

The way that food shortages were drawn into the EU–US trade conflict is illustrated well by an unprecedented exchange of letters between high-level officials in the *Wall Street Journal* in January 2003. On 13 January the *Wall Street Journal* published an article accusing the EU of being 'immoral' in discouraging African nations from accepting GM food aid from the United States. Pascal Lamy (EU Trade Commissioner) and five other European Commissioners wrote a reply which stated, amongst other things:

> You should do a little independent thinking rather than simply repeat the view of U.S. cabinet members . . .
>
> To say Europe is 'bullying Africa into refusing to accept American food aid even though millions are malnourished and starving' is downright irresponsible . . .
>
> Neither Europe nor even the U.S. has the right to tell sovereign African nations what kind of food aid they should accept or not accept. Moreover, choices for developing countries should not be limited to 'accept GM food aid or starve.' The EU's own policy is to source food aid regionally, thus ensuring that the countries in need receive the foodstuffs to which they are accustomed as well as helping local economies. Milling the grains is also a means of ensuring that the concerns expressed by these countries about possible dissemination of GMOs into local crops are addressed while providing much-needed food aid.
>
> Food aid to Southern Africa should be about meeting the urgent humanitarian needs of those who are starving. It should not be about trying to advance the case for GM food, or planting GM crops for export, or finding outlets for domestic surplus. This in turn is immoral.
>
> (Fischler et al., 2003)

Soon the US Trade Representative Robert Zoellick, the most senior US official involved in trade issues, and Pascal Lamy's equivalent, responded to the letter:

I am delighted to read that your Jan. 13 editorial 'Immoral Europe' on European biotech obstructionism has stirred six European Commissioners to mass around an indefensible position . . .

The European fog of misinformation and protectionism resulting from EU biotech policies has had life-and-death consequences. Africans, not Americans, have cited these concerns in refusing to stave off starvation by accepting the same food that Europeans freely eat when they visit the United States. The six commissioners write that they have never asserted that biotech foods are unsafe, yet Europeans block those very foods and threaten African biotech exports. Perhaps this logic is persuasive to Europeans in Brussels, but Americans and Africans find it contradictory. African officials who fear European retribution have told me of Europe's pressure to stymie biotech development. Since Commissioner Nielson asserted in another forum that he only wants the truth, I would propose he start by investigating the activities of the anti-biotech NGOs the commission funds. The truth is that biotech products offer African farmers the promise of higher yields, better nutrition, fewer pesticides and greater resistance of crops to various calamities.

These six commissioners know well that the EU's biotech moratorium is politically motivated, damaging to world trade, and harmful to Africa, Europe, America and the world. I urge them to direct their energies toward the European states that are the cause of the problem, not the Americans who point it out.

(Zoellick, 2003)

These public and highly emotive exchanges introduced new elements into the transatlantic conflict over GMOs. There appears to have been genuine outrage on both sides at the way in which Africa was drawn into the transatlantic dispute. There was also a concerted attempt by the EU and the US to gain the moral high ground. Immorality and famine were discursively linked with other issues like risk, consumer rights, technophobia and sovereignty. The reaction of African states to GM food aid, which was informed to some extent by the European moratorium and concerns, illustrated graphically how Europe could set the regulatory agenda for large parts of the world in the future. The US was concerned not just about European blockages but also about the wider adoption of cautious views towards agricultural biotechnology. This prospect further motivated those arguing for a formal US complaint to the WTO to challenge the EU's regulatory delays. Indeed, within the eventual dispute, the US raised the issue of harm to developing countries done by the EU's moratorium (BRIDGES Trade BioRes, 2004a; USTR, 2004a).

US domestic pressures and European responses

As EU regulatory delays continued, the US government faced greater domestic pressure to submit a formal complaint to the WTO. The decision to do so, however, was always a finely balanced one. At the highest political level the transatlantic dispute over agbiotech products was placed alongside other political and economic priorities in the US at the time. And even within the sector there was considerable political uncertainty. Agbiotech companies were unsure about the possible outcomes of a WTO case. As some realised, such a case could intensify the European backlash against GM products, and even a favourable WTO judgement might not lead to market access anyway; blockages in Europe involved supermarket chains excluding GM grain, not just delays in the approvals process.

Corn was at the centre of the trade conflict and US corn farmers were particularly important in the domestic debate. Representing mainly smaller-scale and family farms, the American Corn Growers Association (ACGA) had a sceptical attitude towards GM corn and 'free trade'. This organisation saw the agbiotech industry as narrowing agricultural research and farmers' options:

> Diversity within this field is imperative to improve genetics and [to] have reasonable pricing of such products which allow for a competitive advantage to corn producers. Therefore the ACGA strongly opposes the further consolidation of the genetic marketing and research industry. . . .
> The ACGA believes that any importing country or company has the right to choose between buying genetically altered commodities or traditional production.
>
> (ACGA, 2003)

From this standpoint, it proposed strict standards for seed purity, as well as liability for 'market disruption caused by genetically altered crops' (ACGA, 2003). Thus, challenging claims that GM crops benefit US farmers, the ACGA drew on the arguments of transatlantic consumer networks, for example, the right to choose and demands for labelling (see TACD Table 3.3).

The ACGA sought links across the Atlantic with others who might hold a similar view. Some members met farmers and others who sought to maintain non-GM alternatives, for example the UK Small and Family Farm Association and Farmers Link in East Anglia. Speaking at a European conference, the ACGA Executive Director described GM crops as an albatross around farmers' necks because of the uncertainties around marketability, cross-pollination, segregation, labelling and so on. He added, 'If anyone ever asks if people have the ability to shape their own world against the power of multi-national corporations, just show them what Europe has done' (Goldberg, 2000: 124). Thus he linked non-GM alternatives and European sovereignty, as a global model and basis for alliances; this language has similarities to TACD demands for sovereign risk assessment and GM labelling (as in Tables 3.2 and 3.3).

By contrast to the ACGA, the National Corn Growers Association (NCGA) promoted GM corn and global access for US exports which included these varieties. One policy was to 'Encourage WTO action against the EU for their illegal moratorium on the approval process of biotech corn'. They also advocated trade negotiations for harmonisation of regulatory standards or at least mutual acceptance of biotech products (NCGA, 2003a). According to their Congressional lobbyist, biotech products are safer than their conventional counterparts. Indeed, 'The detractors of biotechnology hold onto an aesthetic of farming that no longer exists' (Corzine, 2003: 9). Thus NCGA arguments – for example, science-based regulation, regulatory harmonisation and trade liberalisation as inherently beneficial – overlapped with those of the transatlantic business networks (see again TABD Table 2.2). As a practical strategy, the NCGA advised its members to aim production only at US markets or else to plant only varieties that are legally approved in the EU. However, it did not support EC proposals for verifying those varieties in US grain exports, as a means to overcome the 'corn ban' (see Chapter 2 on the TEP).

Like the ACGA, the NCGA also developed transatlantic links in an attempt at 'making allies' (NCGA, 2003b). In September 2003 representatives attended conferences of French and Europe-wide maize farmers. This included a maize producers' association which had been demanding access to GM maize seeds as a means to enhance economic competitiveness and environmental benefits (AGPM, 2005). In a joint mission to Europe with the US Grain Council, an NCGA delegation visited government officials including the French Agriculture Ministry.

In the name of defending US corn farmers, politicians such as US Senator Grassley denounced the EU moratorium as economic protectionism. Partly on this basis the NCGA demanded US action against the EU. According to their officer responsible for trade policy, 'Mainly we see the biotech moratorium – and more recently labelling and traceability requirements – as a way to use SPS {Sanitary and Phytosanitary measures] and TBTs [Technical Barriers to Trade] to disrupt grain flows and to protect markets' (interview, 14 October 2003). He went on to explain their expectations for a WTO dispute against the EU:

> Q: How do you foresee corn growers here ultimately gaining something from the WTO dispute?
> A: I think on two levels. One, what it will do is force the Europeans to abide by their international trading requirements, whether it is WTO, SPS or what have you. Secondly, what it is also designed to do is to show the rest of the world that the United States is very serious about confronting these types of barriers to trade in the international market, and that like the beef hormone case before it, we will very actively litigate in the international arena when we see something as flagrantly violating international agreements [such] as both the beef hormone ban and the biotech moratorium. What it's designed to do is to ensure stable and orderly grain flows or grain markets that aren't impacted adversely by unsound or political decisions.

Q: Drawing on the experience of the hormone beef case, what outcome do you expect?

A: It's true that there are not a lot of beef exports going into the EU despite the US victory in that case, but what it did is prevent similar types of efforts in other countries from being implemented. So what it did is draw a line around the EU and say you've behaved badly but other countries do not follow suit and implemented similar bans. And we see that as one critical part of the biotech moratorium case, showing to the rest of the world we will litigate you if you pursue this path and implement barriers to trade that are not based on sound science.

This exchange illustrates several points. It draws attention to the relatively simple way in which arguments distinguish between politically motivated and scientifically based decision making. It also shows how positions are informed by the WTO case on hormone-treated beef; although the US won that case, the EU opted to pay compensation rather than comply with the judgement.

In demanding a US case under WTO rules, then, the NCGA meant to send a signal to other countries, apparently regardless of the outcome for US–EU trade. The same thinking shaped US government deliberations on the WTO case, particularly against the backdrop of developments in southern Africa. In an interview an official in USTR stated:

We're almost certain to win the biotech case; it seems a pretty open-and-shut argument. But is it going to change anything in Europe? We don't think so. It's not going to make Europeans turn and say, 'Okay, we'll eat this stuff.' . . . What really pushed some to take the case was a clear move by Europe into Africa, spreading the European disease in Africa.

(Interview, 15 October 2003)

Shortly before the US made its complaint to the WTO, EU officials also had a perspective on the growing tension between the EU and the US, and how this was linked to domestic pressure. In the following quote a trade official from the EC reflects on the suggestion that US saw value in making threats rather than seeking a definitive legal judgement from the WTO:

It's not clear that they are reluctant to seek a legal judgement. It's a question of timing. If one of your constituencies in Washington says, 'Please make a threat', sometimes it suits you to do that. Biotech isn't the only issue on Zoellick's agenda but if he gets certain constituencies in Congress saying, 'Please make a threat', then he may want to keep in with them. He needs Congress to legislate WTO-compliant legislation [in other areas] . . . So he's playing a large number of different games with Congress.

(Interview, 2 April 2003)

This comment indicates a broader set of issues around trade liberalisation, within which agricultural biotechnology became a bargaining item.

In a reference to TEP discussions concerning how to overcome the corn ban (see Chapter 2), the same person continued:

> I think the logic that led the USDA and the US corn industry to block the corn process is the same logic that leads them to press for WTO action. A stronger belief than we think is justified that they have a just cause and will win, and a higher degree of pessimism than we think is justified that the cooperative route will produce a commercially viable outcome. So I think that the WTO threats are part and parcel of the stalling of that operational element of the TEP agenda. Those threats make it more difficult to get a positive outcome on corn . . . Also, I think already this aggressive posturing is having a chilling effect on the American position. That logic seeps into their judgement of the issues like corn and what we can do. So it is very hard to run aggression and co-operation tactics in parallel.
>
> (Interview, 2 April 2003)

Moreover, US threats against the EU were backfiring, provoking relatively stricter legislation in the EU system (as noted by the EC interviewee above). In this period the Commission sought to overcome the *de facto* moratorium, by moving forward the EU-wide regulatory procedure and enacting new legislation to accommodate member states, for example on traceability and labelling. Yet its specific proposals were turned into a symbol of EU surrender to the USA. Conversely, whenever the European Parliament voted for more stringent rules than the Commission had proposed, this was widely celebrated as defending sovereignty. Regarding a vote on GM labelling rules, for example, a Green MEP said, 'It's a great victory for consumer choice and a clear message to Tony Blair and his American friends' (Agence Europe, 2002).

The Commission sought to counter those suspicions about external pressures forcing decisions. Eventually the Environment Commissioner portrayed the new EU procedures as a better global model, which therefore must be implemented: 'We have to start because we want to demonstrate to the rest of the world that our way of taking decisions about GMOs works. Otherwise they will not believe us', according to the DG-Environment Commissioner (Margot Wallstr m, Associated Press, 28 January 2004).

The WTO case: from legal to expert arguments

The US threatened repeatedly to bring a case against the EU at the WTO from 1999 onwards. As evidence of EU crimes against trade law, the USTR website quoted the EU's Environment Commissioner. For example: 'We have already waited too long to act. The moratorium is illegal and unjustified . . . the value of biotechnology is poorly appreciated in Europe' (Margot Wallstr m, 13 July 2000). Also, 'I have stopped guessing when the moratorium would be lifted. We have put in place the legal framework . . . but some member states are opposed to GMOs and they will try to move the goal posts. They will try to find another obstacle' (Margot Wallstr m, 17 October 2002). Eventually Commissioners stopped making such public statements about an EU moratorium.

Under standard WTO procedures, on 13 May 2003 the US finally requested consultations with the EU in relation to biotechnology products (USTR, 2003b). Canada and Argentina soon filed similar requests. This dispute settlement case became 'European Communities – Measures Affecting the Approval and Marketing of Biotech Products (DS291, DS292, DS293)', with all three complaints being treated simultaneously. The US complaint had three aspects: (1) the suspension of the EC's approval procedure; (2) the failure of the EC to consider applications already submitted; (3) national marketing and import bans being maintained by some member states. The Ambassador claimed the EU was violating various pieces of trade law, particularly Articles 2 and 5 of the SPS Agreement (US, 2003).

The US announced that it would request a WTO dispute settlement panel (henceforth the Dispute Panel) on 19 June 2003, after consultations with the EC failed to produce a satisfactory outcome (BRIDGES Trade BioRes, 2003a and b). The request was submitted to the WTO shortly after (WTO, 2003). In the rest of this section we identify the main areas of disagreement in the dispute and then analyse US and EC strategies.[1] In relation to EU regulatory delays and blockages since the late 1990s, the antagonists disagreed along the following lines:

- whether agbiotech products come under the SPS Agreement – or rather have a more appropriate forum in other international agreements;
- whether the EU had made a 'moratorium' decision or at least had implemented a *de facto* moratorium as a measure to block approval decisions;
- whether applications to market products in the EU had faced 'undue delays', for example as a way to avoid approval decisions, or, rather, had undergone reasonable delays as means to obtain additional information for a risk assessment;
- whether national bans on EU-approved products were based on risk assessments, in compliance with WTO rules;
- whether the main burden of evidence lay with the defendant or complainants to demonstrate EU compliance or non-compliance with WTO rules;
- whether official EU-level expert advice provided an adequate basis for the Commission and EU member states to approve products in the late 1990s, and therefore an adequate basis for the WTO to judge the dispute;

- whether the WTO needed its own expert advice on the scientific issues and context of the EU's procedural delays in order to evaluate them.

In relation to the final point, neither side suggested that the WTO should attempt to make a definitive judgement on the scientific issues, though the EU and the US gave different reasons for why this was not appropriate.

US strategy: procedural and legalistic

The US strategy at the WTO focused on procedural delays and blockages in the EU system. The US argued that these violated WTO rules and that there was already enough evidence for a judgement. In its first oral statement, for example, the US attacked EU procedural delays, whilst at the same time acknowledging that they were never formalised. The US stated that the EC's moratorium on product approvals ' . . . was not adopted in a transparent manner. Indeed, it was not published in any official journal or otherwise memorialized' (USTR, 2004a: 1). The US went on to say: 'In challenging the EC's moratorium . . . the United States is simply calling on the EC to allow its own approval procedures to run their course' (USTR, 2004a: 2). The US argued later that 'staff-level information exchanges regarding product applications is entirely consistent with a moratorium adopted on a political-level, under which no product was allowed to reach final approval' (USTR, 2004c: 4–5). In this way the US implied that EU procedures were being blocked at the political level, even if they were ongoing at the regulatory level.

As a less obvious procedural argument, the US focused attention on the treatment of risk and uncertainty. The US case acknowledged these as relevant issues but argued that the EU regulatory system was not allowed to deal with them; politicians had taken the decision to block product approvals, so this was a failure of the EU system. In its first oral submission the US argued, for example, that 'Many of the products caught up in the EC moratorium have been positively assessed by the EC's own scientific committees. In this case, the EC can present no scientific basis for its moratorium on approvals' (USTR, 2004a: 2). If there are scientific questions related to GM products, therefore, 'those questions can be and should be addressed within the context of the EC's own approval system, and in a manner consistent with its WTO obligations' (USTR, 2004a: 3). In this way the US acknowledged uncertainty about risk as a potential issue but at the same time it emphasised that these are procedural and political concerns.

With arguments of this kind, the US identified the EU's moratorium as a source of 'undue delay' and inconsistent with the SPS agreement. By emphasising procedural weaknesses and focusing on the SPS Agreement, the US built on aspects of the WTO's judgement in the case of hormone-treated beef. In that case the EU was criticised for not undertaking a focused risk assessment of the banned product. By initially judging the case in this way, the WTO had no need to reach an authoritative judgement on the science involved. In the agbiotech case the US argued that wherever scientific uncertainty and risk were issues, the WTO could rely on the scientific judgements of the EU's own scientific committees, on which the EU failed to act. Given those judgements, the US also argued that there was no need for the WTO to seek expert advice of its own.

Before analysing the EC's case, we discuss two arguments the US made in response to it. As we outline below, the EC claimed that the EU never had a moratorium on approval of GM products. In response the US argued along the following lines: 'To make this claim, the EC asks us to believe . . . that the failure to approve any biotech products between October 1998 and August 2003 was a mere coincidence' (USTR, 2004a: 3). The US also gave numerous examples of EU officials and politicians who referred to the EU 'moratorium' from the late 1990s onwards (see again the beginning of this section). When the EC approved *Bt*-11 maize in May 2004, and claimed that this would not have been possible unless the approval procedure had been moving forward over the period in question, the US dismissed this development. It argued that an approval decision did not show that there never was moratorium, nor that blockages in the EU system were at an end; consequently, it intended to pursue the case regardless, partly as a matter of principle.

As we also discuss below, the EC cited the Biosafety Protocol in its defence. In response the US challenged the EC to establish its relevance. For example:

> . . . the EC discusses the Biosafety Protocol at length. The EC itself, however, acknowledges that the Protocol explicitly provides that parties may *not* [emphasis original] disregard their existing international obligations in their implementation of the Biosafety Protocol. Furthermore, the Biosafety Protocol foresees a functioning regulatory system in each Party country; it does not provide an excuse for refusing to make prompt, transparent decisions.
>
> (USTR, 2004b: 4)

> . . . international law other than the WTO Agreement is only pertinent in so far as it would assist the Panel in interpreting the particular terms of the covered agreements at issue in this dispute. But in this dispute, the EC has not identified how the Biosafety Protocol or a 'Precautionary Principle' would be of relevance to interpreting any particular provision of the WTO Agreement.
>
> (USTR, 2004b: 9)

In the US view, there was no need for the WTO to make judgements about the Precautionary Principle, just as the Appellate Body had refrained from doing in the dispute over hormone-treated beef.

In sum, the US strategy at the WTO was a procedural one. In its view there was no need for the WTO to engage with scientific questions about risks to human health or the environment because these had been (or should have been) addressed by the EU's own regulatory procedures. The US argued instead that the WTO should focus on procedural failures, in particular: the EU's failure to allow its own approvals process to operate; the EU's imposition of a politically motivated moratorium on new GM products; member states being allowed to ban products already approved at EU-level; and expert advice from EU scientific committees being ignored.

This strategy was underpinned by a relatively narrow and legalistic reading of WTO rules. This is seen, for example, in the US criticism of 'undue delay' versus the EC's defence on the same point in the next section. The Commission strategy sought to open up scientific questions around risk and uncertainty, thus interpreting WTO rules more broadly.

EC strategy: scientific uncertainty and interpretive flexibility

In its defence the EC sought to place a greater burden of evidence upon the complainants to demonstrate the EU's non-compliance with WTO rules. From a legal standpoint, it questioned whether the SPS Agreement covered agbiotech products (see earlier section). From a procedural standpoint, it submitted a detailed chronology of how GM product files were handled in EU regulatory procedures. This documentation sought to undermine claims that the EU had a moratorium or undue delays, so that the Dispute Panel would require the complainants to demonstrate such claims in specific cases (CEC–SJ, 2004a).

In its second oral statement, the Commission echoed the political debate about the need to find a legitimate basis on which to make decisions about the future of society. For this argument it drew on the DDT experience: ' . . . [DDT was] praised as a useful tool for agriculture, then withdrawn from the markets for its health consequences, and today, fifty years on, [is] still to be found in human beings and animals – and DDT is just a chemical, not a living organism potentially capable of autonomous reproduction' (CEC–SJ, 2004b: 6). The EC also drew on the EU–US Consultative Forum on Biotechnology (see Chapter 3), whose report had argued that there are many legitimate concerns 'for which science cannot provide answers'. Given that agricultural biotechnology could have far-reaching social consequences, it was necessary to establish forward-looking regulation in advance, in order 'to master these technological developments', argued the EC (CEC–SJ, 2004b: 10).

Most importantly, the EC's strategy linked scientific uncertainty about biotechnological risks with jurisdictional sovereignty and discretion. Near the beginning of its oral statement, the EC argued:

> This is, in the view of the European Communities, a case about regula-
> tors' choices of the appropriate level of protection of public health and

the environment in the face of scientific complexity and uncertainty and in respect of which there is great public interest. It is a case essentially about time. The time allowed to a prudent government to set up and apply a process for effective risk assessment of products which are novel for its territory and ecosystems, and that have the potential of causing irreversible harm to public health and the environment. . . .

The science necessary to assess the risks . . . and in particular any long term, indirect, or delayed effects, has had and is having a hard time to catch up with the rapid development of new GM products. The science traditionally used in risk assessment is deterministic (some say reductionist) by nature, and that means that it had a difficult time to apprehend all the properties of highly complex organisms, the interaction between organisms, and the full picture of the ecosystems and agroecosystems that might be affected.

(CEC–SJ, 2004b: 1–2, 4)

These arguments bear upon appropriate timescales for regulatory decisions. For example, in a context where experts have limited knowledge of scientific methods and risk assessment techniques, what is an 'undue delay'? The EC argued that procedural delays had been linked to requests for additional information and were therefore reasonable. The EC also argued that it had taken only 'provisional measures', as permitted under WTO rules.

In judging criteria like 'undue delay' and 'provisional' measures, the EC emphasised developments in scientific knowledge. In its view, there is no fixed time limit, contrary to an implicit assumption in the US case:

What a reasonable period of time may be in any case depends on all the circumstances. If the assessment is taking place in the context of a very long time frame (as in the present case); in relation to changes that may have a permanent effect (as in the present case); and in relation to changes that are being introduced at an exponential rate compared to the past (as in the present case); then a relatively long period of time may be necessary.

(CEC–SJ, 2004c: 191)

In this way the EC tried to introduce flexible criteria for judging the case.

According to the Commission's argument, moreover, the Dispute Panel would have to engage with scientific uncertainty and therefore would need expert advice. As discussed above, the US argued that this would not be necessary. In its oral statement the EU mocked this idea:

First, we are struck by the fact that all the Complainants, who have the burden of proof, are requesting the Panel NOT to have recourse to scientific and technical advice. The European Communities finds this difficult to understand and cannot believe that the Panel would rule in this case without taking such advice once the issues in dispute are clarified. It is interesting to note that it is only the defendant who is open to a clarification of the facts in this case on the basis of expert advice.

(CEC–SJ, 2004b: 11)

The Commission also argued that judgements of the EU's own expert scientific committees could not exclusively underpin the WTO's judgement. They pointed out, for example, that EU committees overlap with each other, reach different decisions and answer only the specific questions put to them anyway.

For the above arguments about appropriate timescales, the EC also cited the 'mutually supportive' relation between the Biosafety Protocol and other international agreements. It argued that WTO provisions must be interpreted 'in the light of other existing instruments of international law' (CEC–SJ, 2004b: 14). It attacked the US case as 'too simplistic' and 'not tenable' because it focused exclusively on the SPS Agreement. The Commission case drew attention particularly to the Biosafety Protocol and to the Codex Principles for Risk Analysis of Foods Derived from Modern Biotechnology. Among other standards, the latter illustrated the recent, rapid development of scientific knowledge and risk assessment methods. According to the EC, these documents establish an international consensus on key issues that the WTO should keep in mind: regulatory regimes should be tailored to the specific conditions of countries; GMOs should be treated differently from conventional products; GM products should be labelled; there is a need for post-market surveillance; and the 'precautionary principle' is a principle of international law (CEC–SJ, 2004b: 18). Given the complex scientific and legal issues, the US was accused of presenting the issues in an 'excessively simple manner' (CEC–SJ, 2004b: 1).

Another striking feature of the Commission's defence was the argument that there never was a moratorium on GM products in the EU. The Commission's oral statement, given on 2 June 2004, draws attention to the fact that two weeks earlier the EU had authorised *Bt* 11 maize. This, it argued, showed that the approvals process had been moving forward in recent years – a product like this could not simply be authorised in response to the WTO dispute. This point was underlined on 19 July 2004 when the EC authorised Monsanto's NK603 corn. The Commission argued:

Where is there a moratorium in all of this? Can you continue your approval process, authorize products and, at the same time maintain a moratorium? Let me re-phrase: How else can you prove the absence of a moratorium if not through demonstrating that the approval process moves on and results in decisions?

(CEC–SJ, 2004b: 10–11)

From this sketch it is clear that the Commission strategy sought to ensure that the WTO panel engaged with scientific uncertainty. They also wanted to ensure that the SPS Agreement was interpreted in the light of other agreements such as the Biosafety Protocol and relevant Codex standards. More broadly the Commission emphasised flexible criteria for judging the dispute as an alternative to the USA's narrow legalistic approach.

In this section we have emphasised arguments of the EU and the US, because we are primarily interested in interactions between these two jurisdictions. The other complainants made their own submissions taking up scientific issues that the US government regarded as superfluous (e.g. Argentina, 2004; Canada, 2004).

Transatlantic networks criticised the US decision to bring the WTO case, while framing it as an attack on precaution and sovereignty. Shortly beforehand, consumer organisations had urged the US government not to take such action against the EU 'for proceeding in a precautionary manner on approvals' (TACD, 2003a). After the US decision in May 2003, they condemned its implicit aims: to force agbiotech products on an unwilling world, and 'to frighten off other nations' from developing their own safety regulations, especially precautionary ones. As they had stated since 1998, the US and EU should settle their differences 'by adopting an EU-type system' for regulating agbiotech products (TACD, 2003b).

Two different NGO networks eventually submitted *amicus curiae* briefs. One of these was on a transatlantic basis and both attacked the complainants. Likewise a transatlantic academic group criticised the US government model of 'science-based regulation', especially for constraining precaution (Busch et al., 2004; Winickoff et al., 2005). Although these interventions had no clear bearing on the formal dispute, they highlighted the WTO's legitimacy problem in potentially appearing to favour business interests over environmental and consumer protection.

Expert advice as a contested resource

The WTO biotechnology products dispute entered a new phase with the issue of expert advice. As outlined in the previous section, the parties disagreed over whether the Dispute Panel needed expert advice of its own. In this section we discuss related developments in the following areas: how the issue was debated; how questions for experts were set; how experts were chosen; and how their advice was cited.

In all previous WTO disputes involving the SPS Agreement, an expert group advised the Dispute Panel on scientific and technical issues. In the dispute over agricultural biotechnology, the EU was in favour of such a group and the complainants were against. The parties were given until 22 July 2004 to elaborate their reasons. The US largely reiterated earlier arguments: that the case should be judged on procedural grounds, and that the

Dispute Panel could depend on the judgements of the EU's own expert committees if necessary.

In its second written submission, the EC made further arguments in favour of an expert group. The three complainants had approached the scientific issues in somewhat different ways and the Commission argued that this indicated significant scientific uncertainty – the broader context which the Dispute Panel would need to consider in evaluating EU procedural delays. As extra grounds for needing expert advice: 'The European Communities submits that a failure by the Panel to have regard to this broader context will risk undermining the legitimacy of the WTO system' (CEC–SJ, 2004c: 10). In these ways the Commission put pressure on the Dispute Panel not to reach an overall judgement on the case without expert advice. Eventually the Panel invited the Commission to make a formal request for the establishment of an expert group.

On 20 August 2004 the Dispute Panel announced that it would seek scientific and technical advice by establishing an expert group (WTO, 2004). This decision was widely seen as a victory for the EU (BRIDGES Trade BioRes, 2004b); it gave greater scope for Commission arguments about insufficient evidence and scientific uncertainty. It had already argued that member-state objections, the emergence of new issues and conflicting risk assessments justified the EU in not following favourable safety advice from its own experts at the EU level (e.g. CEC–SJ, 2004c). In order to support this argument, the Commission had already documented chronologically the various interactions in the EU's regulatory procedure (e.g. CEC–SJ, 2004a). The Dispute Panel now requested more detail, as a basis for the expert group to judge how regulatory delays involved scientific issues. In response, the Commission laboriously gathered all documents which had been sent between companies, national Competent Authorities and the Commission regarding each GM product.

Following the Dispute Panel's decision to set up an expert group, the parties engaged in further arguments about its role, remit and composition. In October 2004 the WTO issued a draft list of questions for the group. Many of the questions implied the need for the EC to demonstrate evidence of risk. Given the available evidence for each risk issue in the late 1990s, some questions asked whether there was any reason to expect that extra evidence 'would identify an adverse effect that had not been identified in the previous studies'.

The parties responded by proposing extra questions. Although the US continued to argue that expert advice was unnecessary, it was nevertheless drawn into arguments about scientific evidence. According to a further US submission, information available on biotechnology products in the late 1990s could not be regarded as 'insufficient for a risk assessment', as the EC claimed, especially given the positive assessments of the products by the EU's own expert committees (USTR, 2004c: 15). Underlining this argument, the US proposed additional questions about whether additional scientific information could plausibly reveal any risks, especially regarding food safety (USTR, 2004c: 56–7). Apparently the US regarded the evidence as scientifically more straightforward – and thus the EC case weaker – for food safety than for feed and crop uses.

The EC viewed the expert group and its questions as an opportunity to reverse the burden of proof for non-compliance with WTO rules. The complainants should be required to prove that there were 'undue delays' for specific products. And the Dispute Panel should be asked to judge only whether national and EU authorities had acted reasonably in the late 1990s, in the light of scientific debate and available knowledge at that time. Background on the late 1990s was central to this strategy. It was important for the Panel 'to take into account this *d calage* in time between the current scientific knowledge and the scientific knowledge at the time of the alleged "delay"' (CEC–SJ, 2004d: 9). Although the Dispute Panel rejected several questions proposed by the EC, the final list accommodated them to some extent. Many of the Panel's questions opened up the issue of what was not known scientifically in the late 1990s, so that answers could emphasise the evolutionary development of scientific knowledge over recent years.

The parties to the dispute were able to propose organisations that would be asked to nominate members of the expert group. After seeing a preliminary list, the parties also had the opportunity to nominate specific individuals. This process produced a list several times longer than the six individuals being sought for the expert group. As in previous conflicts leading to WTO disputes, the expert group itself would not prepare an overall statement, so nominees were asked whether they would be willing to submit individual responses to the Panel's scientific questions. Each party in the dispute was also invited to state whether they objected to any nominee. Under the WTO rules, if too few nominees survive the rejection process, the Panel can appoint experts despite their rejection by a party. With this possibility in mind, each party may do some second-guessing about the consequences of rejecting too many nominees.

The selection process was contentious, with many nominees being rejected by one or more parties. For its judgement about whom to accept or reject, the US government consulted its regulatory scientific staff. Building on the WTO ruling in the hormone-treated beef case, the EC likewise sought advice for its judgements. But the EC did not need to eliminate all nominees who might be problematic for its case, because its strategy sought to generate and then high-light disagreements amongst experts as a way to establish scientific uncertainty.

After they were chosen the Panel's six experts submitted individual reports. These reports extended earlier disagreements over scientific uncertainty and GM products. Many of the comments addressed the questions put by the Commission which aimed to reverse the burden of evidence – towards demonstrating safety. Such comments drew attention to expert disagreements and knowledge gaps in the late 1990s. Others did not, though they still played a part in indicating differences of opinion. After these submissions the parties consulted their own experts as part of a process of compiling an overall reply to the six reports.

In January 2005 the parties submitted their responses, which established a basis for the next major meeting in Geneva in mid-February. At the Geneva meeting the three complainants and the defendant used the opportunity in different ways. The US government's representatives mainly reiterated their argument that the EU had an illegal moratorium; they said little about the scientific arguments. In contrast, Canada and Argentina called upon their own experts to engage with those arguments. The EC brought six of its own experts and called on them to give a consistent message: that information had been inadequate for a risk assessment in the late 1990s and there were still some ongoing uncertainties about risk.

Drawing on the six expert reports, all the parties cited statements that were favourable to their case. For example, Argentina (2005) selectively quoted statements from two US experts in support of its case – for example, that GM products do not differ inherently from non-GM products, and that member states did not always have strong grounds to reject the safety advice of the EU's scientific committee. The EC cited other statements from the same US experts that drew attention to scientific unknowns in the late 1990s. In this way the EC aimed to highlight expert disagreements and therefore scientific uncertainty.

The WTO Dispute Panel's Interim Findings

On 7 February 2006 the Dispute Panel released its Interim Findings; 1050 pages in length, the document was the longest of its kind in WTO history. The Interim Findings were not made public officially, but the Conclusions and Recommendations were leaked through an NGO website. The Dispute Panel emphasised that it 'did *not* examine: whether biotech products in general are safe' (emphasis in the original). The Panel also dismissed complaints against Europe under all WTO agreements other than the SPS Agreement. Under that agreement it accepted complaints in three areas: 'undue delay' in approving biotechnology products; the lack of a scientific risk assessment to justify trade-related SPS measures; and the application of provisional measures where there is inadequate scientific information for a risk assessment (WTO DP, 2006).

For the period between June 1998 and August 2003, when the Dispute Panel was established, it found that the EC had maintained an illegal *de facto* moratorium on 24 of 27 biotechnology products. These products had been declared safe by EU-level scientific committees and the EC was judged to be violating the 'undue delay' obligation by not approving them. In addition, safeguard measures taken by various member states failed to comply with the SPS Agreement because they were not based on a risk assessment. The Dispute Panel argued that ' . . . in no case was the situation one in which the relevant scientific evidence was insufficient to perform a risk assessment, such that the member State might have had recourse to a provisional measure under Article 5.7 of the SPS Agreement'. Also, 'Although some of the member States did provide scientific studies, in no case did they provide an assessment of the risks to human health and/or the environment meeting the requirements of the SPS Agreement' (WTO DP, 2006: 1031). The Dispute Panel emphasised that EU-level scientific committees did not change their positive assessments of products when they were presented with new arguments and evidence.

The Interim Findings indicate that the Dispute Panel sought to judge the case on procedural rather than scientific grounds, as far as possible. The Dispute Panel explicitly denied making safety assessments of its own. To judge national bans on GM products it used arguments similar to those used against the EU ban on hormone-treated beef (see above; cf. WTO AB, 1998). That said, the Dispute Panel could not avoid implicitly taking a view on whether any missing scientific information mattered for risk assessment of biotechnology products between 1998 and 2003. A negative view is implied in the judgement that there was undue delay in EU-level approval.

Those involved in the dispute interpreted the Interim Findings in an effort to establish their wider significance. Although the Panel had attempted to avoid safety judgements, the US Trade Representative Rob Portman implied that it had found genetic modification to be 'a safe and beneficial technology' (USTR, 2006). The US industry association BIO welcomed the findings and emphasised that farmers around the world were increasingly planting crops 'improved by biotechnology' and that they were reaping 'the benefits of increased productivity and environmental sustainability' (BIO, 2006). According to its European equivalent, EuropaBio, the Panel had upheld the individual's free choice to buy safe products:

> The European biotechnology industry, like the European Commission, supports choice – the choice to grow, import and consume approved GM products. The industry continues to back a science-based regulatory system to ensure farmers have the choice to use sustainable techniques that best meet the needs of their farming operations . . . Countries that do not implement the EU rules, which they themselves put in place, are denying that choice. The dispute over biotech crops is *not about safety*, the crops being grown around the world have passed stringent food, feed and environmental safety standards and are as safe as, or safer than, conventional crops.
>
> (EuropaBio, 2006, emphasis in original)

Consumer organisations emphasised democratic sovereignty over decision making in the face of powerful economic interests. The TACD noted that the findings related to delays in approval and not to EU rules on safety testing, labelling and traceability. They also argued that it was the collapse of the market, not lack of regulatory approval, which had prevented US GM products from entering Europe. Once again civil society groups raised the spectre of the US and biotechnology companies forcing GM food on a reluctant public: 'If the WTO panel rules against the right of individual governments to regulate the use of GM products, the shock waves will be global.' TACD also challenged the legitimacy of the WTO, ' . . . where public interest regulations are regularly ruled against in the name of free trade' (TACD, 2006). Rhoda Karpatkin of the US-based Consumers Union, a member of TACD, said:

> This suit can be seen as a preemptive effort to chill the development of new policies for regulating GM crops around the globe . . . Ironically, the US may have won the battle but it is losing the war. A WTO ruling in favor of the U.S. will only increase consumer suspicion of GM crops and of a global trading system that subsumes the public interest to the interests of giant biotechnology firms.
>
> (TACD, 2006)

The US-based Institute for Agriculture and Trade Policy praised the Dispute Panel for seeking its own expert scientific advice. However, a spokesperson criticised the judgement for limiting precaution: 'Beyond GE crops, the WTO ruling as reported sets a broad precedent to inhibit the ability of WTO member states to set food safety, public health and environmental health measures where there is scientific uncertainty about the adequacy or quality of data submitted for commercialization approvals.' Moreover, according to the IATP Director, 'It is disappointing that the WTO would seek to override democratic decisions at literally all levels of government' (IATP, 2006). As these commentaries illustrate, policy actors interpreted the Interim Findings according to prior framings of the agbiotech issue.

Conclusion

As Chapter 2 showed, the transatlantic trade liberalisation agenda for agbiotech products began to lose momentum and even to fragment in the late 1990s. The TABD–TEP agenda was undermined by regulatory delays in Europe and a commercial boycott of GM grain. As this impasse continued, the TABD-based coalition of agri-food members split, and US–EU inter-governmental cooperation gave way to political competition. As subsequent chapters showed, contending transatlantic coalitions created political pressure for more stringent regulatory criteria on both sides of the Atlantic. This resulted in significant regulatory divergence, rather than the adoption of more stringent regulatory criteria on both sides of the Atlantic. The EC was increasingly pushed towards approaches that constrained or undermined the TABD–TEP agenda.

As this chapter has shown, the earlier trade conflict over hormone-treated beef was extended into various international arenas as the US and EU sought to strengthen their positions in anticipation of a future agbiotech dispute at the WTO. Their trade conflict over agbiotech products became a global contest over legitimate models for the regulation of agricultural biotechnology. This was particularly so as many civil society groups responded by supporting the EU's precautionary model against US government policy on biotechnology in general and its non-regulation of GM food specifically. Against this background we can answer the four narrative questions raised in the Introduction to this book.

How did policy actors try to advance particular policy agendas?

After the Bush administration took office in January 2001, the US government intensified its rhetorical attacks on EU regulatory delays and blockages of agbiotech products. The US increasingly claimed that the EU had a politically motivated moratorium which lacked any scientific basis. Corn exports were at the centre of the trade blockage, so US corn farmers were an important domestic constituency, and their major business organisation demanded that a WTO case be brought against the EU. The NCGA sought to deter other countries from imposing similar blockages elsewhere and in this way hoped to protect other export markets. They did not expect a WTO case to re-open the European corn market.

When famine-struck African countries began to block food aid shipments of US corn in 2002/03, this provided an inflammatory new way of framing the issues involved in the transatlantic conflict. Officials in the US and EU tried to secure the moral high ground. The US government blamed Europeans for encouraging irrational fears and for consigning Africans to death when food aid was available. For the US this graphically illustrated how the EU's precautionary approach could be taken up and implemented more widely around the world. In response, EU representatives attacked the US for exploiting famine to promote agricultural biotechnology and for disrespecting the sovereignty of African nations.

Soon after the southern African famine was drawn into the transatlantic conflict over biotechnology products, the US launched a formal dispute at the WTO. The US government and its co-complainants disagreed with the EU about the nature of the conflict. The US government presented a procedural and narrowly legalistic case, emphasising that EU procedural delays and consequent trade barriers *per se* violated WTO agreements. In response the EC linked those delays with scientific uncertainty about the risks associated with agbiotech products. It also justified interpreting WTO agreements in flexible ways, for example by judging 'undue delay' in relation to long timescales in the spirit of the Biosafety Protocol. The US argued the case on the relatively narrow grounds of illegal barriers to trade, while the EC opened up questions of sovereignty, especially societies' prerogative to make choices about technological futures. The EC also raised the spectre of the WTO's own legitimacy problems in regard to those issues, while alluding to 'anti-globalisation' protest.

How were expertise and knowledge used to influence policy making?

In the WTO agbiotech case, a central issue was the burden of demonstrating whether or not EU authorities had 'insufficient information' to approve GM products in the late 1990s. In the earlier transatlantic dispute over hormone-treated beef, the EC had tried to broaden the interpretation of the SPS Agreement in this regard; it funded new risk research and cited expert disagreements to highlight scientific uncertainty. The EC extended this strategy in the agbiotech dispute. Here the EC successfully argued that the WTO needed its own expert advice to understand the scientific background to the case and to protect its own legitimacy. The EC regarded an expert group as an opportunity to highlight divergent expert opinions. The US argued that such advice was not needed because the case could be judged on procedural grounds alone, and by drawing on the advice of the EU's own scientific committees if necessary. The WTO Dispute Panel eventually accepted the EC's proposal to establish its own expert group.

Following that decision, the parties made further arguments about its appropriate composition and the scientific questions to be answered. Several nominees were rejected by one of the parties; the expert group ultimately included members with diverse viewpoints, thus facilitating the EC's strategy of highlighting expert disagreements and scientific uncertainty. The nature of the questions, however, was also important. They would shape how unknowns in risk assessment would be treated and where the burden of evidence would be placed. As a result of the proposals from the defendant and complainants, the questions that were put to the experts did not simply impose a burden of evidence on the defendant to demonstrate risk; the overall list was relatively more balanced. Complementing the EC's strategy, the questions opened up greater opportunity to explore what was unknown about the risks of agbiotech products in the late 1990s.

For different reasons, none of the parties asked the Dispute Panel to make a definitive judgement on the scientific evidence involved. The US asked the WTO to rely on the risk assessments by the EU's own scientific committees. Some of the statements made by members of the expert group supported the safety claims made by these committees. By contrast, the EC asked the Dispute Panel simply to accept that the EU's regulatory proce-dure had legitimate alternatives to the advice of EU-level advisory committees. The equivalent committees in some member states, for example, had raised issues that were not adequately addressed by the EU's own advisory committees. The WTO Dispute Panel, therefore, was invited to judge whether the EU procedure had plausible alternatives to EU-level expert advice, rather than to make a definitive judgement of its own. To support its case the EC was also able to cite some statements made by members of the Dispute Panel's expert group, particularly where they highlighted what was not known in the late 1990s.

How were regulatory standard-setting processes and trade conflict linked?

Perhaps anticipating the WTO dispute over biotechnology products, the US and the EU competed to influence the wording and practical meaning of international agreements. The US government tried to ensure that any trade barriers must be based on a risk assessment and 'sound science', that is evidence of risk. In contrast, the EU tried to expand the scope for precautionary approaches to scientific uncertainty. This contest arose in the negotiations around the Biosafety Protocol to the UN Convention on Biological Diversity, especially in arguments about how to incorporate precautionary criteria in decision making. In the context of the EU–US trade conflict over agbiotech products, the Biosafety Protocol spanned the boundary between international trade and environmental law. As discussed in Chapter 5, a similar contest took place at the Codex Alimentarius Commission around the Ad Hoc Intergovernmental Task Force on Foods Derived from Biotechnology, though US representatives there accommodated EU proposals for a relatively more stringent wording to some extent.

A turning point for the trade liberalisation period appears to have arrived when the two TEP partners attempted to set up a working group on agricultural biotechnology within the WTO framework in late 1999. EU and US representatives had somewhat conflicting aims for agreeing to such a body, particularly because of their disagreements over whether the SPS Agreement encompassed agbiotech products, and regarding how regulatory procedures should deal with scientific uncertainty. Although the overall Seattle debacle killed the proposal for a WTO Biotechnology Working Group, it nevertheless came to symbolise a general threat to the Biosafety Protocol, which was seen as more amenable to precaution and sovereignty. These developments influenced political strategies and played a role in ensuring that the Biosafety Protocol negotiations ended with agreement shortly after.

The relationship between regulatory standard-setting and trade liberalisation was implicit in all of these interactions because international regulatory standards are a means to avoid, remove, shape or potentially justify trade barriers. The US–EU agbiotech conflict symbolised wider issues such as jurisdictional sovereignty and social legitimacy regarding trade rules. In the interactions associated with the Biosafety Protocol, the Codex Alimentarius and the WTO, there was a tension between agreeing procedures and criteria that might protect jurisdictional sovereignty and enhance social legitimacy, versus those that might not. The EC tried to turn these issues to its advantage in the WTO case by emphasising the WTO's own legitimacy problems.

This was mentioned as an extra reason for its Dispute Panel to interpret the SPS Agreement in ways that would accommodate wider public concerns; these concerns were particularly difficult for the EU, given the popular backlash against GM crops and foods.

How were EU–US interactions and intra-jurisdictional conflicts linked?

Agricultural biotechnology divided US farmers, whose organisations adopted discursive framings similar to those developed by TABD and TACD. One farmers' organisation attacked European trade barriers as a threat to science-based regulation and regulatory harmonisation for GM crops, amongst other things (compare to TABD Table 2.2). Another farmers' organisation characterised the problem as US global imposition of biotechnology products which was denying the right to choose because this depended on non-GM alternatives being available. Their spokespersons welcomed European resistance to agricultural biotechnology as a defence of democratic sovereignty (compare with TACD Table 3.3). From these antagonistic standpoints, both farmers' organisations sought allies across the Atlantic.

The TEP partners sought ways to overcome the trade barriers but they had little scope to do so. GM corn farmers in the US developed segregation measures to help facilitate US corn exports in Europe but they (along with grain traders) did not try to accommodate EU traceability requirements. At the same time the Commission could not relax the burden of evidence upon grain traders to demonstrate the contents of shipments. As a result transatlantic maize shipments did not resume and the 'corn ban' remained as a focus for the transatlantic dispute.

In a political context where the US government was seeking greater authority to negotiate 'free trade' arrangements, many US farmers had doubts about whether trade liberalisation would benefit them in the long term. As a strategic response, advocates of trade liberalisation encouraged farmers to believe that their global market was blocked or threatened by European economic protectionism, which might spread elsewhere in the future; a WTO case against the EU was offered as the solution to this problem. After the US government led the case against the EU, US NGOs joined their European counterparts in denouncing it. They portrayed the US government as a threat to global safety standards; together they issued evidence of scientific uncertainties that could justify regulatory delays.

In Europe there was a different relationship between transatlantic interactions and intra-jurisdictional conflicts. From the late 1990s onwards the US government repeatedly threatened to bring a WTO case against the EU but these threats backfired politically. Whenever the EC tried to move the EU approvals process forward, or tried to provide a new legislative basis to overcome the *de facto* moratorium, it was accused of surrendering to US pressure. Various NGOs and politicians framed the issue as US threats to European sovereignty. Such arguments served to delay regulatory decisions and to introduce relatively more stringent requirements into the EU system. Thus the transatlantic conflict was turned into a discursive resource for potentially delaying or even impeding commercialisation of GM products in Europe.

Eventually the EC changed the arguments it made in an effort to restart the approvals process. Initially it had emphasised the need to avoid a formal dispute with the US at the WTO, but such arguments provoked resentment. After new regulations were in place, the Commission argued that product approvals were necessary to demonstrate that the EU's precautionary system was a viable and functioning alternative. After the WTO dispute began, however, the EC faced a dilemma. Its submissions at the WTO tried to document a scientific basis for regulatory delays in the late 1990s (and possibly even in the present). In an effort to establish the EU's regulatory approach, however, the Commission told member states that they had no valid grounds to delay or obstruct approval of the same GM products.

7 Global governance of agricultural biotechnology

Introduction

We have argued that the EU–US conflict over biotechnology products is an opportunity to study the global governance of a new technology, for several reasons. EU–US interactions, and their regulatory frameworks and standards, have profound implications at the global level. In addition, although the EU and the US often approach the rest of the world with a transatlantic consensus, in this case they found themselves increasingly in conflict. As their dispute intensified, and their regulatory approaches diverged, they began to present competing regulatory models to other countries around the world. This raised the political stakes for transatlantic regulatory differences and for strategies to mediate the conflicts.

The empirical chapters of this book have described key aspects of the dispute, focusing particularly on transatlantic interactions. In Chapters 2 and 3 we described how transatlantic networks of policy actors framed agricultural biotechnology in different ways. They did so to build relationships and in an effort to promote different regulatory standards and frameworks. In Chapters 4 and 5 we examined the regulation of GM crops and GM foods, respectively, to analyse the role of science and transatlantic networks of scientists, in setting regulatory standards. In Chapter 6 we outlined precursors to the US-led complaint against the EU at the World Trade Organization, and the strategies of the main antagonists.

By answering our four narrative questions in the conclusions to Chapters 2–6, we have also begun to analyse many features as governance processes. Our answers have drawn attention to the roles played by contending coalitions of policy actors, operating across the Atlantic and at the international level, in the global governance of agricultural biotechnology. These coalitions framed agricultural biotechnology in competing ways and defined different problems for policy makers. Global governance meant redefining the 'collective problem' that should be the focus of public policy and stakeholder relations. We have also shown that problem-definitions and issue-frames bear upon how potential risks are treated.

In the final chapter of this book, we build further on the earlier analysis to answer the more theoretical questions we raised in Chapter 1 (see particularly Table 1.1). In doing so we draw out key insights with wider relevance, beyond the EU–US conflict over agricultural biotechnology. Global governance is our overarching concern, which we analyse by exploring more specific aspects – collective problems, issue-framing, contending coalitions, standard-setting, regulatory science and so on. For convenience and orientation, we restate our main theoretical questions at the start of each section. These correspond to the ones given in Chapter 1.

Global governance: civil society and collective problems

In Chapter 1 we asked: How did agricultural biotechnology become a governance problem, or a legitimacy problem that required a governance solution? In order to govern GM products, what collective problems have been identified, or how have problems been defined as collective ones?

Transatlantic governance: the NTA, civil society and agbiotech

In Chapter 1 we developed a critical understanding of global governance. To do this we focused on legitimacy problems, which emerged in the late 1990s, but which had their origins in a neoliberal globalisation agenda over the previous decade. The pursuit of this policy agenda weakened earlier forms of political consent (Lipschutz, 1996: 55; citing Gill, 1993: 32–33), provoking resistance which created deep conflicts between governments and civil society. These conflicts in turn created new opportunities for international networks and imperatives for global governance processes, particularly the UN system (Paterson et al., 2003). From this perspective, therefore, global governance involves creating new institutions and processes to accommodate or incorporate critics, and in this way help to restore legitimacy, perhaps on a new basis.

All of the networks discussed in Chapters 2 and 3 owe their existence to the neoliberal policy agenda and transatlantic trade liberalisation. The New Transatlantic Agenda, agreed in 1995, identified 'barriers to transatlantic trade' as the collective problem that EU and US policy makers should focus on, with trade liberalisation as a shared goal that could redefine the transatlantic relationship after the Cold War. The Transatlantic Business Dialogue (TABD), which pre-dated the NTA, helped to define its aims and the overall policy agenda. Its own objective was 'Approved Once, Accepted Everywhere', at least at the transatlantic level, ideally leading to the creation of a New Transatlantic Marketplace. In 1998 the US and EU governments established the Transatlantic Economic Partnership, a network overseen and organised by trade officials in the EU and the US, to promote transatlantic trade liberalisation and to help implement TABD proposals.

We tracked these developments particularly through agricultural biotechnology. In the mid-1990s the TABD identified biotechnology products as a priority area and its members identified pre-market safety assessment as the only regulatory challenge. TABD emphasised the need for a common approach across the Atlantic, and ideally a centralised approval procedure. The liberalisation of trade in biotechnology products was then included on the TEP's agenda. The TEP was designed as a largely technical body and its meetings aimed to identify regulatory differences as a step towards overcoming them. Taking this approach, the TEP intended to conduct a pilot project on simultaneous assessment of a biotechnology product. The US had already done a similar project with Canada as a basis for mutual recognition of safety assessments across that border.

Civil society protests began to challenge the 'free trade' neoliberal agenda in the mid- to late 1990s, through movements widely called 'anti-capitalist' or 'anti-globalisation'. Such protests created the context within which mainstream NGOs could more effectively challenge the NTA–TEP, and especially the close relationship between governments and the TABD. The subsequent legitimacy problem led the US and EU to invite NGOs to establish their own 'transatlantic dialogues' so that they could participate in the NTA–TEP process (see Table 3.1). The TACD and the TAED can therefore be understood as transatlantic governance processes, structuring relations between civil society and the transatlantic trade liberalisation agenda. As some critics warned at the time, 'If NGOs decide to participate . . . they risk contributing to the survival of a project which lacks a popular mandate and could be stopped.' Conversely, the survival of the NTA–TEP may have depended upon such participation and collective self-discipline by NGOs, especially in the agbiotech sector.

Their own 'transatlantic dialogues' created a pressure on NGOs to define shared goals and to agree strategies, even though the views of member organisations differed. Consumer NGOs in the EU and the US, through the Transatlantic Consumer Dialogue, found shared goals in 'consumer rights', such as the 'right to safe products' and the 'right to know and right to choose'. At the same time, however, other issues, where there was less consensus across the Atlantic, were marginalised. In this way the TACD forced consumer groups 'to put on a governance hat', as one US trade official put it. Some TACD members continued to attack the NTA–TEP, thus illustrating tensions within the TACD. Public Citizen, for example, continued their criticism of regulatory harmonisation as a policy agenda for 'levelling down' standards. Many member organisations continued to regard the TACD process with suspicion, particularly as a way for governments to co-opt consumer NGOs into a trade liberalisation process. The TACD therefore played at least two roles at once: it was a transatlantic governance network and the core of a contending policy coalition (see further below).

The case of agricultural biotechnology illustrates the problems and opportunities facing TACD. The 'right to safe products' led TACD to argue for the application of the 'precautionary principle' to GM food safety, something that challenged the TABD's emphasis on 'sound science'. The 'right to know, right to choose' underpinned their demand for labelling of GM foods, even in cases where GM material is no longer detectable. TABD members characterised such labelling as a barrier to trade and as having no scientific basis. However, in the context of the public backlash against GM products in Europe, European politicians and policy makers increasingly accepted these demands. In this way consumer groups provided policy proposals that might help to restore legitimacy, whilst at the same time stimulating EU–US regulatory divergence.

Environmental groups also took part in the NTA–TEP process, but only for a brief period. In 1999 they formed the TAED but there were tensions from the outset. Environmental groups were more antagonistic towards transatlantic trade liberalisation (as compared to TACD members overall), and they saw fewer opportunities to influence it through a transatlantic dialogue. Consequently, when its initial two-year funding ran out, the TAED network disbanded itself. Agricultural biotechnology illustrates this brief history well. TAED included diverse views on GM crops and foods. They were generally more hostile than TACD. TAED members' views were eventually expressed as a demand for proof of safety, something that would never be accommodated in policy, as distinct from consumer demands for stricter safety criteria. Environmental NGOs therefore perceived more opportunities to challenge trade liberalisation and agricultural biotechnology outside TAED.

The EU–US Consultative Forum on Biotechnology was a further experiment in transatlantic governance. It was created to find ways of overcoming conflict around biotechnology, within a shared understanding that government needed to regain public confidence in regulatory frameworks. The Forum included a diverse range of stakeholders; members were selected less as representatives of particular positions and more as mediators of conflict. Although the Forum's final report made some strong recommendations, it was also vague and inconsistent in crucial places. The report served more as a reference point and discursive resource than as a direct influence on policy or means to resolve the conflict. The EC welcomed the Forum report as complementing its own policies and cited it regularly, including in its own defence in the WTO agbiotech dispute. The US likewise welcomed the report, whilst also ignoring any conclusions that challenged US policy. US NGOs used it to criticise their government.

The political shift to the Bush administration left little scope for the Consultative Forum's report to bridge the widening transatlantic gap in relation to agricultural biotechnology. In this new context, the Pew Stakeholder Forum sought ways to govern US domestic conflicts over the regulation of GM products. In part this effort also took place with a view towards enhancing international credibility of US regulation. But this governance initiative foundered because of the contradictory pressures associated with the transatlantic conflict. There was pressure to move towards more stringent and publicly accountable regulatory approaches and safety criteria, particularly in relation to the non-regulation of GM food. At the same time, however, there were fears that change would imply that earlier approaches were deficient, something that was particularly problematic for consumer confidence in products already on the market and for US arguments in the EU–US case at the WTO. The impasse precluded any overall stakeholder consensus on regulatory reform in the US.

Global governance of GM food: redefining the policy problem

The discussion so far has examined global governance as a response to conflicts that accompany trade liberalisation and a neoliberal policy agenda. We can develop this understanding further by examining the role of 'collective problems'. As we discussed in Chapter 1, a functionalist view of global governance suggests that it involves cooperation to deal with collective problems, as if such problems are associated with consensus and self-evident. Policy problems, however, are often associated with conflict and rarely speak for themselves. Some theorists have conceptualised the redefinition of policy problems as 'process management', with problem-definitions expanded or changed through an interactive process encompassing diverse views. One has argued that 'The idea of process management also helps us to grasp the role that regimes can play in deepening or even transforming our understanding of the problems that led to their creation' (Young, 1997: 286). Building on this insight, a more critical understanding of global governance can focus on how stakeholder relations are managed in a legitimacy crisis, and how new problems are defined as collective ones through governance processes, as a way of managing conflict. In Chapter 6 we showed how this happened in the case of GM food, with 'substantial equivalence' being recast partly to regain public confidence in risk assessment.

In the late 1990s agricultural biotechnology was framed in three ways. The pro-agbiotech framing linked it to efficient agriculture, economic growth and benefits to farmers and the environment. Biotechnology members of TABD successfully promoted this framing within government, especially in the NTA and TEP. The anti-agbiotech framing, in contrast, presented the technology as an ominous symbol of economic globalisation and a threat to sustainable agriculture. Product approvals were seen as undemocratic submissions to the US government and multinational companies. Various environmental groups and other critics, particularly in Europe, promoted this view. Mainstream consumer groups, however, presented the third framing. They did not object to the technology in principle but focused instead on improving regulatory frameworks from a consumer rights perspective.

When the potential risks associated with GM foods became a focus for debate, they were elaborated and disputed through these framings. The pro-agbiotech coalition framed GM techniques as more precise than conventional plant-breeding techniques and thus GM food risks as more predictable. Any risks were understood to be readily testable, using tests that could be standardised across countries. The anti-agbiotech coalition framed GM techniques as inherently generating unknown and irreducible risks. Agricultural biotechnology was understood to extend industrial agriculture, something that was already harming health and the environment. Mainstream consumer groups, in contrast, framed the risks as uncertain but reducible: any risks must be (and can be) clarified in the consumer interest. GM food risks were therefore linked to the three main framings in different ways – regulatory efficiency, industrial hazards and consumer rights, respectively.

The three overarching framings constituted the scientific uncertainties around GM food in different ways, with different implications at different times. The pro-agbiotech framing informed early risk assessment and approval procedures in the US and the EU. It also underpinned efforts to harmonise regulatory standards across the Atlantic. The anti-agbiotech framing fundamentally challenged the existing inter-governmental (EU–US) consensus. Greenpeace, for example, argued that application of 'substantial equivalence' would not have protected consumers from the scrapie prion and vCJD; in this way, agbiotech opponents cited the 'mad cow' crisis to draw an analogy with scientific ignorance about GM food. By contrast, mainstream consumer groups accepted that GM foods already on the market were safe but demanded regulatory changes to ensure that this continued to be the case for future products.

As public protest led to commercial and regulatory blockages in Europe, this in turn created pressure to accommodate the mainstream consumer groups. Such accommodation became a way of dealing with the conflict and the legitimacy problems. In this process, the conflict was mediated through risk assessment criteria and regulatory standards. This happened in Europe first, where a new collective problem of 'restoring consumer/public/market confidence' emerged and converged with European expert moves towards more stringent test methods for GM food. Based mainly in Europe, this convergence provided a basis on which to govern the conflict on a national, EU and transatlantic scale. This process also led to a policy/strategic shift by European consumer organisations. In the mid-1990s they had raised doubts about the safety of GM products, especially the Ciba *Bt* maize in 1997, but eventually the mainstream groups no longer questioned the safety of GM food products on the market.

Recasting 'substantial equivalence' in more stringent, flexible and widely acceptable ways facilitated this shift. In effect this opened up risk assessment criteria to being reframed. Various governance processes achieved this reframing. Examples include the EU–US Consultative Forum on Biotechnology (as above) and the Codex Alimentarius Commission's Ad Hoc Intergovernmental Task Force on Foods Derived from Biotechnology. Discussions in these fora also marginalised the criticisms of anti-agbiotech groups, although they pursued their policy agenda, especially to undermine public confidence, in many other fora.

Ultimately 'consumer/public/market confidence' in GM food emerged as the new collective problem that facilitated new common ground between some policy actors. At least in Europe, this collective problem challenged the hegemony of the 'barriers to transatlantic trade' collective problem, which had been emphasised by TABD and taken up by the NTA–TEP. Through this new collective problem, and a new way of framing the issues, stakeholder relations were renegotiated and the conflict was governed. This collective problem did not obviously exist before these interactions, contrary to some political science accounts of governance (cf. Young, 1997). The new Codex standards in particular show how governance results from 'alliances between coalitions in global civil society and the international governance arrangements associated with the UN system' (cf. Lipschutz, 1997: 96).

More generally we can see that a focus on GM food safety helped to separate biophysical risk issues from deeper conflicts over GM food. These deeper concerns – ominous globalisation, trade liberalisation, industrial agriculture – played a central role in the backlash against the technology in Europe. But they were marginalised in the subsequent efforts to govern the conflict. Starting from their own regulatory demands, consumer groups participated in governing the risks of GM products, even though they had not welcomed them in the mid-1990s. At the same time, risk-framings antagonistic to GM food were marginalised, particularly those put forward by environmental protest groups. This happened even when environmental groups participated in relevant governance events and consultations.

Issue-framing: policy making and stakeholder coalitions

In Chapter 1 we asked: In relation to agricultural biotechnology, what role did issue-framing play for actors engaged in the policy process? How did policies for GM crops and foods change?

Contending coalitions framing agricultural biotechnology: beliefs and/or discourses?

Earlier we argued that issue-framing helps to explain relations within contending policy coalitions as well as how coalitions try to influence policy. Sabatier's Advocacy Coalition Framework (ACF), for example, focuses on the beliefs that actors hold. By contrast, Hajer's Discourse Coalition Framework (DCF) emphasises storylines, argument and shared discourse. According to Hajer (1995: 71), these analytical perspectives are incompatible because ' . . . both language and context help to constitute beliefs'. In other words, it must be discourses rather than beliefs that bind actors together in coalitions. Rather than take sides in this theoretical argument, we acknowledged beliefs as relevant but argued that coalitions depend on discourses that condense beliefs (Fischer, 2003). Discourses, therefore, are particularly important for broadening coalitions.

By drawing on Chapters 2 and 3 we can gain further insights into the theoretical challenges involved in understanding policy coalitions through issue-frames. In the conclusions to those chapters we analysed the framing of agricultural biotechnology by the TABD and TACD (compare Tables 2.1, 2.2, 3.2, 3.3). As the tables show, the ACF and the DCF are both useful ways of analysing our case, although for different reasons. The ACF draws attention to the role of beliefs and how specific policy proposals in a given area can be linked to deep core or policy core beliefs. The TACD, for example, have argued that without adequate regulation business activity will tend to ignore consumer rights and be associated with various costs to society. Not surprisingly, therefore, when the TACD outlined their regulatory demands in relation to biotechnology products, they raised a large number of regulatory issues – post-market monitoring, traceability, labelling, time-limited licences, environmental liability and mandatory insurance.

Beyond helping us to understand the regulatory demands of policy coalitions, the ACF also helps us to appreciate relationships within coalitions. Beliefs play an important role in binding actors together within the TABD and TACD (see Chapters 2 and 3). When members of the TABD and TACD were asked about the coherence and functioning of their networks, they regularly referred to something like shared beliefs as an important factor. As a member of the TACD commented, 'People tend to agree on the principles . . . The basis of what we do is still, even though it is not done explicitly, the core consumer principles.' Overall we can make these observations without saying anything about a hierarchy of beliefs, which is an important aspect of the ACF.

As Chapter 1 suggests, the ACF can be challenged by the DCF in various ways. Here we can begin by using DCF to provide additional insights, without entering the debate over how these analytical frameworks relate to each other or which one best explains the coalitions. In the transatlantic debate over GMOs, various storylines have been deployed by the TACD and the TABD (as listed in Tables 2.2 and 3.3). Some key storylines are: 'consumers have a right to make choices about GMOs' – versus 'GMOs will solve environmental and social problems', and 'trade in GMOs will enhance economic growth'. Such arguments have been expressed with discourses such as 'right to know, right to choose' versus 'approved once, accepted everywhere'. We can understand such discourses as condensing beliefs, rather than indicating their irrelevance.

In contrast to the ACF's hierarchy of beliefs, the DCF sees storylines being flexibly combined because there is a 'discursive affinity' between them, not because they go together logically or are consistent with each other at the level of beliefs (Hajer, 1995: 66–7). Thus storylines can be combined simply for tactical or strategic reasons. These arguments draw attention to an important aspect of the GM case. For example, when the TABD argued for a centralised approval process, and that GM products should only need to be approved once in order to be sold in both the EU and the US, it was easy to link this to the argument that science is an objective basis for regulation which applies across borders. In this case there was a discursive affinity between storylines and a strategic reason for combining them. As a similar example, the TACD linked scientific uncertainty with GM food labelling, so that consumers can make their own decisions about risk.

Neither the ACF nor the DCF would suggest that the TABD and TACD are the full extent of policy coalitions, which also involve other organisations or at least key individuals outside. In the agricultural biotechnology policy area, this breadth can be illustrated by the wide range of organisations that took up similar arguments to those deployed by the TACD or TAED. This happened particularly amongst US farmers, as sketched in Chapter 6. For example, the American Corn Growers Association adopted some of the language of NGOs who had been part of the TAED. They celebrated Europe's defence of its sovereignty against the biotechnology industry and economic globalisation. By contrast, the National Corn Growers Association adopted the language of the TABD (and later the US-based AgBiotech Planning Committee) when they blamed EU protectionism for their problems; likewise they counterposed 'science-based regulation' as the solution. These broader policy networks or coalitions can be explained better through shared discourse rather than shared beliefs.

The Consultative Forum presents a more complex example for exploring the role of beliefs and discourses because it involved a diverse range of policy actors but nevertheless produced a consensus document as a final report. Of course, the Consultative Forum was a mediation exercise rather than a policy coalition, and the wording used in the final report included ambiguities that could be interpreted according to incompatible policy views – as the US government did (see below). Nevertheless, TABD and TACD members of the Forum accepted arguments and wordings that apparently conflicted with their coalition's beliefs, especially in the case of the TABD, thus creating an opportunity to build new common discourses. Moreover, participants and the two governments generally welcomed the report as if it were a transatlantic consensus, rather than portraying specific wordings as a 'victory' against opponents.

From the standpoint of ACF, there are three possible explanations for why coalition members appeared to accept wordings inconsistent with their beliefs. First, perhaps deep core beliefs were not involved and only issues at the margins of their belief system were being discussed. Second, perhaps the Forum's final report required members to make statements on issues where previously there had only been strategic silences, and so does not contradict beliefs set out elsewhere. Before 2001, for example, the TABD had not made a clear statement opposing GM food labelling, something the Forum's report raised. Third, it is also possible that Forum members did not contribute TABD or TACD positions because such positions do not exist in individuals but instead distill multiple views. If any of these explanations are true, then the Forum's final report does not challenge the ACF in a significant way because it did not require members to compromise on policy beliefs.

For the DCF the inconsistency between members' views and the Consultative Forum report is less problematic. The DCF's emphasis on argumentation and discourse allows it to explain apparent contradictions with relative ease. Put simply, words can have multiple meanings and this helps a multi-stakeholder group to find a consensus. The DCF also emphasises the generation and combination of discourses, through argument in specific contexts, as a way of overcoming conflicts. Significantly, in the case of the Consultative Forum, members were selected because of their ability to find a compromise. In broad terms, therefore, the DCF is better able to account for the contribution of the EU–US Consultative Forum on Biotechnology.

Changing policy for agbiotech: learning and crisis

The discussion so far helps us to understand how policy coalitions operated across the Atlantic in relation to agricultural biotechnology. We can say that contending coalitions, with business and consumer groups at their core, were held together by shared beliefs that framed the technology in different ways. These beliefs informed policy recommendations, but discursive framings were more important beyond the core of the coalition, especially when members from different coalitions interacted or attracted wider support. Discursive framing helped to enrol additional members into policy coalitions and it allowed apparent consensus to be reached among members of contending coalitions. In the rest of this section we will build on this understanding by exploring more dynamic aspects of policy coalitions.

Chapter 1 outlines how the ACF and the DCF address the issues of policy learning and policy change through crisis. The ACF suggests that policy learning can take place through new experiences, information and analysis; moreover, such learning may lead to new policy recommendations – changes in secondary aspects. The ACF also emphasises that radical changes in policy, which involve changes in core beliefs, may require an external shock to the policy system. As Sabatier (1998: 105) has argued, 'while policy-oriented learning is an important aspect of policy change and can often alter secondary aspects of a coalition's belief system, changes in the policy core aspects of a governmental program require a perturbation in non-cognitive factors external to the subsystem'. In contrast, the DCF argues that policy learning depends on reflexive institutional arrangements. Such arrangements involve the socio-cognitive basis of knowledge and 'can therefore never be based on preconceived problem definitions'. Reflexive practices should 'be oriented towards constructing the social problem' that needs a solution (Hajer, 1995: 285–7).

Transatlantic interactions around agricultural biotechnology give us an opportunity to explore the differences between these theoretical frameworks. A useful starting point is policy responses to the European backlash against biotechnology in the late 1990s. Particularly within Europe, but also at the transatlantic level, policy makers took up many TACD proposals which had previously been kept off the policy agenda. Examples include the need for a precautionary approach to risk assessment and the need for labelling of GM food based on traceability. Policy makers took up these ideas after the backlash partly as a way of managing the conflict. As a result some TACD arguments gained greater attention in official procedures – at the expense of those being made by the TABD.

These headline developments appear to underline the value of the ACF, given that dramatic changes in policy required a shock to the system. In this case the EU embarked on a series of regulatory measures that many feared or claimed were illegal under international trade law. It is not clear, however, that the processes identified by the ACF were actually operating. Shock and crisis are important in the ACF because they can lead to fundamental changes in core beliefs, coalitions and policies. Sabatier has referred to a process similar to 'religious conversion'. In the GM crops and foods case, however, it is not clear that widespread changes of beliefs happened.

Rather we see a necessary response by policy makers and politicians to manage conflict, a process in which discourse clearly played an important role. 'Over-regulation' had been attacked as unfairly and unscientifically stigmatising agbiotech, yet more stringent and precautionary regulation was later accepted as measures necessary for public confidence. Precaution and informed consumer choice were previously counterposed to market integration, yet later those discourses were linked as complementary. Indeed, the EU developed a traceability and labelling regime, partly in the name of protecting the internal market in food, even though it complicated transatlantic trade. These new linkages indicate that the DCF might have more explanatory value.

We can explore the ACF and the DCF further by examining two networks where policy learning and change may have taken place – the TEP and the Consultative Forum. For the TEP the framing of the policy problem was relatively fixed – 'barriers to transatlantic trade'. At least at the outset, its task was understood as a technical one involving trade and regulatory officials and government scientists. They set out to learn from each other how to regulate GMOs in order to overcome barriers to trade. Safety assessment was their primary focus. The Consultative Forum, in contrast, had a much more open brief: the need to find a way to overcome the EU–US trade conflict and public distrust of agricultural biotechnology. The Consultative Forum was understood to be a discursive body, with relatively greater scope to redefine 'the problem'.

From an ACF perspective, the TEP would facilitate policy learning, or at least would provide a technical basis for such learning, while avoiding contentious policy issues. As Fischer (2003: 109) points out, the ACF suggests that 'Scientific debate based on the exchange and comparison of objective findings rather than political deliberation is the means for creating policy consensus.' Sabatier views policy learning as something that is linked to technical expertise of the kind that was involved in the TEP. The Consultative Forum, on the other hand, simply put together actors with wildly different ways of framing the issue, without asking them to engage with technical information. So the latter could not easily result in policy learning, from an ACF perspective. From a DCF perspective, however, the Consultative Forum would be the more likely location for policy learning because it had some scope to explore new problem definitions; in this sense, its final report represents policy learning.

Also at issue, however, are the criteria for what counts as policy learning. As Fischer points out, what comes to be recognised and accepted as 'learning' is a political issue. 'In short, learning for one person may not be learning for another person with a different political ideology,' he argues (Fischer, 2003: 111). Indeed, the US government largely ignored the Consultative Forum's final report. Likewise US officials raised doubts about the value of the TEP process if it was reduced to a mere 'talking shop', unable to deliver concrete results by reconciling regulatory differences. This suggests that the US government officials did not regard the Consultative Forum as a process that would lead to the type of learning that was required. For the EC, by contrast, experience led to policy learning that included complex issues beyond the scientific and technical.

Before moving on, we can now point to a bridge between theoretical perspectives. In this section we built on our earlier discussion of transatlantic and global governance and the definition of collective problems by exploring the role of issue-framing and policy coalitions. As we noted, some accounts of governance acknowledge multiple perspectives on problems but at the same time assume the existence of a collective problem that could be separate from the interactions of policy actors. In the case of GM food, however, we showed that a new collective problem was formulated as a way of dealing with the conflict. We have now linked that analysis with issue-framing and policy coalitions. As a result we are now much clearer about the processes involved, particularly the roles played by beliefs and discourses in policy coalitions, and the dynamics of policy learning. This illustrates the value of linking Political Science and Policy Studies literature.

Standard-setting: regulatory harmonisation and judicial review

In Chapter 1 we asked: In the case of agricultural biotechnology, how have standard-setting and trade liberalisation shaped each other? How have civil society groups used trade liberalisation and trade conflict to stimulate higher regulatory standards for agbiotech products?

Trading up and agricultural biotechnology

As we outlined in Chapters 1 and 3, the relationship between trade liberalisation and regulatory standards has been controversial in recent years.
Debate has focused particularly on whether trade liberalisation is associated with higher or lower standards. Critics suspect that it leads to a
'levelling down'. We have argued, however, that this focus is problematic
because it reifies trade liberalisation as an independent variable; trade liberalisation is seen as something separate, which has effects elsewhere. To avoid
this assumption, we asked questions that open up the black box of trade
liberalisation. For example: How does trade liberalisation take on institutional forms that favour those who advocate or oppose higher standards?
How are institutional forms related to processes of issue-framing and the
definition of collective problems? We are now in a position to answer such
questions.

A trade liberalisation agenda framed the early regulation of biotechnology
products in the mid-1990s. In Chapter 2, for example, we outlined the roles
played by the TABD and the TEP as they promoted regulatory harmonisation across the Atlantic. As part of the New Transatlantic Agenda, these
groups planned to undertake a pilot project on the simultaneous assessment
of a GM product in the US and the EU in the late 1990s. This would have
been an important step towards regulatory harmonisation and may have led
ultimately to a single centralised regulatory procedure. Similarly, although
at the international level, Chapter 5 drew attention to the role of substantial
equivalence in regulatory harmonisation for GM food in the early 1990s. By
the mid-1990s both the EU and the US had included this concept in their
GM food regulations and in this way they created the basis of a harmonised
regulatory regime across the Atlantic. In practice, however, these early
efforts to promote trade liberalisation helped instead to provoke intense
conflict.

The 'trading up' perspective can help us to understand how trade liberalisation and trade conflict have related to regulatory standards. As mentioned
in Chapter 1, Vogel argues that trade liberalisation can create opportunities
for NGOs and others to campaign for higher regulatory standards. Such
pressures may ultimately lead to trading up, namely the adoption of higher
regulatory standards in a context of trade liberalisation. As we outlined,
other scholars have already indicated that such influences have been important for regulatory standards in the case of agricultural biotechnology.
According to Princen (2002: 259–60), for example, trading up has certainly
happened within the EU in part through the influence of NGOs. Young
(2001) extends this point by arguing that there has been a 'transmission of
political mobilisation' across the Atlantic. With this phrase Young means
that European NGOs created greater opportunities for US ones, who in turn
influenced regulatory standards in the US; Young argues that this can be
understood as trading up.

Drawing on our own research, we can extend these observations by analysing the links between trade liberalisation, trade conflict and standard-setting in more subtle ways. As outlined in Chapter 3, the TABD and the NTA–TEP became a focus for NGO criticism in the late 1990s. Multi-sectoral trade liberalisation was a central part of the 1995 New Transatlantic Agenda, and its call for 'science-based' regulation could have been used to justify downward harmonisation of regulatory standards across the Atlantic. As a result NGOs feared that the TABD and the NTA–TEP could be used to 'level down' regulatory standards, or at least to limit higher standards in the EU and elsewhere. They criticised the privileged position of business in the NTA–TEP process and their own exclusion, though they did not necessarily seek to participate within a trade liberalisation agenda. As shown in Chapter 3, in 1998 some critics cited efforts to harmonise regulations for agricultural biotechnology to illustrate the wider threat from trade liberalisation.

As Vogel (1997: 61–2) notes, 'Any effort to harmonize regulations in . . . visible and emotional areas is likely to prove highly divisive, if not fruitless.' Moreover, publicly sensitive areas, such as food and environmental safety, create more opportunities than others for NGOs. Drawing on our case, we have further evidence to support these observations. European consumer and environmental groups, which had already raised concerns about trade liberal-isation and the NTA–TEP process, played a central role in raising public concern about agricultural biotechnology in the late 1990s. They also successfully linked these issues. Along with social movements, they encour-aged the public backlash that eventually led to the unofficial *de facto* moratorium. As part of a campaign strategy, European anti-agbiotech groups targeted US shipments of maize and soybean, partly to highlight the threat posed by trade liberalisation, which was framed as European surrender to the US. As well as a specific development to be contested, therefore, agricultural biotechnology was attacked as an example of neoliberal economic globalisa-tion which should also be resisted for various reasons – undermining government sovereignty, removing consumer choice, polluting the environ-ment and so on.

How did these developments influence regulatory standards? In essence, a controversial technology was linked with a controversial trade liberalisation agenda and actual transatlantic shipments of biotechnology products. When followed by the backlash in Europe, the EU Council's moratorium and the commercial boycott of GM products, this context provided a resource for critics of safety claims. The regulatory standards associated with biotech-nology products then became a focus for the conflict and a way of governing stakeholder relations. Chapters 4 and 5 show how critics were able to chal-lenge the implicit or explicit standards that underlay regulatory decisions and product approvals. There were similarities in the areas of GM crop and GM foods but there were also differences due to the different pressure groups, regulatory agencies and treaty frameworks involved. We will briefly consider each in turn.

The emergence of tighter regulatory standards for *Bt* maize is discussed in Chapter 4 and summarised in the table at the end of that chapter. We see more stringent regulatory standards emerging in the areas of normative judgements, risk assessment and risk management. These changes are particularly clear in the US, and analogous pressures for change were emerging in the EU's new regulatory procedures by 2004. In some cases, criticisms of low standards had their origins in Europe and they crossed to the US via transatlantic networks of critical scientists and NGOs. Other pressures leading to higher standards in the US had more domestic origins. All criticisms were taken more seriously because of the politically charged situation and the EU–US trade conflict over GM maize. In this context, scientific criticisms of safety claims and critics of lax regulations in the US got more attention in expert procedures. As the trade conflict between the EU and the US intensified, and as the divergence of their regulatory systems became clearer on the global stage, there was also increased pressure in the US to ensure that its domestic regulatory framework was scientifically robust and internationally defensible.

Tighter regulatory standards in relation to GM foods emerged through more formal and international processes. As shown in Chapter 5, substantial equivalence was recast in at least three ways. First, it was implicitly redefined through extra phrases in official documents. Second, it was re-interpreted and risk assessment procedures began to engage with more uncertainties and require more evidence of safety than before, especially in Europe. Third, the concept was demoted in EU regulatory procedures. Most recently the concept has been softened further, and some proponents now refer to the 'comparative approach' instead. Many of these changes emerged through formal interactions between jurisdictions. For example, trading up happened within the EU, when judgements or proposals by individual member states were adopted more widely as EU-level standards. At the international level, NGOs played an important role in discussions around the Codex Alimentarius Commission, which eventually agreed a document outlining appropriate test methods for GM foods.

Our analysis has linked changes in regulatory standards with trade conflict – not trade liberalisation per se. Although Vogel's case studies often involve conflicts around trade barriers, his theory of trading up largely focuses on trade liberalisation. In the case of agricultural biotechnology, however, trade liberalisation played an unexpected, contradictory role; transatlantic trade has remained an elusive goal for most GM products (apart from soya). Put simply, our case shows that the TABD and the NTA–TEP process sought to establish common regulatory standards across the Atlantic in order to avoid or overcome trade barriers for biotechnology products. That process inadvertently created a conflict linking both issues. Using the conflict, civil society groups sought more stringent standards, which would establish a more transparent and publicly accountable basis for transatlantic trade. Our study therefore suggests that regulatory standard-setting processes can shape the terms for trade liberalisation in practice; this reverses the relationship implied in Vogel's approach.

Thus the 'trading up' perspective draws our attention to dynamics that might otherwise remain hidden. In undertaking this kind of analysis, however, we have extended the concept in novel ways (as did Princen, 2003). As Chapter 1 shows, 'trading up' literature tends to focus on explicit and formal standards, such as product specifications or the 'burden of proof' for risk or safety. Much of our analysis has focused on a less formal standard-setting processes and regulatory standards which are often implicit. In such situations it is a methodological challenge simply to establish what a regulatory standard is, and a further challenge to establish if it changed, 'upwards' or 'downwards'. To help us do this we have linked standard-setting with regulatory science (discussed below).

Rationality and legitimacy: international agreements and the conflict over GM products

In Chapter 6 we focused on how the EU–US conflict over agricultural biotechnology is being contested and negotiated at the international level. That chapter drew attention to overlapping international agreements and rules in the form of the Biosafety Protocol, the WTO agreements and the standards of the Codex Alimentarius Commission. As it also highlighted, the EU used the US-led agbiotech dispute to link two issues: (1) the role of science and risk assessment in judging trade disputes; (2) the legitimacy problems faced by the WTO in association with its judicial review function (as discussed in Chapter 1). We can explore these issues further here by drawing on the analytical perspectives of Isaac (2002) and Scott (2004).

As outlined in Chapter 1, Isaac (2002) argues that all international agreements have two functions. Their economic function is to improve the efficiency of the market; their social function is to ensure that the results of market activity are consistent with public expectations that exist within jurisdictions. These two 'rationalities' operate in all international agreements. Beyond this schema, Isaac also points out that international agreements understand science and technology differently, and in ways contingent upon their relative basis in economic and social rationalities. For example, international agreements based on economic rationality tend to view new technologies and related products positively and see science as something that can provide an objective risk assessment, which therefore should be accepted by all countries. International agreements based on social rationality, however, favour more sceptical views about the benefits of new technologies and the ability of science to predict risks.

Using these ideas Isaac (2002: 27) distinguishes between international agreements of different kinds, including those involved in the global regulation of agricultural biotechnology. The WTO's SPS Agreement, for example, aims to 'facilitate' economic integration and seeks to achieve this by coordinating national standards within international ones agreed by organisations such as the Codex Alimentarius Commission. The SPS Agreement also presumes the ability of science to determine product risks and it echoes the 'sound science' view endorsed by the US. Here we see economic and scientific rationality working together. The Biosafety Protocol, in contrast, aims 'to develop a global . . . social construct through cooperative, *ex ante* coordination of domestic economic and social regulations' (Isaac, 2002: 27). It includes criteria which license jurisdictions to shape economic integration to favour public goods, for example on the basis of uncertainty about risks. In this case there is an endorsement of precaution, a framework supported by the EU. Here we see a greater influence of social-rationality and scepticism regarding risk assessment.

We can extend this discussion by focusing on the EU–US conflict over biotechnology products, particularly by drawing on the perspective of Scott (2004). She identified the WTO's democratic dilemma as follows: how should the preferences within a jurisdiction be weighed against a country's obligations to those beyond its borders? The WTO is required to judge the agbiotech dispute, in a way that involves science and risk assessment, but its judgement might be perceived as anti-democratic if it overrules decisions that have popular support within the EU. As Scott (2004: 9–10) has argued: '[the WTO's] judicial review function . . . bites also in respect of legislative acts, including those adopted by democratically elected parliaments within the Member States . . . This fact of judicial review at the level of the WTO presents a profound challenge to the legitimacy of this organization from the perspective of democracy.'

All these issues arose in the EU–US dispute over biotechnology products. In the late 1990s the backlash against GM food threatened the food trade and market stability at the global level. 'Market efficiency' then had to be restored based on new socio-political arrangements and technical criteria, and these emerged at the Codex Alimentarius Commission. Subsequently, however, the EU–US dispute at the WTO raised further problems. The transatlantic trade conflict became a global contest over legitimate models for the regulation of agri-biotechnology, especially as many civil society groups supported the EU's precautionary approach against US government policy, and especially against its WTO case. In the formal proceedings, the US argued narrowly and legalistically that the EU had a 'moratorium' which was illegal on procedural grounds and contradicted EU expert advice. In response the EC played upon the WTO's doubts about its legitimacy in ruling against trade restrictions that have popular support. It framed EU procedural delays as a sovereignty issue. The EC also emphasised expert disagreements, uncertainties about risk, the role of risk regulation in deciding societal futures and thus the importance of jurisdictional sovereignty.

In this way, the economic and social rationalities within global rules were the focus for conflict, which the WTO's judicial review had to address in some way. Playing on the WTO's legitimacy problem, the EC's arguments successfully created greater scope for the Dispute Panel to consider expert disagreements, indicating scientific uncertainties and justifying EU procedural delays over biotechnology products. Commission staff had previously described this strategy in reverse: 'uncertainty indicates evidence showing credible scientific disagreements among experts' (Christoforou, 2003: 208). On this basis, the Panel could modestly judge only whether restrictions had a basis in 'plausible scientific alternatives' to the safety claims of EU-level expert committees (Christoforou, 2000).

In this way, social rationality potentially reframed economic rationality. Even WTO procedures could create opportunities to reconcile them, though the US argument tried to keep them separate, for example by questioning the relevance of the Biosafety Protocol. The SPS agreement had been negotiated mainly as an instrument of trade liberalisation; it was expected to favour this agenda and generally does so. However, societal conflict over GM products provided a context out of which WTO judgements might allow greater scope for a jurisdiction to delay decisions. Such longer timescales would be needed to develop regulatory frameworks, to investigate scientific uncertainties and to clarify regulatory standards in more publicly accountable ways.

Here again we see a way that economic and social rationalities might be linked. Such linkages became more compelling in the agbiotech case, which intensified the WTO's democratic dilemma and underlying legitimacy problems. Markets are embedded in normative constructs, so the economic perspective is meaningless if separated from social realities, according to Isaac (2002: 13). Moreover, European regulation was creating new social realities for agbiotech, so the WTO dispute became a global test case for justifying these within international trade law.

Regulatory science: the science-policy boundary and risk assessment

In Chapter 1 we asked: In relation to agricultural biotechnology, how have policy agendas and scientific uncertainties been linked? What is the relationship between the context and content of regulatory science in the case of GM products?

GM food: links between science and policy

As Chapter 5 shows, the concept of substantial equivalence played a central role in demarcating the boundary between science and policy in relation to GM food risks. The concept emerged in 1993 as the outcome of an inter-governmental expert process organised by the OECD. An earlier FAO/ WHO (1991) expert consultation concluded that GM foods could be compared with their non-GM counterparts in order to establish safety – if more rigorous data were obtained on the composition of conventional foods. However, as we have shown, the OECD drew on that report in selective ways. For example, business argued and regulators accepted that substantial equivalence could be demonstrated largely through tests of physical/chemical composition, without the earlier caveat about inadequate data. Thus substantial equivalence limited demands for additional scientific information; it also avoided arguments over methodological problems associated with other types of tests, such as testing whole foods on animals.

In the mid-1990s, therefore, the concept of substantial equivalence played several roles. First, it implied that risk assessment of GM food was entirely separate from policy, almost as if substantial equivalence were itself a 'scientific principle', although officials never explicitly made this claim. Second, by focusing on some safety tests rather than others, the concept justified minimal expert scrutiny and facilitated safety claims. (The concept also achieved this rhetorically by suggesting that GM foods could be readily shown as similar to non-GM foods.) Third, the concept was a vehicle for standardising risk assessment criteria within and across countries. This served the goals of efficient and harmonised regulation, by avoiding duplication or divergence of safety tests, and ultimately trade liberalisation (cf. Newell, 2003). Based on these observations we can say that in the early to mid-1990s we see an effort to scientise policy, or, conversely, to depoliticise policy through science.

Such scientisation had unstable foundations, which were undermined from the mid-1990s onwards, particularly in Europe. When the European controversy over agricultural biotechnology erupted, the concept of substantial equivalence became a prominent target for attack. Critics ridiculed it as a careless, deceptive and pseudo-scientific concept. They argued that it played down the novelty of GM food, facilitated the avoidance of risk assessment, and led to safety claims being accepted too readily. In broad terms, and drawing again on Chapter 1, we can understand these protests as opposing the use of 'scientific rationality' to conceal political choices as technical ones. This development in relation to GM food was similar to previous controversies involving technologies and risk (cf. Nelkin, 1979). As an analogy, 1970s movements against nuclear power had targeted the same anti-democratic tendency.

At least in Europe, protest undermined the public legitimacy of risk assessment procedures and the effort to scientise policy. Drawing further on Chapter 1, we can say that the GM food controversy in Europe eventually stimulated a scientification process, instead of scientisation. Implementation of substantial equivalence had emphasised tests of physical/chemical compositional as a basis for comparison with conventional equivalents, but these were now under attack as insufficient to establish safety. Critics pointed to inadequate baseline information about conventional foods, inconsistent criteria and thus deceptive comparisons.

The 1991 WHO/FAO expert consultation had originally foreseen these limitations, but the 1993 OECD report largely ignored them. It was only in the context of public controversy that available tests and knowledge were recast as being near the frontier of science (cf. Weingart, 1999).

For EU governments, the scientification process meant that risk assessment procedures became more dependent upon scientific progress. Scientific developments, however, produced an abundance of new knowledge, which was in turn open to diverse expert interpretations. Interpretations by every side were vulnerable to the accusation that they based risk assessment on political rather than scientific criteria.

This scientification process, therefore, also created more opportunities to politicise science. In this way the discussion in Chapter 1 is also confirmed by our case. Policy actors on all sides of the debate became engaged in an adversarial competition involving expert claims, the latest research results, new test methods and any weaknesses in inconvenient results. For example, as mentioned above and discussed in Chapter 5, the concept of substantial equivalence had been used to bypass the methodological difficulties associated with testing whole foods on animals. When Arpad Pusztai later gained funds to improve such methods, his unexpected results were used to question the safety of GM foods, leading to polarisation between international expert networks supporting and criticising his test methods. Consumer groups sponsored their own expert reports challenging inconsistencies and weaknesses in the test data submitted by companies. This illustrates how the increased dependency on new knowledge can create more opportunities to politicise science.

In the case of GM food, therefore, we see an early scientisation of policy, followed by a scientification of politics and politicisation of science. Most importantly, the public backlash against agricultural biotechnology in Europe, and the related public controversy, broke the original link between science (risk assessment) and policy in the area of GM foods, while challenging the status of safety claims as 'science'. In time the previous safety assumptions were treated as uncertainties that warranted greater scrutiny and additional knowledge. In these ways, the boundary between science and policy was subtly shifted to encompass more issues than before within policy, rather than science (cf. Jasanoff, 1987).

This boundary shift implied a legitimate scope for non-specialists, that is an expertise broader than those who had taken part in the earlier OECD discussions on substantial equivalence. Their perspectives converged with many scientists who were anyway pressing for more stringent standards of evidence for safety. There remains a practical tension: between re-establishing an 'objective' scientific basis for risk assessment of GM food versus leaving open the criteria for further deliberation with stakeholders as a way of dealing with the conflict. This tension continues around pressures to improve or devise scientific tests (see Table 5.1).

The GM food case also reveals dynamic links between problem-redefinitions, issue-framings and regulatory standards. In the case of GM food, as we noted above, risk issues were initially framed by commercial approval, regulatory harmonisation and trade liberalisation in the early 1990s. However, civil society groups, using the European anti-agbiotech backlash to influence expert discussions, challenged this risk-framing. Recent regulatory changes have responded to this challenge and increased the regulatory burden on producers of GM foods, as our analysis has shown. Risk assessment criteria and regulatory standards mediated the conflict between different policy agendas. This analysis illustrates the value of linking the concept of governance with regulatory science.

Bt *maize: context and content of regulatory science*

In Chapter 4 we described changes in US and EU regulatory standards in relation to *Bt* maize. These changes illustrate dynamic links between the context and content of regulatory science. Before the public controversy over agbiotech and the subsequent trade conflict, there had been little critical discussion of regulatory science and few opportunities for critics to generate such a debate. In this context regulators ignored or denied relevant unknowns about the potential risks associated with *Bt* maize. Later, however, transatlantic networks of critical scientists and NGOs used the public controversy in Europe to generate a critical debate about test methods and risk assessment criteria. By citing novel hazards, they raised concerns about the normative and scientific basis of regulation. In this new context, regulatory officials engaged with more critical views and in some cases accommodated them. They did this partly by changing the regulatory standards associated with risk assessment and risk management.

This case illustrates, therefore, what can happen when the relatively 'private' world of regulatory science is opened up to greater public scrutiny (see Chapter 1 and Irwin et al., 1997). In the case of *Bt* maize, the biotechnology industry made various optimistic assumptions which were initially taken up by regulators. Critical scientists and NGOs challenged these and turned them into issues requiring further research and/or control measures. This happened in three areas – normative judgements, risk assessment and risk management – often in interlinked ways (see Table 4.1). Further research clarified some issues but was also interpreted as highlighting additional sources of uncertainty. There were further arguments about whether experiments adequately simulated conditions in agricultural fields. In such ways, early 'science-based' judgements were contested as lax, thus opening up the standard-setting process.

Contextual features of this case include new technology, public controversy, trade conflict and transatlantic networks of critical scientists and NGOs. In particular, following its critique of regulatory standards in Europe, the EcoStrat consultancy was commissioned by an NGO based in the US to scrutinise the US EPA's risk assessments of *Bt* maize. The EPA's Scientific Advisory Panel then translated such criticisms into more direct pressure on the EPA and companies. In this way US critics appropriated European arguments and used them to shape regulation of *Bt* maize in the US.

The *Bt* maize example also illustrates the relationship between the composition of expert advisory bodies and regulatory science (Jasanoff, 1990; Irwin et al., 1997). Starting in the late 1990s, US expert bodies began to include more critical scientists who took up arguments from NGOs and European scientists. In particular they challenged the EPA's double standards applied to evidence of risk and safety. More critical peer review arose from the changing context of the risk debate and the changing composition of expert bodies. In the EU system some member states and their expert advisors played a peer-review role that was functionally similar to that of US expert bodies.

Drawing on Chapter 4, we analysed links between funding sources and standards of regulatory science. In both the US and the EU, regulatory conflicts led to more publicly funded risk research in relation to *Bt* maize, which favoured more academic scientists. This differed from earlier research that had been mostly conducted or funded by companies, and standards became more stringent in various ways. For example, the EPA began to evaluate a wider range of risks, whilst seeking more sensitive and reliable test methods. As a result, public funding enhanced both the breadth and quality of regulatory science.

More generally the *Bt* maize case illustrates the mutual shaping of the context and content of regulatory science. Content influenced the context, particularly as critics of agricultural biotechnology used new evidence of risk to undermine optimistic assumptions about safety. This led to changes in expert judgements and regulatory science more generally. Following the public backlash in Europe and the transatlantic trade conflict, the new context influenced the content of regulatory science in various ways, particularly by generating more plural forms of advisory expertise and introducing more publicly funded research. More stringent agri-environmental norms and novel methods of testing more complex uncertainties were also outcomes. These dynamics illustrate the hybrid character of regulatory science, linking its content and context (Irwin et al., 1997).

The *Bt* maize case also allows us to build a bridge between analytical perspectives on regulatory science and trading up. The latter drew our attention to contextual influences, particularly the conflict over trade liberalisation, which offered new opportunities for transatlantic networks of civil society actors. They used and transformed that regulatory context, in turn influencing the content of regulatory science. Moreover, European changes in regulatory science had a global significance; the EU played an indirect but central role – as a source of higher standards to be adopted, influenced or anticipated by various policy actors elsewhere.

Conclusion

In this chapter we developed our analysis of the EU–US conflict over agricultural biotechnology by exploring the theoretical perspectives and questions introduced in Chapter 1. Our conclusion will summarise the overall argument of the book by addressing two important questions: In what sense is the US–EU conflict over agricultural biotechnology a transatlantic one? How can the origins and trajectory of the conflict be explained?

The commercialisation of GM crops and foods led to a legitimacy crisis for European policy makers in the late 1990s. In 1999, in an effort to deal with this crisis, European politicians imposed an unofficial *de facto* moratorium on the approval of new GM products. This in turn created a transatlantic trade conflict: US maize shipments, which might have contained 'illegal' GM maize, could not enter the European market. In May 2003 the US finally initiated a multi-country complaint at the World Trade Organization, after years of threatening to do so.

The EU–US conflict over GM products has been widely attributed to regulatory differences across the Atlantic. We are told by some commentators, for example, that the US bases its regulation on 'sound science', while EU restrictions and delays have accommodated the fears of an 'irrational public'. Others have argued that the US government builds safety claims on scientific ignorance and force-feeds the world with GM food, while the EU defends precaution and democratic sovereignty. These arguments are very different, but they have in common their emphasis on transatlantic differences.

Most academic accounts also contrast the US and EU systems. Although this work is more subtle, by focusing on the internal characteristics of jurisdictions, it has nevertheless ignored important transatlantic interactions. In this book we have gone beyond such accounts by analysing the biotechnology conflict through contending coalitions operating and interacting across the Atlantic. Policy actors in business, government and civil society have cooperated in transatlantic networks in an effort to shape regulatory policy for GM products, and coalitions have often framed the policy issues in antagonistic ways.

In the 1990s the EU and the US cooperated to remove 'barriers to transatlantic trade' and thus promote their shared policy agenda of transatlantic trade liberalisation. Biotechnology products were an important part of this agenda. The Transatlantic Business Dialogue and the Transatlantic Economic Partnership formed a policy coalition based on shared beliefs and discourses. Examples include 'approved once, accepted everywhere', at least in principle, and 'sound science' as a basis for product approval. This coalition assumed that avoiding trade barriers was a largely technical exercise and its members focused on overcoming differences in risk assessment criteria.

In practice EU–US efforts to harmonise regulations across the Atlantic had unanticipated consequences, particularly by creating a context in which activists could generate a European backlash against agricultural biotechnology. Opponents turned GM products into a symbol of political-economic globalisation, which threatened to undermine democracy and consumer rights. As the trade conflict began, members of the TABD–TEP coalition warned that the US could bring a WTO case against EU regulatory delays and/or GM labelling rules. These threats backfired, by increasing political pressure in Europe against product approvals and in favour of more stringent rules.

In this book a critical understanding of governance has illuminated how 'collective problems' were redefined to deal with legitimacy problems – in this case, as a way of mediating conflicts between contending coalitions of policy actors. The problem of 'barriers to transatlantic trade' was displaced or supplanted by a new collective problem of 'consumer/public confidence'. Through a convergence with scientists who were seeking more stringent regulatory standards, consumer groups were drawn into a broader policy coalition which could potentially legitimise GM food as safe, even though they did not welcome such products. At the same time, more antagonistic views towards agricultural biotechnology and trade liberalisation were marginalised from official procedures, though the groups that held them could still pursue oppositional agendas in the wider society, especially in Europe.

This governance process helped to manage the conflict over agricultural biotechnology and this was achieved partly through changes in regulatory frameworks and standards. For GM foods, for example, consumer groups emphasised the 'right to know, right to choose', as a basis on which to demand traceability and labelling. They also argued for the application of the 'precautionary principle' and more stringent risk assessment criteria. Through various governance arrangements, such as the Transatlantic Consumer Dialogue and the Codex Alimentarius Commission, consumer groups were able to reshape regulation along these lines in Europe and at the global level. To do this they were also able to take advantage of the transatlantic conflict.

In the US, where there were fewer obvious legitimacy problems, NGOs nevertheless had some success in pressing for more stringent environmental standards for *Bt* insecticidal maize in US EPA procedures. Implicit in the changes was the need to maintain international credibility for US safety claims and its expert status. US NGOs were also, therefore, able to take advantage of the transatlantic conflict. In relation to GM food the transatlantic conflict was used to exert contradictory pressures, ultimately resulting in a continuation of the US FDA's non-regulation policy. With the US involved in a dispute at the WTO, some US policy actors feared that statutory regulation would imply weaknesses in the existing procedures.

At the empirical and methodological levels, therefore, this analysis shows how intra-jurisdictional conflicts and regulatory frameworks have been shaped by transatlantic interactions. In the US these interactions encouraged more stringent environmental standards for some GM crops but a policy impasse over the non-regulation of GM food. In the EU they led to more stringent criteria and rules, partly as a reaction against the US. All these pressures converged at the WTO during the dispute over biotechnology products. These dynamics and outcomes cannot be explained simply by focusing on the internal characteristics of the EU or the US.

This book has also made a broader theoretical contribution by exploring governance in several ways. Governance has meant redefining policy problems as collective ones, as a means to gain legitimacy for regulatory procedures and frameworks. To understand policy coalitions and the definition of collective problems, we focused on 'issue-framing', thus drawing on post-empiricist approaches to policy analysis. To analyse the relationship between trade liberalisation and regulatory standards, we extended available studies of 'trading up' regulatory standards. To explain links between risk assessment and regulatory standards, we extended available studies of 'regulatory science'. In these ways we have gained insights by linking three academic areas: Political Science, Policy Studies and Science and Technology Studies.

Notes

4 Environmental risks of GM crops: the case of *Bt* maize

1 A number of factors help to explain the wider adoption of *Bt* maize as compared with chemical control methods. Insecticides are not very effective after the corn borer larvae have tunnelled inside the plant. Also, corn borers are not a pest in all areas every year, and so chemical control methods are not always used. *Bt* within a plant acts against corn borers in the stalk; because the seeds are planted at the beginning of a season, they do not simply respond to the emergence of a problem during the season.

2 '... any recommendation of refuge size must be based partly on scientific evaluations and partly on a consensus of perceived risk... Because of the uncertainty surrounding several of the model parameters, other interpretations and recommendations could be made' (ILSI, 1999: 6).

3 This experiment involved feeding larvae, in the lab, on milkweed plants that had previously been placed within, and at varying distances from, a *Bt* maize crop shedding pollen.

5 Health risks of GM foods: the concept of 'substantial equivalence'

1 It is worth noting that at this time NGOs unsuccessfully proposed that the FDA should classify GM foods as food additives and on this basis require a risk assessment (Krimsky and Wrubel, 1996: 106–7).

6 The WTO agbiotech dispute as a global contest

1 The US's first written submission was presented to WTO dispute panel on 21 April 2004. The EU defended its position in its first written submission on 17 May 2004. For our purposes, the oral statements made on 2 June 2004 are more interesting (USTR, 2004a; CEC, 2004b). These were an opportunity to refine key points and to challenge the strategy being adopted by the other side. The rest of this chapter emphasises those submissions, with quotes from some others.

References

ABPC – AgBiotech Planning Committee (2001) 'Letter to a US Senator', 18 December 2001. Available HTTP: <http://www.ncga.com> (accessed on 29 April 2005).

ABSTC (2001) 'Amended revised response to EPA's data call-in notice concerning the potential for adverse effects of *Bt* corn on non-target lepidopterans', Agricultural Biotechnology Stewardship Technical Committee (Non-Target Organism Subcommittee) and Novigen Sciences, Inc., 22 June.

ACGA – American Corn Growers Association (2003) 'Statement of policy', February. Available HTTP: <http://www.acga.org/> (accessed 5 June 2005).

ACNFP – Advisory Committee on Novel Foods and Processes (1997) *Annual Report 1996*, London: Ministry of Agriculture, Fisheries and Food (MAFF).

—(1998) *Annual Report 1997*, London: Ministry of Agriculture, Fisheries and Food (MAFF).

—(2001) *Annual Report 2000*, London: Ministry of Agriculture, Fisheries and Food (MAFF).

Afonso, M. (2002) 'The relationship with other international agreements', in C. Bail, R. Falkner and H. Marquard (eds) *The Cartagena Protocol on Biosafety*, London: RIIA/Earthscan. 423–437.

Agence Europe (1997) Commission considers that the firmness of the European Parliament resolution on GM maize is unwarranted, 9 April.

—(2002) 'Parliament strengthens labelling rules on GM food but avoid upsetting balance', 3 July.

AGPM – Association G n rale des Producteurs du Ma s (2005) 'Une production durable, respecteuse de l'environnement'. Available HTTP: <http://www.agpm.com> (accessed 10 August 2005).

AgraFood Biotech (2001) 'US–EU concord on GM regulation to be discarded, says prof', *AgraFood Biotech*, 50 (7 March): 14–15.

—(2002) 'GM crop approvals no nearer in EU', *AgraFood Biotech*, 92 (29 October): 15–16.

Amicus Coalition (2004) 'Information submitted to the panel by non-parties: European Communities – measures affecting the approval and marketing of biotech products (DS291, DS292, DS293)', Geneva, 27 May. Available HTTP: <http://www.genewatch.org/> (accessed 5 June 2005).

Amijee, F. (2002) 'Harmonising substantial equivalence – an industry task towards plant specific consensus documents', in H. Gaugitsch and A. Sp k (eds) *Evaluating Substantial Equivalence: A Step Towards Improving the Risk/Safety Evaluation of GMOs*, Vienna: Federal Environment Agency – Austria. 45–52.

Andow, D. and Alstad, D. (1998) 'F2 screen for rare resistance alleles', *Journal of Economic Ento-mology*, 91, 3: 572–578.

Andow, D. and Hutchison, W. (1998) '*Bt*-corn resistance management', in D. Andow, D. Ferro, F. Gould, W. Hutchison, B. Tabashnik and Mark W. (contributors) *Now or Never? Serious New Plans to Save a Natural Pest Control*, Cambridge, MA: Union of Concerned Scientists. 19–66.

Argentina (2005) 'Second oral statement of the Argentine Republic: European Communities – measures affecting the approval and marketing of biotech products (DS291, DS292, DS293)', Geneva, 21–22 February. Available HTTP: <http://www.genewatch.org/> (accessed 5 June 2005).

B ckstrand, K. (2004) 'Civic science for sustainability', *Global Environmental Politics*, 3, 4: 24–41.

Bail, C., Falkner, R. and Marquard, H. (eds) (2002) *The Cartagena Protocol on Biosafety*, London: RIIA/Earthscan.

Bates, S. (1996) 'Greens attack EU go-ahead for genetically modified crops', *Guardian*, 19 December.

Beck, U. (1992) *Risk Society: Towards a New Modernity*, London: Sage.

—(1996) 'Risk society and the provident state', in S. Lash, B. Szerszynski and B. Wynne (eds) *Risk, Environment and Modernity*, London: Sage. 27–43.

Bernauer, T. (2003) *Genes, Trade and Regulation: The Seeds of Conflict in Food Biotechnology*, Princeton, NJ: Princeton University Press.

Bernauer, T. and Caduff, L. (2004) 'In whose interests? Pressure group politics and environ-mental regulation', *Journal of Public Policy*, 24, 1: 99–126.

BEUC – Bureau Europ en des Unions de Consommateurs (2001) 'GM food and feed: comments on proposed legislation'. Available HTTP: <http://www.beuc.org> (accessed 10 March 2005).

—(2003). 'Risk assessment of GM-plants and derived food and feed'. Available HTTP: <http://www.beuc.org> (accessed 10 March 2005).

BIO (2006) 'BIO statement on WTO case', Washington, DC: Bio-Industry Organization, 7 February. Available HTTP: <http://www.bio.org/news> (accessed 19 February 2006).

Bourguet, D., Chaufaux, J., Seguin, M., Buisson, C., Hinton, J., Stodola, T., Porter, P., Cron-holm, G., Buschman, L. and Andow, D. (2003) 'Frequency of alleles conferring resistance to *Bt* maize in French and US corn belt populations of the European corn borer Ostrinia nubilalis', *Theoretical Applied Genetics*, 106, 7: 1225–1233.

BRIDGES Trade BioRes (2003a) 'US takes next step in EU biotech challenge', BRIDGES Trade BioRes, International Centre for Trade and Sustainable Development, 3, 12 (30 June).

—(2003b) 'US requests WTO panel in US–EU biotech case', BRIDGES Trade BioRes, Inter-national Centre for Trade and Sustainable Development, 3, 14 (25 August).

—(2004a) 'US argues EU biotech moratorium hurts developing countries', BRIDGES Trade BioRes, International Centre for Trade and Sustainable Development, 4, 8 (30 April).

—(2004b) 'Biotech case: scientists to be heard, final decision delayed', BRIDGES Trade BioRes, International Centre for Trade and Sustainable Development, 4, 16 (10 September).

BRIDGES Weekly (1999a) 'WTO members ponder GMO inclusion in talks', BRIDGES Weekly Trade News Digest, International Centre for Trade and Sustainable Development, 3, 42 (25 October).

—(1999b) 'Biotechnology', BRIDGES Weekly Trade News Digest, International Centre for Trade and Sustainable Development, 3, 46 (24 November).

Busch, L., Grove-White, R., Jasanoff, S., Winickoff, D. and Wynne, B. (2004) 'Amicus Curiae brief, submitted to the Dispute Panel of the World Trade Organization in the case of EC:

measures affecting the approval and marketing of biotech products (DS291, DS292, DS293)', Geneva, 30 April. Available HTTP: <http://www.genewatch.org/> (accessed 5 June 2005).

Buttel, F. (2000) 'GMOs: the Achilles heel of the globalization regime?', a paper prepared for the annual meeting of the Rural Sociological Society, Washington, DC, August.

BWG/CoC – Biotechnology Working Group/President's Council on Competitiveness (1991) *Report on National Biotechnology Policy*, Washington, DC: President's Council on Competitiveness, Biotechnology Working Group, chaired by Vice-President Quayle.

CAC – Codex Alimentarius Commission (2000) 'Report of the first session of the Codex Ad Hoc Intergovernmental Task Force on Foods Derived From Biotechnology', Chiba (Tokyo), March.

—(2001) 'Report of the second session of the Codex Ad Hoc Intergovernmental Task Force on Foods Derived From Biotechnology', Chiba (Tokyo), 25–29 March. Available HTTP: <ftp://ftp.fao.org/codex/alinorm01/al0134ae.pdf> (accessed 10 March 2005).

—(2003) *Codex Principles and Guidelines on Foods Derived from Biotechnology*, Codex Alimentarius Commission (FAO/WHO). Available HTTP: <ftp://ftp.fao.org/codex/standard/en/CodexTextsBiotechFoods.pdf> (accessed 10 March 2005).

Canada (2004) 'First written submission of Canada: European Communities – measures affecting the approval and marketing of biotech products (DS291, DS292, DS293)', Geneva, 21 April.

CCC – Consumers Choice Council (1999) 'GMOs/LMOs and labeling in the context of the Biosafety Protocol negotiations', letter to the FDA from Consumers Choice Council and several NGOs. Available HTTP: <www.consumerscouncil.org/gmo/loy2999.htm> (accessed 10 March 2005).

CEC – Commission of the European Communities (1995) 'Further information on the EU–US New Transatlantic Agenda'. Available HTTP: <http://europa.eu.int/en/agenda/tr04a.html> (accessed 14 January 2005).

—(1997a) 'Commission decision of 23 January 1997 concerning the placing on the market of genetically modified maize (Zea mays L.) with the combined modification for insecticidal properties conferred by the *Bt*-endotoxin gene and increased tolerance to the herbicide glufosinate ammonium pursuant to Council Directive 90/220/EEC', *Official Journal*, L 031, 1 February: 69–70.

—(1997b) 'Regulation 97/258/EC of 27 January 1997 concerning novel foods and novel food ingredients', *Official Journal of the European Communities*, L 43, 14 February: 1–6.

—(1998a) 'Fourth TABD conference to boost transatlantic marketplace, Charlotte, 5–7 November 1998', press release, 5 November, No. 93/98.

—(1998b) 'Commission decision of 22 April 1998 concerning the placing on the market of genetically modified maize (Zea mays L. line MON 810), pursuant to Council Directive 90/220/EEC', *Official Journal*, L 131, 5 May: 32–33.

—(1999) Sir Leon Brittan's Address at the Transatlantic Environmental Dialogue Launch, Brussels, 3 May. Available HTTP: <http://europa.eu.int/comm/external_relations/us/environment/slb0305.htm> (accessed 6 May 2005).

—(2001a) 'The EU–US Consultative Forum on Biotechnology', Commentary on the report from the Commission services. Available HTTP:<http://europa.eu.int/comm/external_relations/us/biotech/ec_commentary.htm> (accessed 6 May 2005).

—(2001b) 'European Parliament and Council Directive 2001/18/EC of 12 March on the deliberate release into the environment of genetically modified organisms and repealing Council Directive 90/220/EEC', *Official Journal*, L 106, 17 April: 1–38.

—(2001c) 'Proposal for a regulation on genetically modified food and feed', COM 2001 – 425 final. Available HTTP: <http://europa.eu.int/comm/food/fs/biotech/biotech08_en.pdf> (accessed 11 March 2005).

—(2002a) 'Commission decision of 3 October establishing guidance notes supplementing Annex VII to European Parliament and Council Directive 2001/18/EC on the deliberate release into the environment of genetically modified organisms and repealing Council Directive 90/220/EEC', *Official Journal*, L 280, 18 October: 27–36.

—(2002b) 'Commission decision of 24 July establishing guidance notes supplementing Annex II to European Parliament and Council Directive 2001/18/EC on the deliberate release into the environment of genetically modified organisms and repealing Council Directive 90/220/EEC', *Official Journal*, L 200, 30 July: 22–30.

—(2003a) *Towards a Strategic Vision of Biotechnology and the Life Sciences: Progress Report and Future Orientations*, 5 March, Brussels: CEC.

—(2003b) 'Regulation 1829/2003 of 22 September 2003 on genetically modified food and feed', *Official Journal of the European Communities*, L268/1–23 (18 October).

CEC–SJ – Commission of the European Communities–Service Juridique (2004a) 'First written submission by the European Communities: European Communities – measures affecting the approval and marketing of biotech products (DS291, DS292, DS293)', Geneva, 17 May. Available HTTP: <http://www.europa.eu.int/comm/trade/> (accessed 5 June 2005).

—(2004b) 'Oral statement of the European Communities at the first meeting of the Panel with the Parties, European Communities – measures affecting the approval and marketing of biotech products (DS291, DS292, DS293)', Geneva, 2 June. Available HTTP: <http://www.europa.eu.int/comm/trade/> (accessed 5 June 2005).

—(2004c) 'Second written submission by the European Communities: European Communities – measures affecting the approval and marketing of biotech products (DS291, DS292, DS293)', Geneva, 19 July. Available HTTP: <http://www.europa.eu.int/comm/trade/> (accessed 5 June 2005).

—(2004d) 'Supplementary rebuttal submission by the European Communities: European Communities – measures affecting the approval and marketing of biotech products (DS291, DS292, DS293)', Geneva, 15 November. Available HTTP: <http://www.europa. eu.int/comm/trade/> (accessed 5 June 2005).

CEO – Corporate Europe Observatory (1998) 'EU–US trade deregulation: the TEP of the iceberg – how the New Transatlantic Marketplace became the Transatlantic Economic Partnership', *Corporate Europe Observer*, 2 (October). Available HTTP: <http://www.corporateeurope. org/> (accessed 4 May 2005).

CGG – Commission on Global Governance (1995) *Our Global Neighborhood*, Oxford: Oxford University Press.

Christoforou, T. (2000) 'Settlement of science-based trade disputes in the WTO: a critical review of the developing case law in the face of scientific uncertainty', *N.Y.U. Environmental Law Journal*, 8: 622–648.

—(2003) 'The precautionary principle and democratising expertise: a European legal perspective', *Science & Public Policy*, 30, 3: 205–211.

CI – Consumers International (1996) 'Genetic engineering and food safety: the consumer interests', London: Consumers International, Global Policy and Campaigns Unit.

—(2000a) 'Building the capacity of consumer organisations for improved participation in Codex', Conference Room document, agenda item 4.3.b, January.

—(2000b) 'Consumers International's Response to CL 2000/50-FBT: Proposed Draft Principles for the Risk Analysis of Foods Derived from Modern Biotechnology and the Proposed Draft Guideline for the Conduct of Safety Assessment of Foods Derived from Plants Obtained Through Modern Biotechnology', at Step 3 of the Codex process, London: Consumers International.

—(2002) 'The global voice for consumers', leaflet (June), London: Consumers International.

CIEL et al. – Center for International Environmental Law and others (2004) 'Information submitted to the Panel by Non-Parties: EC – measures affecting the approval and marketing of biotech products (DS291, DS292, DS293)', Geneva, 1 June, Center for International Environmental Law (and others). Available HTTP: <http://www.genewatch.org/> (accessed 5 June 2005).

Claybrook, J. (1999) Speech at 23 April TACD meeting by the President of Public Citizen. Available HTTP: <http://www.tacd.org> (accessed 5 July 2005).

Cohen, P. (1997) 'Science: can DNA in food find its way into cells?', *New Scientist*, 4 (January): 8.

Corzine, L. (2003) Testimony to Congress from the Chairman of the Biotechnology Working Group, National Corn Growers Association (26 March).

CSPI – Center for Science in the Public Interest (2003) *Holes in the Biotech Safety Net: FDA Policy Does Not Assure the Safety of Genetically Engineered Foods*, Washington, DC: CSPI.

Cutler, K. (1991) '*Bt* resistance: a cause for concern? Industry says: no need for panic', *Ag Biotech News*, January/February: 7.

Dawkins, K. (2000) 'The international food fight: from Seattle to Montreal', *Multinational Monitor*, Biotech Futures, 21, 1&2 (January–February).

De Marchi, B. and Ravetz, J. (1999) 'Risk management and governance: a post-normal science approach', *Futures*, 31: 743–757.

DeSombre, E. and Barkin, J. (2002) 'Turtles and trade: the WTO's acceptance of environmental trade restrictions', *Global Environmental Politics*, 2, 1 (February): 12–18.

DG Research (2003) Cell Factory. Summaries of Cell Factory research and demonstration projects (Brussels: European Commission) (See also http://europa.eu.int/comm/research/quality-of-life/cell-factory/volume2/index_en.html).

Donabauer, B. and Valenta, R. (2002) 'An assessment of the principle of substantial equivalence regarding evaluation of allergenic effects of genetically modified organisms', in H. Gaugitsch and A. Sp k (eds) *Evaluating Substantial Equivalence: A Step Towards Improving the Risk/Safety Evaluation of GMOs*, Vienna: Federal Environment Agency – Austria. 67–68.

Dratwa, J. (2002) 'Taking risks with the precautionary principle', *Journal of Environmental Policy and Planning*, 4: 197–213.

EcoStrat (Hilbeck, A., Meier, M. and Raps, A.) (2000) *Review on Non-Target Organisms and Bt Plants*, Zurich, Switzerland: EcoStrat GmbH.

EcoStrat (Hilbeck, A. and Meier, M.) (2001) *Critique of EPA's Environmental Risk Assessment of Bt Crops*, Zurich, Switzerland: EcoStrat GmbH.

'Editorial' (1999) 'Health risks of GM foods', *The Lancet*, 353: 1811.

EEC – European Economic Community (1990) 'Council Directive 90/220 on the deliberate release to the environment of genetically modified organisms', *Official Journal of the European Communities*, L 117, 8 May: 15–27.

EFSA (European Food Standards Agency) GMO Panel (2005) Scientific Panel on GMOs: Opinion on notification C/ES/01/01, *Bt* insect-protected maize 1507; Opinion on notification C/F/96/05–10, *Bt* 11 insect-protected maize. Available HTTP: <http://www.eu.efsa.int> (accessed 5 July 2005).

ENDS (1997) 'EC marketing consent fails to still controversy over Ciba maize', *The ENDS Report*, 264 (January): 41.

—(2003) 'US mounts WTO challenge over EU moratorium on GMOs', *The ENDS Report*, 340 (May): 59.

EuropaBio (2001) 'Safety assessment of GM crops: substantial equivalence', Brussels: EuropaBio, Technical Advisory Group of Plant Biotechnology Unit.

—(2002) 'Safety Assessment of GM Crops (Document 3.2): Monitoring of Insect-Resistant *Bt*-Crops'. Available HTTP: <http://www.europabio.org> (accessed 5 June 2005).

—(2006) 'EuropaBio statement on WTO ruling on biotech crops', 8 February. Available HTTP: <http://www.europabio.org/> (accessed 19 February 2006).

EU–US Biotechnology Consultative Forum (2000) 'Final Report', December. Available HTTP: <http://europa.eu.int/comm/external_relations/us/biotech/report.pdf> (accessed 6 May 2005).

Falkner, R. (2000) 'Regulating biotech trade: the Cartagena Protocol on Biosafety', *International Affairs*, 76, 2: 299–313.

FAO/WHO – Food and Agriculture Organization/World Health Organization (1991) 'Strategies for assessing the safety of foods produced by biotechnology: Report of a joint FAO/ WHO consultation', Geneva: World Health Organization.

—(2000) 'Safety aspects of genetically modified foods of plant origin', Report of a Joint FAO/ WHO Expert Consultation on Foods Derived from Biotechnology, 29 May–2 June.

—(2001) 'Evaluation of allergenicity of genetically modified foods', Report of a Joint FAO/ WHO Expert Consultation on Foods Derived from Biotechnology, 22–25 January.

Fischer, F. (2003) *Reframing Public Policy: Discursive Politics and Deliberative Practices*, Oxford: Oxford University Press.

Fischler, F., Nielson, P., Byrne, D., Wallstr m, M. and Patten, C. (2003) 'Letter to the Editor', *Wall Street Journal*, 21 January (F. Fischler, Agriculture and Fisheries Commissioner; P. Nielson, Development and Humanitarian Aid Commissioner; D. Byrne, Health and Consumer Protection Commissioner; M. Wallstr m, Environment Commissioner; C. Patten, External Relations Commissioner).

FoEE – Friends of the Earth Europe (1999) *FoEE Biotech Mailout*, 5, 5 (31 July).

—(2005) 'New EU moratorium on GM cultivation', *FoEE Biotech Mailout*, July: 1–4. Available HTTP: <http://www.foeeurope.org/GMOs> (accessed 21 July 2005).

Fox, G. (2004) 'NAS issues mixed message on unintended effects of GM food', *Nature Biotechnology*, 22, 9: 1062.

Funtowicz, S. and Ravetz, J. (1993) 'Science for the post-normal age', *Futures*, 25, 7: 735–755.

Gieryn, T. (1995) 'Boundaries of science', in S. Jasanoff, G. E. Markle, J. C. Petersen and T. Pinch (eds) *Handbook of Science and Technology Studies*, London: Sage. 343–360.

Gill, S. (1993) *Gramsci, Historical Materialism and International Relations*, Cambridge: Cambridge University Press.

Goldberg, G. (2000) 'GM crops and the American agricultural producer: a farmers perspective', in *Eursafe 2000: 2nd Congress of the European Society for Agricultural and Food Ethics*, Preprints, Copenhagen: Centre for Bioethics and Risk Assessment. 121–124.

Graff, L. (2002) 'The precautionary principle', in C. Bail, R. Falkner and H. Marquard (eds) *The Cartagena Protocol on Biosafety*, London: RIIA/Earthscan. 410–422.

Greenpeace (1997a) 'Genetic engineering: too good to go wrong?', Greenpeace.

—(1997b) 'From BSE to genetically modified organisms: science, uncertainty and the Precautionary Principle', Greenpeace.

Hajer, M. (1995) *The Politics of Environmental Discourse*, Oxford: Oxford University Press.

Hajer, M and Wagenaar, H. (2003) (eds) *Deliberative Policy Analysis: Understanding Governance in the Network Society*, Cambridge: Cambridge University Press.

Hansen-Jesse, L. and Obrycki, J. (2000) 'Field deposition of *Bt* transgenic corn pollen: lethal effects on the Monarch Butterfly', *Oecologia*, 125, 2: 241–248.

Haslberger, A. (2002) 'Safety assessment of GM-Foods: the substantial equivalence and environmental influences', in H. Gaugitsch and A. Sp k (eds) *Evaluating Substantial Equivalence: A Step Towards Improving the Risk/Safety Evaluation of GMOs*, Vienna: Federal Environment Agency – Austria. 53–56.

—(2003) 'Codex guidelines for GM foods include the analyses of unintended effects', *Nature Biotechnology*, 21, 7: 739–41.

Head, G. (2000) 'Reconciling science, economics and practicality in resistance management for transgenic insect-protected crops', in J. Schieman (ed.) *Proceedings of the 5th International Symposium on the Biosafety Results of Field Tests of Genetically Modified Plants and Micro-Organisms*, Braunschweig, 6–10 September 1998: 225–230.

Hellmich, R., Siegfried, B., Sears, M., Stanley-Horn, D., Daniels, M., Mattila, H., Spencer, T., Bidne, K. and Lewis, L. (2001) 'Monarch larvae sensitivity to *Bacillus thuringiensis* purified proteins and pollen', *Proc. Natl. Acad. Sci.*, 98 (9 October): 11937–11942.

Hilbeck, A., Baumgartner, M., Fried, P. and Bigler, F. (1998a) 'Effects of transgenic *Bt* corn-fed prey on mortality and development time of immature *Chrysoperla carnea*', *Environmental Entomology*, 27, 2: 480–487.

Hilbeck, A., Moar, W., Pusztai-Carey, M., Filippini, A. and Bigler, F. (1998b) 'Toxicity of *Bt* Cry 1 Ab toxin to the predator *Chrysoperla carnea*', *Environmental Entomology*, 27, 5: 1255–1263.

Ho, M.-W. and Steinbrecher, R. (1997) 'Fatal flaws in food safety assessment: a critical response to the joint FAO/WHO Biotechnology and Food Safety Report'. Penang/London: Third World Network.

Hodgson, G. (1999) 'European biotechnology governance seizes up', *Nature Biotechnology*, 17: 418.

Hodgson, J. (1999) 'Monarch *Bt*-corn paper questioned', *Nature Biotechnology*, 17: 627.

Huang, F., Buschman, L., Higgins, R. A. and Li, H. (2002) 'Survival of Kansas dipel-resistant European corn borer (Lepidoptera: Crambidae) on *Bt* and non-*Bt* corn hybrids', *Journal of Economic Entomology*, 95: 614–621.

Hutchison, W. and Andow, D. (2000) 'Resistance management for *Bt* corn: progress and challenges to consensus in US policy', in J. Schieman (ed.) *Proceedings of the 5th International Symposium on the Biosafety Results of Field Tests of Genetically Modified Plants and Micro-Organisms*, Braunschweig, 6–10 September 1998: 231–238.

IATD (2006) 'WTO ruling on genetically engineered crops would override international, national and local protection', 7 February. Available HTTP: <http://www.tradeobservatory. org> (accessed 19 February 2006).

ILSI – International Life Sciences Institute (1999) *An Evaluation of IRM in Bt Field Corn: A Science-Based Framework for Risk Assessment and Risk Management*, Washington, DC: International Life Sciences Institute. Available HTTP: <http://www.ilsi.org> (accessed 5 June 2005).

Irwin, A., Rothstein, H., Yearley, S. and McCarthy, E. (1997) 'Regulatory science – towards a sociological framework', *Futures*, 29, 1: 17–31.

Isaac, G. (2002) *Agricultural Biotechnology and Transatlantic Trade*, Oxford: CABI Publishing.

Jasanoff, S. (1990) *The Fifth Branch: Science Advisors as Policy Makers*, Cambridge, MA: Harvard University Press.

—(1993) 'Bridging the two cultures of risk analysis', *Risk Analysis*, 13, 2: 123–129.

—(2005) *Designs on Nature: Science and Democracy in Europe and the United States*, Princeton, NJ: Princeton University Press.

Kearns, P. (2002) 'The concept of substantial equivalence – the rise of a decision tool', in H. Gaugitsch and A. Sp k (eds) *Evaluating Substantial Equivalence: A Step Towards Improving the Risk/Safety Evaluation of GMOs*, Vienna: Federal Environment Agency – Austria. 11–14.

Kearns, P. and Mayers, P. (1999) 'Substantial equivalence is a useful tool', *Nature*, 401 (14 October): 640.

Kessler, C. and Economidis, I. (eds) (2001) *A Review of Results: EC-Sponsored Research on Safety of GMOs*, Brussels: DG Research, European Commission.

Kuiper, H., Noteborn, H. and Peijnenburg, A. (1999) 'Commentary: adequacy of methods for testing the safety of genetically modified foods', *The Lancet*, 354: 1315–1316.

Kuiper, H., Kleter, G., Noteborn, H. and Kok, E. (2001). 'Assessment of the food safety issues related to genetically modified foods', *The Plant Journal*, 27, 6: 503–528.

Laws, D. and Rein, M. (2003) 'Reframing in practice', in M. Hajer and H. Wagenaar (eds) *Deliberative Policy Analysis: Understanding Governance in the Network Society*, Cambridge: Cambridge University Press. 172–206.

Levidow, L. (2002). 'Ignorance-based risk assessment? Scientific controversy over GM food safety', *Science as Culture*, 11, 1: 61–67.

Levidow, L. and Bijman, J. (2002) 'Farm inputs under pressure from the European food industry', *Food Policy*, 27, 1: 31–45.

Levidow, L. and Carr, S. (2000) 'Normalizing novelty: regulating biotechnological risk at the US EPA', *Risk – Health, Safety and Environment*, 11, 1: 61–86.

Levidow, L., Murphy, J., Carr, S. (forthcoming) 'Recasting "substantial equivalence": transatlantic governance of GM food', *Science Technology and Human Values*.

Levy, A. S. and Derby, B. M. (2000) 'Report on consumer focus groups on biotechnology', Washington, DC: FDA Center for Food Safety and Applied Nutrition.

Lipschutz, R. D. (1996) *Global Civil Society and Global Environmental Governance: the Politics of Nature from Place to Planet*, New York: SUNY.

—(1997) 'From place to planet: local knowledge and global environmental governance', *Global Governance*, 3, 1: 83–102.

Losey, J., Rayor, L. and Carter, M. (1999) 'Transgenic pollen harms Monarch larvae', *Nature*, 399 (20 May): 214.

McGarity, T. O. and Hansen, P. I. (2001) 'Breeding distrust: an assessment and recommendations for improving the regulation of plant-derived GM foods', a report prepared for the Food Policy Institute, Consumer Federation of America. Available HTTP: <http://www.consumerfed.org/gmsummary.pdf> (accessed 11 March 2005).

McKechnie, S. (1999) 'Food fright', *Guardian*, 10 February [Director of the Consumers Association].

Millstone, E., Brunner, E. and Mayer, S. (1999) 'Beyond "substantial equivalence"', *Nature*, 401, 7: 525–526.

Murphy, J. and Chataway, J. (2005) 'The challenges of policy integration from an international perspective: the case of GMOs', in C. Lyall and J. Tait (eds) *New Modes of Governance*, Aldershot: Ashgate. 159–176.

Murphy, J., Levidow, L. and Carr, S. (2006) 'Regulatory standards for environmental risks: understanding the US–EU conflict over GM crops', *Social Studies of Science*, 36, 1. 133–160.

Murphy, J. and Yanacopulos, H. (2005) 'Understanding governance and networks: EU–US interactions and the regulation of genetically modified organisms', *Geoforum*, 36, 5: 593–606.

NCGA – National Corn Growers Association (2003a) 'Position: biotechnology', March. Available HTTP: <http://www.ncga.org/> (accessed 5 June 2005).

—(2003b) 'Corn growers make allies, discuss importance of commodity corn in France', September. Available HTTP: <http://www.ncga.org/> (accessed 5 June 2005).

Nelkin, D. (1979) 'Science, technology and political conflict', in D. Nelkin (ed.) *Controversy: Politics of Technical Decisions*, London: Sage. 9–24.

Nester, E., Thomashow, L., Metz, M. and Gordon, M. (2002) '100 years of Bacillus thuringiensis: a critical scientific assessment', a report from the American Academy of Microbiology.

Nestle, M. (2003) *Safe Food: Bacteria, Biotechnology and Bioterrorism*, Los Angeles: University of California Press.

Newell, P. (2003) 'Globalization and the governance of biotechnology', *Global Environmental Politics*, 3, 2: 56–71.

Noteborn, H. J. P. M., Lommen, A., Van der Jagt, R. C. and Weseman, J. M. (2000) 'Chemical fingerprinting for the evaluation of unintended secondary metabolic changes in transgenic food crops', *Journal of Biotechnology*, 77: 103–114.

NRC – National Research Council (2000) *Genetically Modified Pest-Protected Plants: Science and Regulation*, Washington, DC: National Academy Press.

—(2002) *Environmental Effects of Transgenic Plants: The Scope and Adequacy of Regulation*, Washington, DC: National Academy Press.

Obrycki, J., Losey, J. and Oberhauser, K. (2001b) 'Letter to OPP–EPA on registrations for *Bt* plant-pesticides', 11 September.

Obrycki, J., Losey, J., Taylor, O and Jesse, L. (2001a) 'Transgenic insecticidal corn: beyond insecticidal toxicity to ecological complexity', *BioScience*, 51, 5: 353–561.

OECD – Organization for Economic Cooperation and Development (1993) 'Safety evaluation of foods derived by modern biotechnology: concepts and principles', Paris: OECD.

OSTP – Office of Science and Technology Policy (1986) 'Coordinated framework for regulation of biotechnology: announcement of policy and notice for public comment', *Federal Register*, 51 (26 June): 23302–23393.

Paterson, M., Humphreys, D. and Pettiford, L. (2003) 'Conceptualizaing global environmental governance: from interstate regimes to counter-hegemonic struggles', *Global Environmental Politics*, 3, 2 (May): 1–10.

Pettauer, D. (2002) 'Interpretation of substantial equivalence in the EU', in H. Gaugitsch and A. Sp k (eds) *Evaluating Substantial Equivalence: A Step Towards Improving the Risk/ Safety Evaluation of GMOs*, Vienna: Federal Environment Agency – Austria. 15–24.

Pew (2003a) 'U.S. vs. EU: an examination of the trade issues surrounding genetically modified food', Pew Initiative on Food and Biotechnology.

—(2003b) 'The stakeholder forum on agricultural biotechnology: an overview of the process', Pew Initiative on Food and Biotechnology.

—(2003c) 'Stakeholder forum concludes work, issues closing report', Pew Initiative on Food and Biotechnology.

Pollack, A. (2001) 'FDA plans new scrutiny in areas of biotechnology', *New York Times*, 18 January.

Powell, K. (2003) 'Concerns over refuge size for US EPA-approved *Bt* corn', *Nature Biotechnology*, 21, 5 (May): 467–468.

Princen, S. (2002) *EU Regulation and Transatlantic Trade*, London: Kluwer Law International.

Raman, S. (2003) 'The significance of political rationality in governance: assessing the energizing of UK building regulations, 1990–2002', PhD Thesis, The Graduate School of Public and International Affairs, University of Pittsburgh.

Rautenberg, O. (1999a) 'Image bad, all bad: *Bt*-corn is again under eco-logical criticism', 28 May. Available HTTP: <http://www.bio-scope.org> (accessed on 1 October 2004).

—(1999b) 'Do *Bt* crops pose a threat to the 'colourful world of butterflies?', 3 July. Available HTTP: <http://www.bio-scope.org> (accessed on 1 October 2004).

Reuters (2000) 'UN experts work on genetically modified food standards', 16 March.

—(2003) 'US consumer groups slam biotech firms for ending talks', 31 May.

Rich, A. (1997) 'Apr s la vache folle, r cidive sur le ma s transg nique', page 1; 'Pourquoi ce ma s transg nique et quelles garanties sanitaires', page 8; '"Une d cision r fl chie" ou "Une d cision dans l'urgence"'?, page 8, *Le Soir*, Brussels, 27 January

Riddick, E. W. and Barbosa, P. (1998) 'Impact of Cry3A intoxicated *Leptinotarsa decemlineata* (*Coleoptera: Chrysomelidae*) and pollen on consumption, development, and fecundity of

Coleomegilla maculata (Coleoptera: Coccinellidae)', *Annals of the Entomological Society of America*, 91, 3: 303–307.

Roqueplo, P. (1995) 'Scientific expertise among political powers, administrations and public opinion', *Science & Public Policy*, 22, 3: 175–182.

Royal Society (1999) 'Review of data on possible toxicity of GM potatoes', London: Royal Society.

—(2002) 'Genetically modified plants for food use and human health – an update', London: Royal Society.

Sabatier, P. (1988) 'An advocacy coalition framework of policy change and the role of policy-oriented learning therein', *Policy Sciences*, 21: 129–168.

—(1998) 'The advocacy coalition framework: revisions and relevance for Europe', *Journal of European Public Policy*, 5, 1: 98–130.

Sabatier, P. and Jenkins-Smith, H. (eds) (1993) *Policy Change and Learning: An Advocacy Coalition Approach*, Boulder, CO: Westview Press.

SAP – Scientific Advisory Panel (1998) *Final Report of the FIFRA Scientific Advisory Subpanel on Bacillus thuringiensis (Bt) Plant-Pesticides and Resistance Management*, Docket Number: OPPTS-00231.

—(2000) *Characterization and Non-Target Organism Data Requirements for Protein Plant-Pesticides*, Report No: 1999–06, from FIFRA Scientific Advisory Panel Meeting, December 1999. Available HTTP: <http://www.epa.gov/scipoly/sap/1999> (accessed on 10 October 2004).

—(2001) *Bt Plant-Pesticides Risk and Benefit Assessment*, Report No. 2000–2007, from FIFRA Scientific Advisory Panel Meeting, October 2000. Available HTTP: <http://www.epa.gov/scipoly/sap/2000> (accessed on 10 October 2004).

—(2002) 'A set of scientific issues being considered by the Environmental Protection Agency regarding: corn rootworm plant-incorporated protectant', Meeting Minutes No. 2002–5, August. Available HTTP: <http://www.epa.gov/scipoly/sap/2002> (accessed on 10 October 2004).

SBC – Schenkelaars Biotechnology Consultancy (2001) 'GM food crops and application of substantial equivalence in the European Union', a report by Schenkelaars Biotechnology Consultancy, commissioned by Consumers International & BEUC.

SCF – Scientific Committee for Food (1997) 'Food Science and Techniques: Reports of the Scientific Committee for Food (forty-first series)', Brussels: European Commission. Available HTTP: <http://europa.eu.int/comm/food/fs/sc/scf/reports/scf_41.pdf> (accessed 6 June 2005).

SCF – Scientific Committee on Food (2002) 'Opinion of the Scientific Committee on Food on the safety assessment of the genetically modified maize line GA21, with tolerance to the herbicide glyphosate', 27 February. Available HTTP: <http://europa.eu.int/comm/food/fs/sc/scf/index_en.html> (accessed 11 March 2005).

Schenkelaars, P. (2002) 'Food crops and substantial equivalence in the EU', in H. Gaugitsch and A. Sp k (eds) *Evaluating Substantial Equivalence: A Step Towards Improving the Risk/Safety Evaluation of GMOs*, Vienna: Federal Environment Agency – Austria. 57–62.

Scott, J. (2000) 'On kith and kine (and crustaceans): trade and environment in the EU and the WTO', in J. Weiler (ed.) *The EU, the WTO and NAFTA: Towards and Common Law of International Trade*, Oxford: Oxford University Press: 125–167.

—(2004) 'European regulation of GMOs: thinking about 'Judicial Review' in the WTO', Jean Monnet Working Paper 04/04, New York: NYU School of Law.

SCP – Scientific Committee on Plants (1998) 'Opinion of the Scientific Committee on Plants Regarding Pioneer's MON9 *Bt* Glyphosate-Tolerant Maize', notification C/F/95/12–01/B,

19 May. Available HTTP: <http://europa.eu.int/comm/food/fs/sc/scp/out10_en.html> (accessed 15 October 2004).

—(1999) 'Opinion on *Bt* resistance monitoring'. Available HTTP: <http://europa.eu.int/comm/food/fs/sc/scp/out35_en.html> (accessed 15 October 2004).

—(2000) 'Opinion on the invocation by Germany of Article 16 of Council 90/220/EEC regarding the genetically modified BT-MAIZE LINE CG 00256–176 notified by CIBA-GEIGY (now NOVARTIS)', notification C/F/94/11–03 (SCP/GMO/276Final – 9 November 2000) (Opinion adopted by written procedure following the SCP meeting of 22 September 2000). Available HTTP: <http://europa.eu.int/comm/food/fs/sc/scp/outcome_gmo_en.html> (accessed 15 October 2004).

Shiva, V. (1999) 'Campaign on biosafety issues for Seattle', Dr Vandana Shiva, 4 November 1999. Available HTTP: <http://www.biotech-info/seattle_issues.html> (accessed16 May 2005).

SSC – Scientific Steering Committee (2002) Joint SCF/SCP/SCAN GM/NF WG, Guidance document on the information needed for the risk assessment of genetically modified plants and derived food and feed, GM-NF, Opinions of the Scientific Steering Committee, 12 April, WG/Guide/005-rev21.

—(2003) 'Opinion of the Scientific Steering Committee accompanying the guidance document for the risk assessment of genetically modified plants and derived food and feed', 6–7 March. Available HTTP: <http://europa.eu.int/comm/food/fs/sc/ssc/out327_en.pdf.> (accessed 20 July 2005).

Starr, A. (2000) *Naming the Enemy: Anti-Coporate Movements Confront Globalization*, London: Zed Books.

StCF – Standing Committee on Foodstuffs (2000) 'Summary record of 78th meeting', Standing Committee on Foodstuffs, 18–19 October. Available HTTP: <http://europa.eu.int/comm/food/fs/rc/scfs/rap02_en.html> (accessed 11 March 2005).

Suppan, S. (2006) 'An initial analysis of the WTO's biotech dispute', Institute for Agriculture and Trade Policy, Minneapolis, Minnesota. 9 February. Available HTTP: <http://www.tradeobservatory.org> (accessed on 19 February 2006).

Surel, Y. (2000) 'The role of cognitive and normative frames in policy-making', *Journal of European Public Policy*, 7, 4 (October): 495–512.

Tabashnik, B., Carri re, Y. Dennehy, T. Morin, S. Sisterson, M. Roush, R. Shelton, A. and Zhao, J.(2003) 'Insect resistance to transgenic *Bt* crops: lessons from the laboratory and field', *Journal of Economic Entomology*, 96: 1031–1038.

TABD – Transatlantic Business Dialogue (1996) 'Chicago declaration', CEO Conference, Chicago, 9 November.

—(1997) 'Rome Communiqu ', CEO Conference, Rome, 7 November.

—(1998) 'Statement of Conclusions', CEO Conference, Charlotte.

—(1999) 'Conference Conclusions', CEO Conference, Berlin, 29–30 October.

—(2004) 'TABD co-chairs urge leaders to pursue barrier-free transatlantic market', press release, 26 June. Available HTTP: <http://www.tabd.com> (accessed 29 April 2005).

—(2005) 'About TABD', background information. Available HTTP: <http://www.tabd.com> (accessed 29 April 2005).

TACD – Transatlantic Consumer Dialogue (1999a) 'Annual Report 1999'. Available HTTP: <http://www.tacd.org/> (accessed 6 May 2005).

—(1999b) 'Genetically Modified Organisms (GMOs)', TACD position paper, Doc No. FOOD-5-99, April. Available HTTP: <http://www.tacd.org/> (accessed 6 May 2005).

—(2000) 'Consumer concerns about biotechnology and genetically modified organisms (GMOs)', TACD position paper, Doc No. FOOD-5PP-00, February. Available HTTP: <http://www.tacd.org/> (accessed 6 May 2005).

—(2003) TACD priorities for government action 2003–4, April. Available HTTP: <http://www.tacd.org> (accessed 20 July 2005).

—(2004) Transatlantic consumer groups call upon US government to drop WTO GMO, 24 June.

—(2006) 'TACD statement on WTO decision on genetically modified foods'. Available HTTP: <http://www.tacd.org/docs> (accessed 19 February 2006).

TAED – Transatlantic Environmental Dialogue (1999) Press release announcing the launch of TAED. Available HTTP: <http://www.eeb.org/press/launch_of_the_transatlantic_envi.htm> (accessed 29 January 2004).

—(2000) Press release announcing the suspension of TAED. Available HTTP: <http://www.eeb.org/press/TAED_suspends_activities.htm> (accessed 29 January 2004).

Tappeser, B. and von Weizsacker, C. (1996) 'Biodiversity Convention-COP3 Briefing no.4: Monsanto's genetech-soybeans safe for consumers? Safe for the environment? Gap analysis and flaw identification in Monsanto's testing', Penang: Third World Network.

TEP – Transatlantic Economic Partnership (1998a) 'The Declaration on the Transatlantic Economic Partnership', EU–US Summit, London, 18 May.

—(1998b) Transatlantic Economic Partnership Action Plan.

—(2000) 'Report of Transatlantic Economic Partnership Steering Group'. Report made to the meeting of trade and economic ministers at the US–EU Summit in Washington, 18 December.

Toke, D. (2004) *The Politics of GM Food: A Comparative Study of the UK, USA and EU*, London: Routledge.

US Dept of State (2000) 'Fact Sheet: Report of the U.S.–EU Biotechnology Consultative Forum', US Department of State, Office of the Spokesman, 19 December.

UCS – Union of Concerned Scientists (1998) *Now or Never? Serious New Plans to Save a Natural Pest Control*, Cambridge, MA.: Union of Concerned Scientists.

—(2001) 'Comments to the Environmental Protection Agency on the renewal of *Bt*-crop registrations, Docket OPP-0067B', 10 September, Cambridge, MA.: Union of Concerned Scientists.

—(2002) 'To EPA on Monsanto's application to register rootworm-resistant *Bt* Corn', May, Cambridge, MA.: Union of Concerned Scientists.

US EPA – United States Environmental Protection Agency (1998) '*Bt* CryIA(b) Delta-Endo-toxin and the genetic material necessary for its production in corn: update to include popcorn use' [for Novartis/Mycogen], pesticide fact sheet, April; also, '*Bt* Cry9C protein and the genetic material necessary for its production in corn: new active ingredient' [for Plant Genetic Systems (America)], pesticide fact sheet, May, Washington, DC: US EPA Office of Pollution Prevention and Toxic Substances.

—(2001) '*Bacillus thuringiensis* plant-incorporated potectants', Biopesticide Registration Action Document, Washington, DC: US EPA Office of Pesticide Programs.

—(2003) 'Fact sheet: *Bt* Cry3Bb1 Protein and the GM material necessary for its production in MON863 Corn', March, Washington, DC: US EPA.

US FDA – US Food and Drug Administration (1992) 'Statement of policy: foods derived from new plant varieties', *Federal Register*, 57, 104 (29 May): 22984–23005. Available HTTP: <http://www.cfsan.fda.gov/~lrd/bio1992.html> (accessed 11 March 2005).

—(1997) 'Guidance on consultation procedures: foods derived from new plant varieties', US Food and Drug Administration.

—(2001) 'Premarket notice concerning bioengineered foods, proposed rule', *Federal Register*, 66, 12 (18 January): 4706–4738.

—(2002) 'List of completed consultations on bioengineered foods', US Food and Drug Administration, Center for Food Safety & Applied Nutrition, Office of Food Additive Safety.

USDA–GIPSA (2002) USDA Grain Inspection, Packers and Stockyards Administration, GIPSA's Biotechnology Program. Available HTTP: <http://www.usda.gov/gipsa> (accessed 8 October 2003).

USTR – Office of the US Trade Representative (2003a) 'Factsheet: USTR says regulation assures safe biotech products', 13 May, Washington DC: USTR.

—(2003b) 'Letter from US Ambassador to the WTO', 13 May.

—(2004a) 'Oral statement of the United States, European Communities – measures affecting the approval and marketing of biotech products (WT/DS291, 292, and 293)', 2 June.

—(2004b) 'Rebuttal submission of the United States: European Communities – measures affecting the approval and marketing of biotech products (WT/DS291, 292, and 293)', 19 July.

—(2004c) 'Supplementary rebuttal submission of the United States: European Communities – measures affecting the approval and marketing of biotech products (WT/ DS291, 292, and 293)', 15 November.

—(2006) 'US Trade Representative Rob Portman and U.S. Agriculture Secretary Mike Johanns on agricultural biotechnology and the WTO', Press Release, 7 February. Available HTTP: <http://www.ustr.gov/Document_Library/Press_Releases/2006/February/> (accessed 22 February 2006).

Vogel, D. (1995) *Trading Up: Consumer and Environmental Regulation in a Global Economy*, Cambridge, MA: Harvard University Press.

—(1997) *Barriers or Benefits: Regulation in Transatlantic Trade*, Washington, DC: Brookings Institution Press.

von Schomberg, R. (2000) 'Agricultural biotechnology in the trade–environment interface', in D. Barben and G. Abels (ed.) *Biotechnologie – Globalisierung – Demokratie*, Berlin: Sigma. pp.111–27.

Weinberg, A. M. (1985) 'Science and its limits: the regulator's dilemma', *Issues in Science and Technology*, 2, 1: 59–72.

Weingart, P. (1999) Scientific expertise and political accountability: paradoxes of science in politics, *Science & Public Policy*, 26, 3: 151–161.

Winickoff, D., Jasanoff, S., Busch, L., Grove-White, R. and Wynne, B. (2005) 'Adjudicating the GM food wars: science, risk, and democracy', *Yale Journal of International Law*, 30: 81–123.

WTO – World Trade Organization (2003) 'European Communities – measures affecting the approval and marketing of biotech products. request for the establishment of a Panel by the United States'. WT/DS291/23, 8 August 2003, (03–4170). Available HTTP: <http://www.wto.org> (accessed 13 August 2005).

—(2004) 'European Communities – measures affecting the approval and marketing of biotech products. communication from the Chairman of the Panel'. WT/DS291/26, WT/ DS292/20, WT/DS293/20, 20 August, (04–3484). Available HTTP: <http://www.wto.org> (accessed 13 August 2005).

WTO AB – World Trade Organization Appellate Body (1998) 'EC – Hormones Appellate Body Report: EC measures concerning meat and meat products (Hormones) (WT/DS26/ AB/R, WT/DS48/AB/R)', adopted 13 February, DSR 1998: I, 135.

WTO DP – World Trade Organisation Dispute Panel (2006) Conclusions and Recommendations, WT/DS291/Interim, WT/DS292/Interim, WT/DS293/Interim, 7 February. Available HTTP: <http://www.tradeobservatory.org> (accessed 19 February 2006).

Yearley, S. (1991) *The Green Case: A Sociology of Environmental Issues, Arguments and Politics*, London: Routledge.

Young, A. (2001) 'Trading up or trading blows? US politics and transatlantic trade in genetically modified food', EUI (European University Institute) Working Paper, Robert Schuman Centre for Advanced Study, RSC No. 2001/30.

Young, O. R. (1994) *International Governance: Protecting the Environment in a Stateless Society*. Ithaca, NY: Cornell University Press.

Young, O. R. (ed.) (1997) *Global Governance: Drawing Insights from the Environmental Experience*, Cambridge, MA: MIT Press.

Zerbe, N. (2004) 'Feeding the famine? American food aid and the GMO debate in Southern Africa', *Food Policy*, 29: 593–608.

Zoellick, R. (2003) 'Letter to the Editor', *Wall Street Journal*, 24 January.

Index

Lightning Source UK Ltd.
Milton Keynes UK
UKOW042115180412

191011UK00005B/16/P